D1610536

TRIP OF A LIFETIME

Trip of a

Paul Grescoe

Lifetime

THE MAKING OF THE ROCKY MOUNTAINEER

HURRICANE PRESS

A Tribute Book

Hurricane Press
A Tribute Book
Vancouver, British Columbia

Canadian Cataloguing in Publication Data
Grescoe, Paul, 1939–
Trip of a lifetime: the making of the Rocky Mountaineer
ISBN 0-9698845-3-2
1. Rocky Mountaineer Railtours—History.
2. Railroad travel—Rocky Mountains, Canadian (B.C. and Alta.)—History.
3. Railroads—British Columbia—History. I. Title.
HE2810.R63G74 2000   385'.06'5711   C00-900012-7

Jacket and text design: Peter Cocking
Proofreading: Paper Trail Publishing
Jacket photographs: train by Scott Rowed;
portraits by Stuart McCall/North Light Images;
author photo by Peter Timmermans
Printed and bound in Canada by Friesens

Photo credits:
Unless otherwise indicated, photographs in this book are courtesy
of the Great Canadian Railtour Company.
p. 4: McCord Museum; p. 7: National Archives of Canada PA-26438;
p. 8: Canadian Pacific Archives NS.431; p. 11: Canadian Pacific Archives A.11416;
p. 12: McCord Museum; p. 15: Canadian Pacific Archives NS.13833;
p. 16: Vancouver Public Library 1773; p. 19: Canadian Pacific Archives NS.1340;
p. 20: Vancouver Public Library 1092; p. 21: National Archives of Canada PA-25529;
p. 22: Peter Timmermans; p. 25: *Vancouver Sun*; p. 26: Roy Peterson/*Vancouver Sun*;
pp. 30, 146: Canadian Press; p. 34: Stuart McCall/North Light Images;
centre colour photo section: opening page courtesy Travel Alberta;
last page courtesy Tourism BC.

This book is dedicated to all those people who over the past
10 years supported the Great Canadian Railtour Company and the
Rocky Mountaineer as employees, suppliers, consultants and
friends, including the many hundreds of well-wishers who just quietly
cheered on the Little Train That Could—and Did.

CONTENTS

Welcome Aboard!
The People Who Made the

Mountaineer ¶ The story of the *Rocky Mountaineer*—and its glorious rail route carved through Canada's western mountains—is equal parts historical pageant, business drama and travel adventure. That story unfolds on the following pages, mostly in the words of the people who participated in the making of our remarkable railroad. This oral history marks the 10th anniversary of my assuming control, with four others, of the *Rocky Mountaineer*. In early 1990 we acquired the operations

. . .

Left: Janice Kurylowich welcomes aboard another group of Mountaineer *guests.*

of the innovative all-daylight train service, which the Canadian government's VIA Rail had launched less than two years earlier. It was a time of great transition in the national transportation industry, and the *Rocky Mountaineer*, as this chronicle reveals, played a central role in the drama.

As it turned out, I was only one of many players who were to appear on the stage. The characters you'll encounter here often propel the action as stars; others are relatively brief walk-ons. Their words can brim with comedy or take on overtones of tragedy, but above all, they collectively tell a dramatic, entertaining tale. Many of their stories were a surprise even to me—and I've lived through all the ups and downs of our rocky rail odyssey.

You'll hear the voices of the original visionaries and labourers who created the first railroad through the Rockies; the men and women who reinvented the dream a century later; the employees, colleagues and suppliers, consultants and advisors who got the *Rocky Mountaineer* on the rails and keep our service running so smoothly; and the ever-growing number of passengers and media representatives who have made it such a success today (reflected in the fact that North American travel journalists not long ago named us Best International Attraction).

Sometimes you are lucky; sometimes you're born lucky. I was lucky to be born into a supportive family. My older brother, Bev, has been a tremendous support to me in this venture and in others that were not so successful. My older sister, Joy, was always willing to work no matter how short the notice. And my mother, Kitty, while rolling her eyes, never lost confidence that somehow I would pull it all off. I have also been lucky to add to my family a strong and understanding wife, Wendy, and three great kids—Ashley, Chelsea and Tristan—who are individually smarter than their dad. And Wendy's parents and sister, Kelly, have been there for us all along, right down to the mandatory greeting from my father-in-law, Geoff Robinson, every time I see him: "So, how are the loads?" Without this type of support, the impossible is not possible. While my dad, David, never lived to see Bev and me working together, I know he would have been proud of what we have accomplished together.

In researching and writing this book, author Paul Grescoe has had access to our company files, past and present employees, and many others who played a role in the history of our company. Paul has been given a free hand to tell the story as he saw fit. We wanted this to be more than just a "corporate story"—we wanted to chronicle an oral history from those who made the company.

This book has been conceived as a gift to all these many participants in an often-epic story—all those who gave of their time, energy and best wishes. I hope in some small way it shows my appreciation for your contributions.

In the end, the *Rocky Mountaineer* is so much more than impressive scenery and an exciting train journey. It's the enterprising people who shaped it, the ones who now serve its legacy so well and those who have supported it so enthusiastically for the past decade, our first 10 years. It's time to celebrate a bit, but we begin our second decade with a trainload of fresh challenges. For all of us, it will continue to be the Trip of a Lifetime.

PETER R. B. ARMSTRONG
President and CEO
Great Canadian Railtour Company

Building the Dream:

The Visionaries and the Labourers

Two great men, a Canadian and an American, shared an astonishing

vision in the final quarter of the 19th century: to construct the longest

transcontinental railroad in North America through an impossible land.

In one of the world's greatest engineering feats, the fabulous enterprise

would plant rails of steel in endless empty plains and pathless forests,

across wide roiling rivers, and over and around and through barricades

of almighty mountains. And all of the efforts would have the grand,

. . .

Left: William Cornelius Van Horne, Boss of everything.

if brazen, goal of linking a loose collection of scattered settlements—some of them a tempting target for an American takeover—into a single northern nation.

Sir John A. Macdonald was the first prime minister of Canada, and William Cornelius Van Horne was the American railwayman who became the first general manager of the Canadian Pacific Railway. Together the dreamer and the builder made the railroad that united a country from the Atlantic to the Pacific coasts, 5,300 miles in all. And it was their audacity that drove the vision that drove the tracks across the imposing mountains—where, more than a century later, the trains of the *Rocky Mountaineer* have taken tens of thousands of passengers on a once-in-a-lifetime, once-in-a-world journey.

The original impetus behind the transcontinental railroad was the desire expressed as early as the 1820s to locate such a land route across British North America to transport the bounty of Asia to Europe. Later a purely political motivation arose: the founding fathers of Canada, which came into being in 1867, were well aware of the possibility that some of the western reaches of their new nation would be easy plucking for their neighbours to the south. The United States had purchased Alaska from Russia the same year the Dominion of Canada was founded. Two years later, the U.S. finished building *its* first transcontinental railroad.

The British colony of British Columbia, perched on the Pacific coast above the 49th parallel and below Alaska, was a sitting duck for the acquisitive Americans. B.C.—its white population of 12,000 floundering economically after a flurry of gold-rush fever had subsided—agreed to join Confederation in 1871 on the condition that a Canadian transcontinental line would bind it to the rest of Canada. When progress on the project ebbed, the cocky young province threatened to fly into the willing arms of the Yankees. The stage was set for one of the fundamental dramas of Canadian history.

FINDING THE WAY
The first task was to survey the best route for the railroad, particularly through the wicked terrain of the western mountain ranges: the Rockies, Monashees, Selkirks, Purcells and the Coast Mountains. Sir Sandford Fleming, a Scottish civil engineer, became 19th-century Canada's pre-em-

inent railway surveyor and construction engineer (and later the inventor of international standard time). Fleming oversaw the monumental survey of the proposed cross-country line, employing 2,000 men at a time.

They battled numbing cold, torrid heat, and maddening mosquitoes and flies; 38 of the men died. Among the survivors was hard-driving professional engineer Walter Moberly, who surveyed the route through the Rockies and B.C.

R. M. RYLATT, an ex-sergeant with the British Royal Engineers in B.C., led Moberly's survey crew through treacherous Howse Pass in the Rockies, starting in 1871, and later reported (eccentric spelling and all) to an audience back home: It would be difficult for you, in England, to form any conception of American forests; of the density of the undergroth; the great size of the trees; for though their original position is an upright one, many of these towering giants lay prostrate, either broken off by storms, or torn up by the roots. Often piled one upon another, forming a massive network, and the tough and thorny underbrush, adds greatly to the difficulty of cutting a passage for the loaded ani-

Sir Sandford Fleming

mals. At times the trail winds round the steep sides of mountains, through swamps roughly bridged or corderoyed by the limbs and branches of trees, and where many a poor cayoosh horse or mule mires deep, and at times is left to his fate, his pack stripped off him, and the additional burden borne by his fellows. . . .

Upon starting, our party consisted of 4 officers (surveyors), 16 men, principally axeman about one half of them Canadian, 8 Mexican and Indian Packers, and one hunter for the party—a Bavarian. There were 45 animals in the Pack Train, each carrying about 300 pounds. . . .

I am suffering somewhat from Scurvy [on April 15, 1873]; my mouth is in a dreadful state, the gums being black, the teeth loose, and when pressed against any substance, they prick at the roots like needles; at times the gums swell, almost covering the teeth; to chew food is out of

A CPR survey camp near Selkirk, B.C.

the question, and so have to bolt it without mastication. My legs are also becoming black below the knee, although they appear to give me no uneasiness beyond the knowledge their symptoms bear. My breath likewise is somewhat offensive, and I am troubled with a dry cough. In fact I feel like an old man, and have a disinclination for anything like exertion. The quantity of blood discharged somewhat alarms me, while the eyes are dull, and the cheeks hollow.

'THIS MAD PROJECT'

While the surveying continued, scurvy and all, the Conservative government of Sir John A. Macdonald wooed Montreal steamship tycoon Hugh Allan to launch the Canadian Pacific Railway. When it emerged that Allan was secretly courting American backers and had bribed the

Tory party with $350,000 in campaign funds, the government fell in the subsequent Pacific Scandal of 1873, taking the first incarnation of the CPR down with it. The Liberal administration of Alexander Mackenzie had no will for a national railway, especially during the economic depression that plagued its single term in office. In 1878 the Macdonald government returned to power, preaching a strong nationalism.

SIR JOHN A. MACDONALD: It is quite evident to me that the United States Government is resolved to do all it can, short of war, to get possession of the western territory, and we must take immediate and vigorous steps to counteract it. One of the first things to be done is to show unmistakably our resolve to build the Pacific Railway.

Macdonald, a Glaswegian immigrant who became a criminal lawyer, was among Canada's few major statesmen—despite what one commentator called "an inclination to conviviality that at times of crisis would tip into alcoholic incapacity." The Macdonald government found a syndicate of financiers and experienced railroad builders to carry out the immense project. George Stephen was the president of the Bank of Montreal, and his cousin Donald A. Smith had been chief commissioner of the Hudson's Bay Company, the vast trading enterprise that had once owned 40 percent of what became Canada. Their partner was James Hill, a pioneering Canadian transportation magnate. Together they had made a success of a floundering American railroad. Now they re-established the CPR, promising to complete a cross-Canada line within 10 years—in return for a government subsidy of $25 million and a land grant of 25 million acres. Of that total, $10 million was being raised on the financial markets. Skeptics abounded, especially in Britain.

HENRY LABOUCHÈRE, editor of the London weekly *Truth*, writing in 1881: A group of Montreal and New York bankers have undertaken to float $10 million worth of the company's land grant bonds. . . . The New Yorkers are keen enough gamblers, and reckless enough at times I admit, and yet it is impossible to believe that they are such fools as to put their money into this mad project. I would as soon credit them with willingness to subscribe hard cash in support of a scheme for the utilization of icebergs. The Canadian Pacific Railway will run, if it is ever finished, through a country frost bound for seven or eight months in the year, and will connect with the western part of the Dominion a province which embraces about as forbidding a country as any on the face of the earth. British Columbia, they say, has forced on the execution of this part of the contract under which they become incorporated with the Dominion, and believe that prosperity will come to them when the line is made. This is a delusion on their part. British Columbia is a barren, cold, mountain country that is not worth keeping. It would never have been inhabited at all, unless by trappers of the Hudson's Bay Company, had the "gold fever" not taken a part of mining adventurers there, and ever since that fever died down, the place has been going from bad to worse. Fifty railroads would not galvanize it into prosperity.

'GORGES, CANYONS AND PLUNGING CATARACTS'

But the financing was raised, and construction began in earnest in 1881. Americans were involved from the beginning: James Hill hired Major A. B. Rogers, a railway survey engineer from New England, to seek a more southerly route for the CPR than the one Sandford Fleming had recommended through the Yellowhead Pass. That first year, Rogers took a party over the Selkirk Mountains.

J. H. E. SECRETAN, an English surveyor who had worked for Fleming, describes "Hell's Bells" Rogers: A rough and ready engineer, or rather pathfinder. A short, snappy little chap with long Dundreary whiskers [fashionable silky side-whiskers, named for a character in an English play]. He was a master of picturesque profanity, who continually chewed tobacco and was an artist in expectoration.

TOM WILSON, a 22-year-old supply packer who responded to Major Rogers's request for a volunteer to accompany him to survey camps: Silence greeted his request; there were good reasons for it. Every man present had learned in three days to hate the Major with a real hatred. He had no mercy on his horses or men; he had none on himself. The labourers hated him for the way he drove them and the packers for the way he abused the horses; he never gave their needs a thought. When no one volunteered I thought I might as well take a chance so took him up.

ALBERT ROGERS, Major Rogers's nephew, reporting on the survey along the south fork of the Illecillewaet River in the Selkirks: Being gaunt as greyhounds, with lungs and muscles of the best, we soon reached the timber-line, where the climbing became very difficult. We

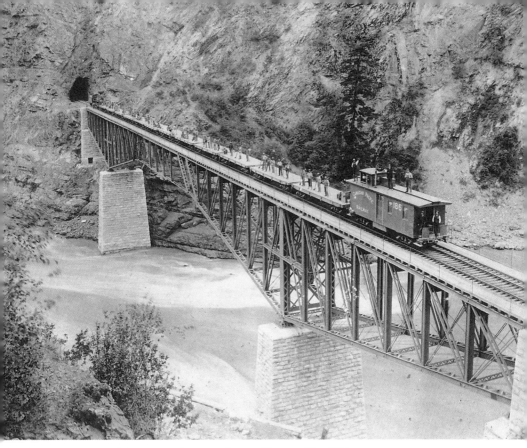

CPR construction crews posed on a cantilever bridge near Cisco, B.C.

crawled along the ledges, getting a toe-hold here and a finger-hold there, keeping in the shade as much as possible and kicking toe-holds in the snow-crust. When several hundred feet above the timber-line, we followed a narrow ledge around a point that was exposed to the sun. (Here four Indians fell over the ledge.) It was late in the evening when we reached the summit, very much exhausted.

Another American engineer, Andrew Onderdonk, had been contracted earlier to push the rail line through the jarring anarchy of rock and jungle of cliffs that are the Fraser and Thompson River canyons between Yale and Kamloops in B.C.

HENRY CAMBIE, a Canadian government engineer supervising construction from Emory's Bar to Boston Bar: Onderdonk found that the white labour that he had got from San Francisco—the only source of supply at the moment—consisted for the most part of clerks out of employment, broken-down bartenders and others of that ilk, men who had never handled a shovel before and who often appeared on the scene attired in fashionable garments in a rather tattered state. . . . so he determined to import a lot of Chinamen—the first large number of Chinese coolies to be imported into this country at one time—and he got two ship loads, 1,000 men in each. They came in very bad weather and had to be kept below hatches most of the way, so as soon as they got upon the work and began to take violent exercise, they developed scurvy and were decimated, fully one-tenth of their number dying.

CHITTENDEN'S GUIDE, reporting on the construction in B.C.: For nearly 60 miles from Yale to Lytton, the river has cut through this lofty

CPR tunnel gangs in the Fraser Canyon worked in tiers, sometimes dodging boulders that threatened their lives.

range, thousands of feet below the summits. Mountain spurs of granite rock, with perpendicular faces hundreds of feet in height, project at short intervals along the entire passage. Between them are deep, lateral gorges, canyons and plunging cataracts. On this 60 miles of tunnels, rock work and bridges, the greater portion of Mr. Onderdonk's construction army of 7,000 men have been engaged since 1880. The loud roar of enormous discharges of giant powder has almost constantly reverberated among the mountains. Fifteen tunnels have been bored, one 1,600 feet in length, and millions of tons of rock blasted and rolled with the noise of an avalanche into the rushing, boiling Fraser; workmen have been suspended by ropes hundreds of feet down the perpendicular sides of the mountains to blast a foot hold; supplies have been packed in upon the backs of mules and horses, over trails where the Indians were accustomed to use ladders, and building materials landed upon the opposite bank of the river at an enormous expense, and crossed in Indian canoes. It is estimated that portions of this work have cost $300,000 to the mile.

'BOSS OF EVERYBODY AND EVERYTHING'
By the end of 1881 the CPR, spending millions of dollars with no imminent returns, was near financial collapse. James Hill, one of the desperate partners, went to the only man he believed could save the company by accelerating construction of the rail line: William Van Horne, who had revived several American railroads facing ruin. Van Horne, Illinois-born of Dutch extraction, started with the railways as a telegrapher. When he came to the CPR as general manager on January 1, 1882, he had been running the 2,200 miles of the Chicago, Milwaukee and St. Paul Railroad. At $15,000 a year, the 38-year-old became the highest-paid GM in North American railwaydom and the most legendary in Canadian history. "He looks harmless," the *Winnipeg Sun* reported, "but so does a buzzsaw."

WILLIAM VAN HORNE: If you want anything done, name the day when it must be finished. If I order a thing done in a specified time and the man to whom I give the order says it is impossible to carry it out— then he must go.

J. H E. SECRETAN: We did not like Van Horne when he first came up to Winnipeg as General Boss of Everybody and Everything. His ways were not our ways and he did not hesitate to let us know what he

thought of the bunch in a general way. At first he had no use for English-
men or Canadians especially Engineers and told me once if he could only
teach a Section Man to run a transit he wouldn't have a single d——d
Engineer about the place.

I was one of the few who got to know him and to know him was to
like him and then admire his extraordinary versatility. He seemed to
know everything and in spite of being a very busy man with awful responsibilities, he always had lots of time to talk on any conceivable sub-
ject, would sit in his office and smoke a cigar a foot long while he talked
and at the same time make a splendid etching on the blotting pad in front
of him, all the time apparently thinking of something else, and probably
gazing at a map on the wall. He was a great big man with a gigantic intel-
lect, a generous soul with an enormous capacity for both food and work.

CROWFOOT, chief of the great Blackfoot Indian Confederacy—
whom Van Horne shrewdly cultivated by awarding him a perpetual pass
on the railway—would over the years come to rue the enthusiasm with
which he responded to the gift:

Great Chief of the Railway:
I salute you, O Chief, O Great.
I am pleased with railway key,
Opening road free to me.
The chains and rich covering of
your name, its wonderful power
to open the road, shows the greatness
of your Chiefness.
I have done.
     His
Crow (X) Foot
    Mark

Van Horne was above all a martinet, driving his men to record feats
of track-laying with assembly-line construction that completed a remarkable 480 miles through the Prairies in the short summer of 1882.

STEPHEN PARDOE, a labourer during that season, recalling the
efficient system that Van Horne oversaw: In places the track was laid so
rapidly that there was not time to set up camps. Large two-story boarding
cars were built for the use of the men. In the upper story the men slept,

Kamloops, 1880: Awaiting the boom that the CPR would bring.

and in the lower they had their mess. Each car held sleeping accommodation for 80 men. These cars, together with the cooking, inspector's, and workshop cars, were permanent portions of the construction train, and were always left at the front. The rest of the train consisted of 21 flat cars (or trucks), and was backed up by the engine, which never had to go more than eight miles for supplies. The sleepers or ties (laid 2,640 to a mile) were packed 33 to a car, and the rails (which were 30 feet long) were 30 pairs to a car, together with five boxes of spikes, 60 pairs of fish-plates, and one box of bolts. The sleepers were loaded on to carts and taken ahead on the dump, distributed, spaced, and lined well ahead of the track-layers. In order to unload the rails the train was backed up to the end of the track, and the rails then thrown off the cars, 15 pairs on each side. The engine then drew off, and the 15 pairs were loaded on to a trolley drawn by horses, together with the necessary fish-plates, bolts, and spikes. When the trolley reached the last laid rail, a pair of rails was dropped, gauged, and the trolley run forward over them. A gang followed to affix the fish-plates, and was in turn succeeded by the spikers. When the load was finished, the trolley was thrown off the rails to make place for another.

Chinese labourers were the backbone of the crews that cut the railway through the Rockies.

MORLEY ROBERTS, a British novelist chronicling the relentless laying of track through the Rockies by 12,000 men during the summer of 1884: Round me, I saw the primaeval forest torn down, cut and hewed and hacked, pine and cedar and hemlock. Here and there lay piles of ties, and near them, closely stacked, thousands of rails. The brute power of man's organized civilization had fought with Nature and had for the time vanquished her. Here lay the trophies of that battle.

DEATH AND OTHER DISASTERS

THE *INLAND SENTINEL* of Yale, B.C., December 21, 1882: ANOTHER CHINESE DIFFICULTY.—Last Thursday at Seabird Bluff, 10 miles below Hope, a blast was let off at the rock cut, and a piece of rock was thrown a considerable distance and struck a Chinaman, cutting his head completely off. Those in the same gang and the next one started on a run for Miller, the Foreman of the rock work, and he had to run for his life; finding himself hotly pursued he ran into the river up to his breast, and was followed some distance into water by some of the Chinamen while others remained upon the bank throwing stones at him. At this crisis in Miller's history Mr. Jno. Garvin, who has a contract at Tunnel work below Hope, appeared in a boat and forgetting all danger to himself amid a shower of stones reached Miller and hauled him into the boat and started for Maria Island. Just then two shots were fired from the Chinamen on the bank, the balls striking the water close to the boat . . . [Garvin] reached the Island and landed Miller who remained there two days . . .

DR. GEORGE W. CAMPBELL, chief timekeeper under Andrew Onderdonk, describing the Caucasian labourers in youthful Yale: [They were] any kind of a human being who could handle a pick and shovel; and as the best of wages were paid, the line was flooded with some of the toughest characters on the coast, not a few of them being men who had done time at St. Quentin. Police protection was an unknown quantity, Jack Kirkup being the one man who was to be depended upon to hold the lawless element in check. Of course there were gamblers and other loose characters hanging on the tail of the work, and as everything ran "wide open" at Yale, the town was the scene of many a riotous night, and not a few men found death or injury as a consequence.

JAMES ROSS, the CPR's manager of construction in the West, writing to Van Horne in February 1885 about the avalanches that had buried seven men and killed two: The men are frightened. I find the snowslides on the Selkirks much more serious than I anticipated, and I think are quite beyond your ideas of their magnitude and danger to the line.

ROSS, communicating two months later about a general strike where the famous Sam Steele (later Sir Samuel) of the North-West Mounted Police rode up to the rescue: While I knew it was necessary to pay the men this and next week for January and February, I had no idea that we would be met by them with such a determined stand as we have had to encounter. . . . The Police could do nothing, and matters looked very serious, the men being well armed and firing indiscriminately. . . .

Yesterday (Tuesday) after our track layers were paid off, I sent them out and the Paymaster went to Mountain Creek, with an escort, on the understanding I would meet them there in the morning; the devils knew it was the track and Mountain Creek bridge I wanted going, if the grading did stop. 150 men met the track laying gang and drove them back here, with the police. I then took charge myself, and told Captain Steele I intended laying the track and expected him to protect me by reading the Riot Act, and if necessary firing into the crowd, who were led by a desperate character, a former contractor, whom I had turned off. I told our men I would be the first to commence work, and did not want them to risk their lives. We succeeded this time, arrested the ring leaders and the Police shot one man who interfered with the arrest.

PORT MOODY GAZETTE, October 10, 1885, describing the day when engineering contractor Andrew Onderdonk completed his final section of track, on the west slope of Eagle Pass: The scene at Yale on Saturday beggars description. A thousand white men lately employed on the railroad rushed out of the cars and into the saloons. In two hours the streets were full of lunatics; they roared and raved and attempted to force their way into private houses. Chinese arrived by the same train and went into the woods, and cooked their rice. It is amusing to see the difference between Pagans and Christians.

'THE WORK HAS BEEN DONE WELL'

The uncertain financial fortunes of the CPR would begin to reverse after William Van Horne arranged to transport 3,000 troops by train from Montreal to Winnipeg to quell Métis leader Louis Riel's North-West rebels in April 1885. The value of the railroad was suddenly self-evident. Within six months Van Horne finished building the transcontinental line—in a fleet four years, six fewer than the federal government had promised. On November 7, 1885, Donald Smith, one of the original trio of investors, drove the last spike of the Canadian Pacific Railway, linking the tracks from the west and the east. The ceremony at Craigellachie, the western entrance to Eagle Pass in B.C.'s Monashee Mountains—although it would become one of the symbols of Canadian nationhood—was deliberately low-key.

VAN HORNE, speaking to a reporter for the Winnipeg *Manitoban* during a refuelling stop on the rail journey to Craigellachie: Our trip has nothing to do with the opening of the road. It is just the plainest kind of business trip. Just the usual trip of inspection before the winter sets in. There has always got to be a general clearing up before winter comes on. We intend going to British Columbia, but cannot say whether we will pass over the line before or after the last spike, about which you appear to

The CPR workers had their own "Last Spike" ceremony on November 7, 1885.

be so anxious, is driven. No, I can't say who will drive the last spike. It may be Tom Malarky or Joe Tubby, and the only ceremony I fancy may occur will be the damning of the foreman for not driving it quicker. There will be no concluding ceremony, no nonsense.

In fact, Donald Smith hit the first spike a glancing blow and bent its head. A roadmaster pulled it out of the rail and replaced it with another—the *last* spike—that Smith then tapped in cautiously.

SANDFORD FLEMING, by now retired from government service but knighted and serving as a CPR director, was one of the few luminaries present: It was indeed no ordinary occasion. The scene was in every respect noteworthy, from the groups which composed it and the circumstances which had brought together so many human beings in this spot in the heart of the mountains, until recently an untracked solitude. The engineers, the workmen, every one present, appeared deeply impressed by what was taking place. It was felt by all to be the moment of triumph....

The first through passenger train from Montreal to Vancouver arrives at Coal Harbour, on May 23, 1887, the eve of Queen Victoria's Golden Jubilee.

The spike driven home, the silence for a moment or two remained unbroken. It seemed as if the act now performed had worked a spell on all present. Each was absorbed in his own thoughts. The silence was, however, of short duration. The pent-up feelings found vent in a spontaneous cheer, the echoes of which will long be remembered in association with Craigellachie.

VAN HORNE: All I can say is that the work has been done well in every way.

CONDUCTOR: All aboard for the Pacific!

SIDE TRIP: LADY ON THE COWCATCHER

LADY MACDONALD, WIFE OF Canada's first prime minister, Sir John A.,
made one of the most daring trips through the Rocky Mountains during the CPR's first season in June 1886. Rather than riding with her
husband in the cushioned, silk-curtained, thick-carpeted luxury of their
private car, Agnes Macdonald insisted on sitting outdoors under a
blanket on the inclined frame on the front of
the steam locomotive—the cowcatcher. As she
exclaimed: "This is lovely, quite lovely; I shall
travel on this cowcatcher from summit to sea."
She rode from Laggan station in the Rockies
for 600 miles. In an excerpt from her own
account of the trip, she mentions meeting a
group of young English hunters and their
Indian paddlers:

Lady S. Agnes Macdonald

Just imagine the feeling with which these
well-regulated young men beheld a lady, bare-
headed and with an umbrella, seated in front of an engine at the mouth
of a tunnel in the Gold Range of British Columbia [at Eagle Pass]! I am
sorely afraid I laughed outright at the blank amazement of their rosy
faces, and longed to tell them what fun it was; but not being introduced,
you know, I contented myself with acknowledging their presence by a
solemn little bow which was quite irresistible under the circumstances!

CHAPTER 2

Reinventing the Vision:
The New Dreamers and Builders

Exactly a century after the last spike was driven to launch the first

transcontinental railroad across Canada, Pat Crowley and Harry Home

acted on a thrilling dream they shared. Crowley was a major tourism op-

erator in Jasper, Alberta, and Home a train engineer based in the resort

town. After Expo 86, the world's fair in Vancouver, drew global atten-

tion to western Canada, they dreamed of running an all-daylight train

service through the Rockies—Jasper by Daylight. They even incorporated

. . .

Left: Expo 86—the transportation world's fair.

a company called Rocky Mountain Rail. They planned to use diesel loco-motives and a restored steam engine—the famous *Bullet Nose Betty* of 1944—to carry coaches of tourists between Jasper and the West Coast, stopping in Kamloops overnight.

Home actually took the scheme to his bosses at Canadian National Railways, the rail-freight operation run as a Crown corporation. CN passed him on to VIA Rail, the operator of Canada's passenger trains. "They never replied to us," he says. "And suddenly VIA made a hurry-up announcement that they were going to run this train from Jasper to Vancouver. The schedule, the timing, the sleeping-over in Kamloops ho-tels, even a lot of the little details—the whole thing was everything we'd thought of. We wrote letters, to no avail. We did consider going to court, but even though I knew we'd been done a terrible injustice, I couldn't see us taking on VIA Rail and the government of Canada."

The manager at VIA who did turn the idea into reality would later compete with a young Vancouver entrepreneur named Peter Armstrong to acquire the *Rocky Mountaineer*—and then resurface to haunt him in years to come. Both men were vying for one of perhaps only two poten-tially profitable routes remaining in the beleaguered Canadian passen-ger-rail business. In the 100 years since rail companies had started moving people across the country, traffic had shrivelled—especially after the Second World War, when the convenience of cars and the speed of airplanes made trains much less efficient as a point-to-point mode of transportation. As Ottawa had to heavily subsidize intercity passenger rail, it began shutting down many of the train services, and in 1977 it formed VIA Rail Canada, a Crown corporation that ran the surviving operations under contract for the federal government. VIA owned only the trains and employed only some of its staff, buying the rest of its ser-vices from CN and the CPR. By 1982, a year after 20 percent of VIA's runs were cut, the cost to government of serving seven million-plus passen-gers was an unnerving $450 million a year—and rising. Only one of two transcontinental trains, the *Canadian*, survived the slashing.

It was no wonder that throughout the 1980s, VIA management des-perately sought ways to staunch the hemorrhaging. While their Toronto-to-Vancouver passenger train was nicely busy in summer, when tourists took the leisurely trip, traffic through the snows of winter was

A young Peter Armstrong helped Gray Line capitalize on Expo 86.

appallingly low. Aside from the Windsor-Montreal corridor straddling Ontario and Quebec, the only other area of likely growth was through one of the world's most magnificent landscapes: the series of ranges that ran from the Rockies outside Calgary to the Coast Mountains looming over Vancouver. Unfortunately, the train travelled half the route in darkness. "For years, as long as I could remember," recalls Jim Roche, who was then VIA Rail's vice-president of corporate planning, "there would always be letters about the fact that people were travelling through mountains in the dark."

It was the visionaries Pat Crowley and Harry Home who not only posed the question—why not take travellers through all the mountains in broad daylight?—but first made an attempt to create a business

based on the concept. Unfortunately, there were others with more influence to cash in on the concept. The closest Home ever came to capitalizing on it was to drive the *Rocky Mountaineer* in the last couple of years before he retired as an engineer.

AN IDEA WHOSE TIME HAD COME

Murray Jackson is the VIA manager credited with developing the idea of daylight mountain train tours. After six years with Trimac Limited of Calgary, which ran Canada's largest tractor-trailer fleet, he joined the railway in 1986 as vice-president of marketing and sales. Making his first cross-country rail trip for the company, Jackson was soon struck by the fact that the summer runs through the ranges of Alberta and B.C. were solidly booked.

MURRAY JACKSON: My mandate was to try to build the ridership, which had been declining for a number of years, and in a number of areas of the country we were really struggling at that time and were operating trains that were half-full. And here is a situation where the trains were full and there was more business than we could handle. I came back from that trip convinced that we had to find a way to add capacity through the mountains during the peak summer tourist season. . . .

When it became clear that the only equipment that was going to be available to us were conventional cars with seats, we talked about how we could do this. Quickly it became clear that we have to stop the train overnight, take the people off the train, and then put them back on. There were some people at VIA who were conditioned to think in terms of the transcontinental service—that wouldn't fly very well [with them] because it's going to take an awful lot longer and it will be awkward getting people on and off. I felt that "No, this can actually be a positive." And I had in my brief time at VIA already received several letters from customers who had taken the transcontinental service with the idea that they were going to experience all of the mountains and were disappointed to learn that a portion of the journey was in darkness.

CHRISTENA KEON-SIRSLY was VIA's director of marketing planning and business development at the time: Murray had already heard that there was this idea out there called the Rockies by Daylight. I can't remember the fellow's name [whose idea it was], but he was a tour operator in Vancouver. It was some individual that Murray had some discussions with [or perhaps a female tourism operator in Jasper?] and came back and said, "This is the only thing we can do, because it's the only equipment we have available." These were cars that had no feeding capability at all. We looked at them; they were pretty rough. For a reasonable amount of money (in our railway terms), it seemed clear that we would be able to get them into reasonable shape, fix up the seats and the interiors. We put in small galleys—just for storage, really. We would be able to operate, initially, one trip a week, and eventually would be able to increase the frequency.

MICHAEL SHAMAN, VIA's Winnipeg-based regional manager of operations in 1988, describes his role in the project: Basically configuring the equipment to make it suitable for daylight viewing, prepare it for safety, ride quality, comfort, service design. We were dealing with a variety of vintage equipment built to Pullman standards [dating back to 1955], with old air-conditioning systems. I'm not trying to paint the equipment as in bad shape, but it needed tender loving care. It was an extremely tough job. There was a lot of interfacing with both Canadian National and Canadian Pacific because of the train scheduling with the hours of operation that were required for daylight travel. There were also some obstacles to overcome in parking the equipment at certain layover locations. In Kamloops it was the old station, preparing the site to facilitate train arrivals and departures, layover locations, establishing a location where you can do safety inspections, servicing the equipment, accommodating buses in and out of the station to receive passengers on the train, detrain passengers. So there was a lot of logistics to put in place and a real tight time frame. I mean, we did this in just a few months.

Barry Dane

JACKSON, meanwhile, was dealing with his masters at VIA: The skepticism was financial. VIA had made a number of financial missteps and, actually just before I joined, they had attempted to introduce a new service through the mountains. The name of the train was *Par Excellence*. It was a continuous trip, using sleeping-car equipment, operating between Calgary and Vancouver. It did not work, it was priced too high, and operationally it just didn't fit with everything else VIA was doing. I would have to say it was done as an Expo-related project. But the idea was that if this worked, it would be the springboard to develop something else. And so one of the early decisions that I had to make was that we would not try to continue with this service in the future. It was priced at several thousand dollars for the trip.

Barry Dane, a Liverpudlian who later became travel and tourism manager of the Calgary Stampede, was then manager of VIA Tours. Jackson had him visit Kamloops to see if the city's hoteliers could support the new service with as many as 19,000 room nights a season.

BARRY DANE: Some felt they were already so busy they didn't need the extra business. But other ones saw the future and a consistent level of almost guaranteed business. A week later there were seven hotels that submitted proposals to us that we accepted. . . . It was such a natural, it was a hit from Day One. And because it was daylight and we were able to put the capacity at around 500 on the train—there's no sleeping cars, no dining cars because you would serve meals at the seat—it became economically feasible to run the train. Especially compared with sleepers that only had a capacity of 25 people and required a dining car and all the attendants that go with it.

On June 5, 1988—just over a year after serious planning began—VIA Rail launched its first all-daylight trains between Vancouver and either Calgary (via Banff) or Jasper. The 10-coach consists (arrangements of railcars) were the first new passenger-rail service in western Canada since the Crown corporation had been created more than a decade earlier.

JACKSON: I was on the first trip, along with our president, Denis de Belleval, and a number of senior managers from VIA rode on that first journey—and it was an instant hit. We invited many of our contacts in the industry, including Peter Armstrong [see *Side Trip: Busman's Holiday*, page 32]. The reaction was very positive and our forecast was 10,000 passengers; we came very close to that. The second year our target was 15,000 and we would have achieved that—but partway through, the government announced plans to privatize.

REMAKING THE ROCKY MOUNTAINEER
In its first year, VIA's new service had been called Canadian Rockies by Daylight, which prompted people to wonder when else the trains would ever go through the mountains. ("It was awful," Christena Keon-Sirsly says of the name.) VIA's advertising director and an assistant came up with several alternative names, from which Murray Jackson chose the *Rocky Mountaineer*. It wasn't a new monicker: during the 1930s the Soo Line Railroad in the United States and its majority owner, the CPR, had a sleeping-car tourist rail service that ran from Chicago to Banff under that name. The current train had a new logo showing a Rocky Mountain sheep on a peak—although such an animal was a stranger amid the southern ranges where the *Mountaineer* ran. However, all of this revamping of image became academic for the people at VIA Rail when in 1989 Ottawa announced a massive downsizing of the company. The number of trains per week was cut by more than half and staff by more than a

Ron Lawless

third. The *Canadian*, its regular transcontinental train, was gone (its name given to a reduced service), and the government hinted strongly at the possible privatizing of the *Mountaineer*.

JIM ROCHE, who later became chief operating officer before leaving to become a government lobbyist in 1994: When the massacre happened, they decided on a number of things. First of all, we had to reduce the network to match the funding. I was vice-president of planning, so that was my job. . . . [The *Mountaineer*] was almost like a political showpiece to sell off. Really there weren't any that could be sold except that one on a straight transaction basis, because all of the others lost money. Only this one didn't lose money. Even that's a moot point because it depends upon whether you're talking about an operating profit or about a contribution to capital. It was using a fixed plant that was already there, in terms of stations and equipment. But the equipment was old and would soon have to be replaced. So the operation was not contributing to that capital cost.

I wasn't happy. First of all, this was a very exciting, even entrepreneurial experiment. We were out to make it succeed and we felt it was just being handed over as sort of a sacrificial lamb to satisfy the gods of privatization. Like, nothing else could be privatized, so here, take this thing. It could have been so easily not sold. I don't even think in the end the government cared that much ... the boys, the trustees, were in charge: [president and CEO Ron] Lawless and Marc [le François, chairman]. They didn't have an affinity to the company. They spent their entire career at Canadian National hating passenger rail and many times screwing passenger rail.

RON LAWLESS: I was a career railroader with Canadian National. When I finally got the presidency, we were a freight railroad and by then, while I participated, we had clearly made a separation between passenger and freight services. The main relationship between VIA and CN before and during my time was as a contractor. We had written up contracts that VIA ran over our tracks and a long-ago established formula was agreed to, and that's the way they were charged. It was a very, very unhappy, uneasy and difficult relationship with VIA, simply because VIA was losing hundreds of millions of dollars. . . . Have in mind that there was a very, very bad taste in the mouth of VIA people like Jim Roche and others who had put together a Rocky Mountain service that they were so proud of, that they felt was one of the few things they were doing that wasn't losing barrelfuls of money. . . . Nobody ever called it privatization. . . . Truth to tell, it was the very first privatization of passenger service in this era.

Amid widespread speculation that the federal government would soon be calling for tenders to take over the *Rocky Mountaineer*, two men got together in the summer of 1989 to discuss the possibility of pooling their resources to make a bid. One of them was a private-sector entrepreneur in Vancouver, the other still a Crown-corporation employee with VIA Rail in Montreal. Peter Armstrong and Murray Jackson were about to embark on a brief but controversial relationship that would create lingering repercussions.

SIDE TRIP: BUSMAN'S HOLIDAY

ON THE INAUGURAL RUN in June 1988 of what became the *Rocky Mountaineer*, one of the fascinated guests was a Vancouver tour-bus company partner named Peter Armstrong. The 35-year-old executive vice-president of corporate development at Gray Line prophetically told an American reporter from *Sunset Travel Review*, "In five years, you'll have to beg to get on this new VIA Rail service because it's going to be so successful." He was a little off on the timing, but what he didn't realize was that by then he would be running the service as a principal in a successful private company, Great Canadian Railtour.

Peter Armstrong started in the hospitality industry as a wide-smiled, strapping six-foot-four doorman at the Hotel Vancouver. That's where he and fellow bellman Mike Miller noted in the summer of 1973 that on many days the local Gray Line tour-bus operation, then run by BC Hydro, was turning away hundreds of possible customers. They opened their own business, Spotlight Tours, with two 23-seat tour buses bought with money from their own savings and family, including Peter's brother, Bev. Miller pulled out after the first unprofitable season and Peter had to enlist new partners, Tom MacDonald and Don Baxter; by the third year Spotlight was in a position to buy majority control of a failing scheduled-route operator and local charter and airport bus company, Trailways of BC.

PETER ARMSTRONG: The first two and a half years were very tough. As the airport contract came up [for rebidding] in September of 1979, we first had to address the morale issue with our staff. There were things that I did and attitudes that I had that were just awful. I was just a young kid who had a very little business that all of a sudden went very big, and I had this grandiose idea that I was good. And I was arrogant, belligerent—and they were my best attributes.

In 1979 Gray Line came up for bid, the province's first Crown corporation to be privatized. Peter had worked on deputy premier Grace McCarthy's Social Credit campaign and she agreed he shouldn't be competing with a money-losing, government-owned bus company. Trailways won the bid to purchase Gray Line after some quiet lobbying, and Peter, holding about 20 percent of the shares, became the first president of the privatized company. When Tom MacDonald later decided to replace him in that post, Peter became executive VP. This was his position in 1988 when he was a guest on the very first all-daylight run through the Rockies.

PETER: Within 15 minutes of being on the train, I understood what was going on. People were comfortable and relaxed. They could stick their heads out from the vestibule and watch some of the most spectacular scenery pass by. I never saw such happy people pour off a train.

CHAPTER 3

Setting the Wheels in Motion: The Race for the

Rocky Mountaineer ¶ Peter Armstrong needed a job. He had

spent a decade running Vancouver's Gray Line tour-bus operation, build-

ing it up into a profitable business. The company flourished during Expo

86; he'd been the first to purchase tickets to the world's fair in 1984, even-

tually buying 200,000 while shrewdly prebooking 40,000 hotel-room

nights. But once the fair ended, his senior partner, Tom MacDonald,

began to squeeze him out. It took Peter three years to fashion a deal to

. . .

Left: Rocky Mountaineer *pioneers (left to right) Mac Norris, Arnold Sturgeon, Peter Armstrong and Dick O'Rourke reliving the heady early days.*

sell out to MacDonald, three years when he was serving as an executive vice-president rather than the president he'd been. "It was the worst time of my life," he recalls. "Unfortunately, I wasn't made to be an employee." In 1989 he left the company and looked for a fresh future—maybe he could find another role in the hospitality industry or even get into manufacturing.

Or maybe, just maybe, he could make a bid for the *Rocky Mountaineer*. The bubbling rumour mill said the feds were going to force VIA Rail to unload the train service into the private sector. Ever since he'd taken the inaugural trip on the *Mountaineer* as a representative of Gray Line (which was doing about $1 million a year in tour and sightseeing trade with VIA's passengers), he'd been convinced of its potential if the train were marketed effectively. Dugal Smith, then a senior management consultant at Price Waterhouse (now PricewaterhouseCoopers) in Vancouver, remembers, "It was sort of an offhand idea; he had this dream of maybe running the *Rocky Mountaineer*, and it was almost a throwaway." Yet Peter was intrigued enough to go to Alaska in early June 1989 with Tom Togus, then vice-president of transportation of Westours, to look at the cruise-line tourist trains run there by the Holland America subsidiary and by Princess Tours—perhaps the only private trains in the world making any money at the time.

And then one day in mid-July, Peter had a call from his friends Barry Dane, manager of VIA Tours, and Barry Gleason, the Crown corporation's director of marketing: could they all get together for dinner? Peter invited them over for a barbecue at his West Vancouver home and they brought along a man he'd met only once before: Murray Jackson, VIA's vice-president of marketing and sales. It would prove to be a fateful meeting in the brief but exciting business drama that ensued over the next few months.

ACT 1

PETER: Over that barbecue I said to the guys: with all these changes, would the VIA management group be putting in a proposal? They all said no. I said I'd be into a privatization of the *Rocky Mountaineer*. A couple of days later Jackson called me out of the blue:"I didn't want to say anything, but I'm putting together a group. Would you be interested in seeing what we're doing?"

Jackson had already quietly informed his VIA superiors about his intention to bid if the *Mountaineer* came on the market (and was told he'd have to resign if he did so). He then approached VIA's director of marketing planning and business development, Christena Keon-Sirsly, and its vice-president of operations, the veteran Bert Guiney—both of whom were interested in being part of his bid. While drawing up a business plan and registering his company in Alberta, Jackson cast about for other partners. (He would eventually line up a Toronto venture-capital company and, at the last minute, the Japan Travel Bureau as potential investors. "It wouldn't have been enough, in retrospect," Keon-Sirsly says now.) Among those he initially approached were Peter Armstrong and Tom Rader, a former vice-president of Westours' cruise-tour division, who had become the owner of a railcar manufacturing company in Oregon that built dome coaches, which were hauled by the state-owned Alaska Railroad. Rader and Peter knew one another from the bus-tour business more than a decade before.

TOM RADER: There were several meetings that we had in Vancouver and Montreal over a six-month period of time [in 1989] when Murray Jackson and crew were trying to figure out a way to buy the service without having it have to go out to public bid. Or at least having their position well defined so that when it came out to bid, they'd be the only ones who would have all the information. We had several meetings and, as I recall, Murray and Christena had actually talked to me about building cars for them. I think I may have even gone to the first meeting without a relationship with Peter.

PETER, recounting the first get-together with the Jackson group that he attended with Rader, in the Mount Stephen Club in Montreal: So we go to the meeting and I'm contributing ideas and so is Tom and we're having great dialogue and trying to help build a new business plan. But it was obvious to us they were way over their heads. We were just dumbfounded by the things that they didn't know. They didn't even know how to structure a deal or when the shareholders were going to be in. . . . They promised us this was a first draft and it would be much better—and to come back.

Murray is really pushing to see if Tom would provide financing on building railcars, so we were called back in October. Tom doesn't want to come. I got on the phone and convinced Tom to hop on a plane and fly up to Montreal. Unfortunately, it was more of the same. The deal that they offered me, I would have been better to put my money into a savings bond. It was all about how much money Murray, Bert and Christena would make, yet I was going to come in with most of the money. A big chunk of money. They were going to come in with nothing. And then they shock us by saying, "We have given an undertaking to the senior VP of VIA"—who was on loan from CN, when they fired the president—"that we will not do anything like organize a business plan or take advantage of the information we have. And we are not even allowed to have a meeting, but we're having it anyway." And I am thinking, here we are going into a partnership with people who have made an undertaking to their employers, using their material, their information, and we are supposed to put our money up for these people.

Tom and I hash it around and we come to the realization that they didn't have the managerial ability, they didn't want to take any advice from us, and there wouldn't really be any role for us. "Other people will be the board members, but please put up your money." We meet the next day with Murray Jackson in the dining-lounge room of the Delta Montreal and he says, "Tom, are you becoming an investor?"

Tom says, "I don't think so, but I would be happy to provide equipment to you if you get financing for it."

"Peter, are you going to be an investor?"

"No, I'm not going to be an investor."

"I'm sorry," Murray says, "that is unfortunate. Do you mind signing a letter of confidentiality?"

"Why would I do that? You know I've always had an interest in this train."

"Well, you are a man of dishonour and I knew you would lie to me . . ."

It got really ugly—yelling and screaming—and Murray walked out. And then there were phone calls from Christena and meetings with her. She says Murray wants to meet, but he wants to bring a court reporter. I finally phoned a friend of mine in Vancouver who said, "Get the hell out of there, they're lunatics!"

So I go away and I don't think about the train for a while.

WENDY ARMSTRONG, Peter's wife of 10 years (and girlfriend for seven years before that), had left her career teaching at Crofton House School for Girls to care for their three children—Ashley and Chelsea, both then 7, and Tristan, 4. She remembers that summer as a happy one: I wasn't worried financially. It was nice to be letting go of Gray Line, Peter had a good settlement, I was coming out of a great career, and he was going to start up something new. The kids were fine, we were comfortable—so things at that moment were not too tough.

ACT 2

But in the early fall of 1989, Peter Armstrong once again thought seriously about the *Rocky Mountaineer* when Ottawa officially announced that it was to be put out to public tender. By then he had been talking about the idea to some key advisors. Among them was his elder brother, Beverley, who was president of Pacific Western Realty, a Vancouver real-estate development firm, and chairman of the 11-location Canadian chain of Red Robin Restaurants. Bev brought Peter together with his two partners: Richard (Rick) Browning, executive vice-president of Pac West and president of a subsidiary; and James (Jim) Houston, chairman and a principal of the Urban Projects Group, which had developed 8,000 housing units and 1.5 million square feet of commercial properties on the West Coast. Together they had a net worth of $30 million-plus, and in 1989 their companies grossed more than $120 million.

JIM HOUSTON, who had met Peter long before: He was having trouble with his relationship at Gray Line and wanted to exit, and so Bev suggested he come and talk to me as a mentor. Peter and I talked about what he should do and at the same time we started looking for other business opportunities. My relationship with Bev had been quite successful, and we'd done some pretty exciting things in the development business. And then Peter one day [in June 1989] had this idea of bidding on the *Rocky Mountaineer*.

I was impressed with his attention to detail, his acumen and the way that he went about things—and he was very aggressive. The idea of getting into a business that was outside of real-estate development was very attractive. Because in the development business, by its nature, things

Jim Houston and wife Jackie (bottom row, third and fourth from left).

come in on an ad hoc basis: You find a deal, you do a deal, it takes a year or two. So the idea of having something that produced money every year was kind of exciting. It wasn't the railway business; this was the tourist business. It was something that Peter knew something about. He had made a lot of money for Gray Line, dealing in tours and at Expo.

He put together some figures and, of course, based on the information that he had, they probably were realistic. What we didn't understand at the time was that the people at VIA might have been bent upon sabotaging the whole thing and they had it appears (and I am sure they will deny it) to have very carefully structured the thing in such a way that it was bound to fail. And they were almost successful. On the other hand, my original assessment of Peter turned out to be the thing that they didn't count on: he had been suckered, but he put his head down and he bowed his neck and he just kept on going—just sheer force of will. If you say to Peter, "I wonder where the president of CPR is today?" Peter will say, "Well, where shall we try him—his home, his cottage, his personal number, his cellular number or his private railway car?"

BEV ARMSTRONG, remembering how he and his partners came to be Peter's partners, first harks back to their childhood: We used to fight the way most siblings fight. I remember fighting with him quite regularly until he got to be my size—and larger—and then it wasn't quite as much fun, so we stopped that in our mid-teens. But we always had a relationship; he was always interested in talking to me.... My partners and I started out by just giving him advice and sort of got involved very, very gradually. Our initial involvement was giving him an office to work out of and secretarial assistance. We were skeptical, but I wasn't really thinking that I was going to be involved, either. I had seen what he had done with Spotlight Tours and how he had taken what most people would have considered a career-ending disaster and turned that into Gray Line, and so I knew that he was a survivor. And he couldn't get into too much trouble because he didn't have very much money.

RICK BROWNING: Bev was a fraternity brother and so was his younger brother, Peter, who worked for two fraternity brothers of mine at Gray Line, Tom MacDonald and Don Baxter. Bev and I were strategizing one day about what we were going to do next. We had made a lot of money and had paid Jim back. Bev says to me, "Well, Peter is thinking about making a bid on the *Rocky Mountaineer*."

I said, "That sounds kind of interesting, but what do we know about the railroad and travel business?" We both looked at each other and laughed.

"Oh," Bev said, "as much as we knew about the restaurant business."

Early on, Peter had also been discussing the *Mountaineer* with a corporate/commercial lawyer friend in Vancouver, the politically well connected George Hungerford, then of Hungerford Simon. The distinguished-looking Hungerford (formerly a Canadian Olympic rower) would become his legal mentor over the next decade. A director of Eldorado Nuclear Limited when Ottawa privatized that Crown uranium refiner, he was wary of Peter's partners at first.

GEORGE HUNGERFORD: I said, "Peter, your partners have got to be strong, they have got to have the same vision, and when you have unequal financial abilities going into a partnership, then it often leads to stress and strain. And where you have nothing and they have all the money and they are used to getting into a real-estate deal and then flipping—you know, I hope you have got the right group." His brother, Bev, was far stronger than I ever realized (because I didn't know him). I didn't know his strengths and I didn't know how much time he was ultimately going to spend counselling Peter and supporting him through this whole process.

BEV ARMSTRONG: We continued to provide assistance as Peter got into it. Ultimately, when it came time to put the bid in—and there were a lot of dollars involved in putting it together—we did agree to underwrite those costs [totalling about $375,000]. He was pretty much putting all of his bid team's travel on my Visa card.

PETER: The first offices we had, starting that fall, were shared with Doug Day at First Cambridge on the 10th floor of Bentall 3: one small office with a desk, and my very first employee, Carolyn Rogers, had a workstation outside in a secretarial pool. Carolyn was a unique, high-powered Aussie; she was with us the first year. We got her through an agency and she immediately threw herself into this project and would work incredible hours. She spent many a weekend and late night typing the original proposal and subsequent submissions—and never complained once. Carolyn lived across the street from Bentall 3 in the YWCA. She said she could get up and be at work in 15 minutes.

Another advisor Peter had approached was Jess Ketchum, who'd been vice-president of communications at Expo 86, where he had gotten to know the man who had bought $100,000 worth of the fair's first tickets. Earlier, Jesse D. Ketchum had been a senior advisor to the government of British Columbia and the provincial minister of transportation and highways and managed one of B.C.'s nine regional tourism associations.

JESS KETCHUM: Peter phoned me and asked me if I would have breakfast with him at the Park Royal Hotel. He always has the eggs Benedict, therefore forcing me to do the same, and the two of us sit there and feel guilty. And then he said, "I've got an idea: I want to start a new company that will take on a struggling business, and the name of this dynamic new company is No. 245 Dynamic Endeavours Inc." He grabbed a napkin and started sketching out a structure of a company, and it took a few minutes for the light to go on as to what he was really talking about. I think he was doing that on purpose just to have a little fun with me, because it became clear that it was transportation-oriented and then tourism-related. And then it became more clear about rail and then of course it became clear—maybe after he told me for the third time—that he wanted to take over part of VIA Rail.

I said, "Passenger rail?" I wasn't familiar with the *Rocky Mountaineer*, but I certainly knew that passenger rail in Canada, and in British

Legal advisor George Hungerford (left) and Peter celebrate.

Columbia in particular, had been a dismal failure. When Peter explained that it was the *Mountaineer* that he wanted to turn into a land-based cruise through the Rockies, it all made sense to me. My initial role was to primarily deal with the strategy of ensuring we had support not only in Victoria but in Ottawa on the government-relations side.

Jess Ketchum

Working with only about $60,000 of his own money, Peter would assemble a team of investors—his brother and Bev's two partners—who formed a company called Mountain Vistas Railtour Services. (Jim Houston jokes about how his wife, Jackie, tells people that Peter called her up and asked if she'd like to own a train. She says, "I thought he was talking about one of those ones with diamonds and gold that you buy at Nieman Marcus, so I said, 'Sure, I would love to have one'—and he said, 'Well, you've got one.'") Rick Browning became chairman and Peter was president. An old friend was consulting to him: Rob Hamilton, formerly a chartered accountant with Arthur Andersen & Co. And Peter began using his connections in relevant industries to form advisory committees. Lawyer George Hungerford chaired one on business; Anna Pollock—a tourism consultant whose clients included Tourism Canada and the western provinces' tourist ministries—headed another on tourism and hospitality. (Jess Ketchum says, "In coming up with the projections on passenger service and marketing and all those other aspects of this business, Anna contributed a lot.")

It was all designed to suitably impress—as it did—the executive consultant who had been hired to select the winning bid. Charlie Armstrong (no relation to Peter) was a career railroader and economist who had retired early in 1982 as president of CN Holdings, which controlled all of the railway's nonrail assets, such as hotels and marine and trucking services. On an executive level with CN Rail's Ron Lawless, he had no bias against privatizing rail operations; as he'd say later, "I have never held the view that the government had to be in the railway business." So in the summer of 1989, when Lawless asked him to become project leader of the privatization process, he felt knowledgeable and independent enough to take on the task.

PETER: Once I'd decided that I was going to meet with Charlie, I recognized quite early that I did not have any real rail expertise. I had been working with Dick O'Rourke on the B.C. Chamber of Commerce transportation committee. He had been the assistant VP for Western Canada for CN Rail; he was the only railroader I ever met. So I hopped on a ferry to Nanaimo and had breakfast with him in the Bastion Hotel. It was about a four-hour meeting, and he said, "Peter, railroading is like no other business," and he gave me the history and a feeling for it.

So we hit it off, and he said, "I know somebody at CP Rail who has just retired—Howard Lyttle—and maybe you can get him on board." Meanwhile, Dugal Smith and an old friend from Social Credit political battles, Bob McMillin [director of executive search services for Price Waterhouse Management Consultants], had been working on a strategy for me on how to get Mac Norris to join our team.

Mac Norris had recently retired as president and CEO of BC Rail, the successful provincial Crown corporation. A graduate of CP Rail, the 44-year rail veteran had spent the previous two decades at BC Rail, having taken the company from a $58-million-a-year loss to a $65-million profit.

BOB MCMILLIN: Peter asked me if we could help him augment his business plan. He had lots of strength with respect to marketing. He sure knew how to do inbound tour packaging and how to respond to and field the wholesale tour packages in Europe and Asia and America. That was the front end of the business. What he didn't have was train operations and logistics—all of the back end. He asked me if there was anything that we could do, and I got in touch with the vice-chairman of BC Rail, Bev Ellis, who worked for us as the senior tax director. I asked her what was going on with Mac Norris, who had just retired from BC Rail and was itching to do something. So Bev introduced us to Mac and we introduced Mac to Peter.

PETER: Bob, Bev, Dugal Smith and Tom Chambers—managing partner in Price Waterhouse's B.C. office—had told Mac all about me and set me up for success. I met Mac for dinner at the Park Royal Hotel in West Vancouver in December. There were a couple of times I've been fearful of meetings, and this was one of them. I got to know everything I could about BC Rail and Mac Norris, who had turned the company around. He was a rough, tough guy, he didn't suffer fools, and he had very strong opinions about everything. He had a lot of things he wanted to get involved in with Rotary and his church, and he'd just married Clara. But I found him to be very supportive and keenly interested once he got over his natural concerns.

JESS KETCHUM: When I was manager of the Cariboo Tourist Association, I used to fight tooth and nail with Mac Norris and his guys at BC Rail. To the point at one time where Mac had to bring his entire board up to my hometown in Quesnel and hold a board meeting so that they could publicly give me a bad time for not knowing what I was talking about. Peter desperately needed someone with Mac's deep knowledge of the industry—and his toughness.

MAC NORRIS, recollecting the day he met Peter: I thought, *What the hell, I'd be interested to see what it's all about.* Peter told me what he was up to and I was sort of intrigued by it. I had a poor opinion of VIA, like most railroaders. I figured privatization and an entrepreneurial outlook would probably have possibilities. I was listening to this young fellow; I thought he was bright. I also wanted to know who the backers were, and it was important that I meet them. So I more or less just listened. And then I thought, *Well, I'd spent a long time building a reputation; I don't want to get into something that would fail.* So I did a little research, not anything tremendously deep. I wanted to know that it was true what Peter told me about his background.

PETER: I think I sweated at least a couple of gallons away, but I got Mac to commit to at least look at our plan and meet my partners. He said, "I'll look at what you have got—I'm not giving you any commitment—and if I see anything I don't like, I'm out of there." So he looked at it and a couple of days later he was meeting with Arnold Sturgeon, who was VP of sales and marketing and former VP of operations at BC Rail.

NORRIS: Having met his partners—and Jim Houston particularly is very impressive—I began to feel fairly comfortable with these guys. They had financial resources; they had business acumen that was certainly worth respecting. They wanted me to head up a rail advisory

The Park Royal Hotel was the scene of many crucial early organizational meetings.

committee. But I specified that I wanted to become a member of the board. He had a list of guys he thought might fit, and I started to meet with them and get their commitment. Arnold Sturgeon was one of them; he'd retired ahead of me [in 1989, as senior vice-president of marketing and sales operations].

ARNOLD STURGEON: When this all came to me through a breakfast meeting with Peter, I was skeptical—you know, the passenger business was very difficult. And I was skeptical because I didn't think that they had the resources and the wherewithal to put it together because they were real-estate people and Peter was a bus guy. He and I had a lot of disagreements, mainly on how to run a railway—because I'm from the old school and, of course, he was a young whipper-snapper who knew nothing about railroads and we didn't trust him. . . . Anyway, I said to Mac, "Well, what have we got to lose?"

Peter, Mac Norris and consulting accountant Rob Hamilton then met with Howard Lyttle, whom Dick O'Rourke had suggested as a member of the rail advisory committee.

PETER: Howard is the doubting Thomas of all time. He had been a senior executive for CP Rail out here. The first time that we meet him it's at the old Peppi's Restaurant in West Vancouver. The lunch doesn't go well.

Rob [Hamilton] and I are there and he's asking questions—"Do you have this? Do you understand operating procedures? Do you understand contracts?" And we're trying to answer, but we're just sinking into the quagmire, not knowing what we're talking about. I am watching this guy and how he's chopping us up. And Rob is getting more angry at him at every moment and I can see this is going to be a real bad thing, so I look Howard in the eye and say, "We don't have the answers to these questions. I'll be honest with you, we don't even know how to ask these questions. I don't know what our success is going to be, but it will be a lot better if we have somebody like you asking these types of questions."

HOWARD LYTTLE, who decided to get involved after all: I told Peter he'd lose his shirt. Well, he had no knowledge of railways. But it was the presence of the other fellows from the other railways, Mac and Dick and Arnold [that convinced him to participate]. Rob showed me five-year figures in a kind of rough plan, and it impressed me with the money that could be made.

On December 18, Peter, Rob Hamilton and tourism consultant Anna Pollock met with the four former railroaders to name Mac Norris chairman of the rail advisory committee and assign Dick O'Rourke to draft an action-plan report.

DICK O'ROURKE, describing the kinds of questions they had to answer: What equipment will we get from VIA? What equipment is available anywhere else? What kind of schedule would we operate on? (How long does it take to get from here to there?) Over whose track would we be operating? Rob, for the longest while, was not convinced that the only place to operate from was the CN station in downtown Vancouver. He wanted us to look at a station out in Fort Langley somewhere and the CPR station out in Coquitlam—you know, ridiculous places because it did not take care of the rest of the operation. When the train comes into the station and unloads people, you have got to have an organization there that will pull the train away, service it, turn it around, bring it back and park it ready to go on the next trip. We knew before we started that this was not going to work, but we had to convince Rob. He doesn't convince that easy.

NORRIS: The time frame was so incredibly short. We had to get an operating plan and cost it. Our first meetings were held around a little desk, and we spent a lot of time meeting at my house and at Park Royal and in the Avalon Hotel [on the North Shore], and borrowing offices. We had to figure out the crew costs, the maintenance of cars, all the costs of that train. I thought, *Well, we need a pro to look at this*, so I got hold of our cost man at BC Rail in a private contract to check out the costing. And we had some ways of looking at CP's costs and comparing them to our own. So there was some reality. The other thing is that you wanted to know what shape those [*Mountaineer*] cars were in. I had George Kelly, chief mechanical officer at BC Rail, take a professional look at the fleet. They were in pretty good shape—it depends on what you consider "pretty good". Mechanically they could be fixed, but they needed a lot of upgrading. Right away, too, we started preparing the initial submission.

GEORGE HUNGERFORD: We are now moving from concept to implementation. Peter is having to worry about the banking side and having some good lines of credit in place. We had to get the [operational liability] insurance, and people like Mac Norris and Rob Hamilton were very helpful to Peter in finding it. There turned out to be only two insurers in the world who would insure us. Finally, through Mac, there was a fellow at BC Rail who helped plug Peter in to the right person in the right insurance group. I could review it, but it wasn't a matter of negotiating with other insurance companies. We only had the choice of the two, and we had about 24 hours to get the stuff in place—so you just have to take it. There was a lot of blind faith here that things were going to work out. There wasn't time to overlawyer the documents or the transactions, because if you thought too seriously about the liability, the whole thing never would have taken place. . . .

So, yes, there was some contractual work, but Peter didn't have any cards to play. He was pretty much on his knees, and people were telling him what he would have to accept. From a lawyer's point of view, I could look at these documents and Peter would say, "These are just terrible. Where do I sign?" Peter really had to take what was offered, because they all really didn't think that he would survive.

PETER: We'd already had a couple of meetings with Charlie Armstrong. I believe he was meeting us out of obligation, and I felt we didn't have any credibility with him at all. Then we had met with him again near the end of the first phase of the bidding [on January 30, 1990], and that's when he read the riot act to us and said, "You're not good enough to be a railroad." It wasn't quite that direct, but he was going to scare off anybody that was fly-by-night and I think he did a good job of it. I was pretty scared.

DICK O'ROURKE: Charlie is a really smart cookie. He gave no indication as to who the other bidders were—or even how many.

There were 11 expressions of interest in the *Rocky Mountaineer*, mostly from travel organizations, including some cruise lines. Privatization consultant Charlie Armstrong then narrowed the field down to five, representing six different groups (two of them consolidated their bids), and finally to three: Peter Armstrong's group, Murray Jackson's and—the only foreign bidder—Westours, the arm of Holland America, owned by gigantic Carnival Cruise Lines. Now Peter and his people had to get even more serious about solidifying a final bid, lobbying key politicians and negotiating track usage and other rail issues with Canadian Pacific and Canadian National.

NORRIS: Peter and I were meeting with provincial ministers in Victoria and in Edmonton and mayors and council members all over the place. One of the things that became evident when we were dealing with CP and CN was that they liked us; they liked dealing with railroaders. We met with them right away because we had to devise the operating plan and establish our credibility.

PETER: On my first visit to CP headquarters at Windsor Station [February 12] with Mac and Howard, we sat through a 20-minute, scaremongering lecture. "This is the way it's going to be: we're going to decide who's going to be the operator, you're going to have to prove to us that

Mac Norris in his later BC Rail days.

you can do it, we're going to run it the way we want to run it." I've dealt with the Teamsters and the other union groups—I've been in a lot of tough situations—but this one actually scared me. We spent the next two hours trying to build up a rapport and ask questions.

Mac and I, at the end of the meeting, excused ourselves to use the washroom. And over the urinal he said—and he's ex-CPR—"Holy shit, that was awful. I've never been through anything like that before."

And we came out of the washroom and Howard Lyttle came up between the two of us, put his arm around us and said, "God, that was great. They love us."

I came to the quick realization that if that's how they liked us, I never want them to not like us. But my impression of CP Rail over the years changed dramatically. I learned what they were trying to do then was to make sure they got the best value for the railroad and their shareholders on the contract and make sure they were going to deal with a credible operator—and in their eyes, on paper, I wasn't very credible. My relationship with CP has since been fabulous—other than for that first 20 minutes. Actually, for the next couple of days I kept saying to our group: "Should we just pack our bags and go?" 'Cause I didn't think we could win on the bid.

DICK O'ROURKE: For a brief while we thought, Gee, maybe the way to deal with CP—because they were really being rigid in their price— would be for Peter and Mac and Howard to just say, "Sorry, guys, we just keep doing the numbers and we can't meet your figure. If you can't come down a little bit, we're just going to have to drop the whole schmear." I guess they tried it and CP said, "Well, too bad." And then they talked their way out of that. It turned out not to have been the best idea in the world.

ACT 3

Peter Armstrong had been unduly pessimistic. Although his group was scrambling to put its bid together, so were his competitors, challenged by the frightening fact that the winner had to be capable of operating the *Rocky Mountaineer* by spring, just a few weeks away. The criteria for the selection process were demanding (see *The Rules of the Game*, page 58).

CHARLIE ARMSTRONG: I knew it was going to be an absolutely transparent process. So I decided that it would combine more than my own opinion—that it would be comprised of three people. One was David Todd, then the CN's vice-president of public relations and our government liaison man in Ottawa, who I felt was very capable, very neutral, understood the political scene, and if necessary could assist me in protecting us from any political interference. We then asked for an outside consultant, and we were recommended a man by the name of Tom Currie. He was then a management consultant on the outside, and we invited him in and said that this was a process we want to go through in a very structured way. . . .

When this went to the board of directors, no officer in VIA, including Mr. Lawless, and none of the board knew the identity of the candidates. The complete report to the board was on the basis of candidates C, D and E, and I made it clear when I entered the board [meeting], I expected a decision to be made without knowledge of the players.

Two issues did not loom as large in the decision-making process as outsiders might have assumed: the amount of money being offered and the fact that Murray Jackson's group had lately been employed by VIA. Charlie Armstrong made it clear to both Ron Lawless and Jackson himself that previous experience of running and marketing the *Mountaineer* would not in itself be a deciding factor.

BARRY DANE, the VIA Tours manager who would go to the Calgary Stampede as travel and tourism manager in 1991, reflects on the challenge Charlie Armstrong faced: Because Murray, Christena and a couple of others in VIA Rail were part of the process, I often wondered whether there would be, from the government's perspective, a perception of unfair advantage. Here is a product being privatized from the Crown corporation and who gets it but a bunch of executives from the Crown corporation? I think Murray was always behind the eight ball because of the fact that, although he had resigned from VIA Rail, there would still be those who would say, "Well, of course." Whereas Peter and his consortium being just private taxpayers, one could argue they didn't get the same level playing field.

CHARLIE ARMSTRONG, speaking delicately of Murray Jackson and Christena Keon-Sirsly: One of the officers at VIA had left the corporation to form something that would take [the *Mountaineer*] over—potentially. He therefore had inherited all the marketing knowledge; one woman had already left to go with him. There was some evidence that he had operating support in the group and was probably going to be a very well qualified competitor. I have no doubt about that, and in fact that proved to be the case. I made it clear to [Jackson] that this doesn't cut any water with me: "We are out here looking for an ideal that fits certain parameters. If you are the top person in this, I should be delighted to carry this to the board. If you are not, then I should have no concern in recommending someone else." We did have that discussion and it was not an unpleasant discussion. It was purely a statement of where we were coming from.

And I knew from the beginning that money was not the issue. Because VIA Rail was literally not selling anything. It was selling an established concept; it was not selling the right to operate on either Canadian National or Canadian Pacific lines, because it did not have that by contract. It was not selling exclusivity, because either of the railways could have . . . produced exactly the same service. They were buying some used equipment.

BEV ARMSTRONG and the rest of his brother's group, however, believed money would be an issue: We have done lots of real-estate bidding. Some people try putting in the lowest possible price that they can get something for; they want to get a bargain. And our approach was if the deal is a good deal and you are satisfied that you want this deal, put in a price that is going to get the deal. If the deal makes sense at the price that you are bidding at . . . We were advising Peter about that over a series of meetings, but it ultimately came down to a meeting in the boardroom of Pac West on the 15th floor of the CIBC building.

RICK BROWNING: The spies out there had told us that "you guys are not number one, so you had better do something about it."

BEV ARMSTRONG: That's when we did actually juice the bid—added a few of the kickers to it. Some of the overrides where VIA was going to participate on the passenger counts and some other incentives. It gave the appearance that the bid was much bigger than it really was in terms of upfront money. And we ultimately ended up providing all the initial cash to make the bid and close the transaction. We settled on about $2.3 or $2.5 million. I mean, the bid was $7.2 million, but the rest was subject to future earnings.

PETER: We offered approximately $800,000 for the equipment, which is what they wanted. We offered about $205,000 in marketing money, to pay out any commissions they had paid, which was fair. We wanted two extra baggage cars; that came to $75,000 total. We also offered $20,000 for their senior manager to be available to help with the transition. And we offered them a royalty: 3 percent of what we thought the future earnings were going to be for several years. We felt that they needed to get a rate of return from their investments, and we also thought it would encourage them to look on us as not a problem but a revenue source. That was a bit naive on our part, but the overall package came to something like $7.2 million. We understand now that the other bids were all dramatically lower.

GEORGE HUNGERFORD, his legal advisor: Peter probably overpaid, but it was a crapshoot and we really knew that we had to bid high. Because if the bids were at all close, then they were going to go with the so-called experienced operators, the VIA insider group. So we had to go high; there was no point in going low and losing.

RICK BROWNING: We thought we were making a financial decision. We didn't think we were making a decision about how we would live our lives for the next four or five years.

Another decision loomed at the very last minute, on the day the final bid was to be tendered. Vancouver labour and employment lawyer Israel Chafetz had been advising them regarding the possibility that the winning bidder would have to assume the union contract covering the *Mountaineer*'s VIA employees. ("We essentially told the union we wouldn't fight them on that," Chafetz recalls. "We would recognize them as being the bargaining agent, but we wanted a new deal to reflect the new business"—which is what ultimately happened.) But Chafetz also had opinions on the rest of the draft proposal, which he expressed to the assembled investors and their consultants the morning of the submission.

ISRAEL CHAFETZ: I said, "This document doesn't have a sense of vision as to what you're attempting to accomplish. What you have is a bunch of numbers and facts and statistics, but you haven't really told the story of what you want to do. It seems to me it's deficient in a fundamental way." You remember: I was just a labour lawyer and there were all these guys there who knew about these things, which I knew nothing about, who were quite content with the document. As I went through the pages—"I don't know why you say this here" and "This strikes me as very odd"—I wasn't particularly complimentary. I think Peter and [Mac] Norris picked up on it and ultimately they came around to it. . . . It was kind of like reading a Tom Clancy novel, like trying to impress upon you how much technical knowledge you know, but the story isn't that great. . . . And it created a big commotion. [Rob] Hamilton was not happy with me at all. But I wasn't there to make people happy. So I left and I think they did a major rewrite—and I remember Peter called me to thank me for keeping it on track.

PETER: Rob Hamilton was bouncing up and down. He was pretty angry, and a lot of other people were pretty frustrated to bring this up at this late hour. But it was a very good point, so we agreed we were going to put vision in the proposal.

TOM RADER, the railcar builder, was optimistic about Mountain Vistas' bid, which included the over-optimistic hope of having a dome-car service within two years: We had a low-level dome-car design and drew

Charlie Armstrong

up an illustration of that design in Peter's colours, which he used as part of his presentation when he made his bid. We were confident that he would succeed. Westours weren't very serious about it; I don't think they considered it worth a large risk. They weren't willing to really put out substantial funds to get the business, nor were they willing to commit to a long-term percentage relationship to VIA.

CHARLIE ARMSTRONG, reflecting a decade later on the factors that led to his final decision: [Holland America's Westours, which ran tourist trains in Alaska] were cut off for a variety of reasons. They have competent international management—you take a big tour outfit, they can produce a railway specialist or [another] kind of specialist. But we [VIA] weren't interested in being combined with their Alaska operation or something of this nature. We wanted somebody who we felt was focused for this operation. . . .

In terms of equity balance, availability of funds and reserves, [the Jackson group] were not as strong as the other group. But in the analysis I presented to the board, I didn't disable them for that. Because they were quite capable—it would have been a stretch, but they could have done it. They had potential to assemble a team, but the team was not assembled. We were faced with the fact that their chief operating officer hadn't yet resigned his day work . . . he had not even given any notice to VIA Rail. The team was shaped but was not in place, and we had serious doubts that on April 1, it would be a well-oiled machine.

There was no doubt in the other case [the Peter Armstrong group]. They had worked for six months on their submission, they had gotten everything right down to the hotels they were going to use at Kamloops. They had figured out the day they needed baggage cars to handle the baggage—which the other group hadn't even thought about yet. . . . They did their homework.

In the case of the monetary offer, one candidate [Armstrong's group] came out superior. Little bit higher on the cash up front, which is an immediate return that VIA was going to get. Secondly, they were quite a bit more imaginative in terms of the value of future considerations. One of the things they recognized is that anybody that takes this over is likely going to lose money on your first year, particularly if you absorb your organizational and set-up costs. You are going to lose money. So don't start giving away money up front: put part of your offer into future considerations, share train revenues or some method of saying to the people from whom you're purchasing that "if I make money, you'll make money."

On March 26, 1990, Charlie Armstrong went to the VIA board of directors with his decision to reject the Westours and Jackson bids. (Murray Jackson, who never returned to the railway, said recently, "I believe we got a fair hearing." Within a few years, however, he would rear up again in Peter's life.) The privatization consultant gave the directors "an unqualified recommendation"—which they accepted—that Peter Armstrong's Mountain Vistas Railtour Services be named the new owner of the *Rocky Mountaineer*. "There was no question that this was the group," Charlie Armstrong told the board, "and that prompt action should be taken so that they could in fact operate."

Operate, in fact, in time for a special pre-season junket that VIA had arranged for a few hundred travel professionals—a trip that was scheduled to depart within only a month from Edmonton, a city where the *Mountaineer* had never run before.

CHARLIE ARMSTRONG—a railroader with three decades' experience, most of it in high-level management—used a complex 300-point matrix of criteria to judge who should run the *Rocky Mountaineer*. Here's how he remembers the benchmarks that the three finalists were measured against:

Do they have initial funding adequate to satisfy any offer to VIA Rail and to finance start-up costs? Do they appear to have reserves available to cover the unexpected operating contingencies, unscheduled equipment repairs, et cetera, and do they certify that these funds are actually now in place or are immediately available? We weren't interested in phantom money. Is there evidence of a reasonable debt-to-equity ratio? Is there reasonable assurance of the capital needed to support future expansion plans? The last thing we wanted was to put somebody out there that would be a limping operation.

Next question was organizational capability—determine whether the candidate has in place, or can establish almost immediately, a well-planned, balanced organization staffed by people with the experience and qualifications needed to make the venture work. Will the resources committed to this operation be located in Canada or close to the scenes of operations? We were not so much concerned about who they were, but that they were on site.

Then we went to quality of the operating plan—that the candidate has a comprehensive knowledge of the operational and marketing service as it was then configured. And is, in fact, in a position to begin an immediate transfer of responsibility for the service, with a minimum requirement for ongoing staff support from VIA Rail—are they prepared to stand on their feet? Do they know about car stocking, interior cleaning, refuse disposal, inspection maintenance requirements? We had one outfit that was extremely aggressive and wasn't satisfied unless they had an answer in every area. That became part of the decision process later.

Does the original submission display a real understanding of the marketing program now in place? Have there been any requests for additional information indicating that the candidates have looked closely at the ongoing sales, marketing activity, status reports, details of advertising program, et cetera?

Then the marketing plan: their longer-term plans for the service and the prospects for a concerted, well-integrated effort to fully exploit the potential of what's involved—which we thought was a great potential.

And how does the man who made the decision think Peter Armstrong's company has since run the *Rocky Mountaineer*?

CHARLIE ARMSTRONG: To the best of my knowledge, the group that acquired the license to operate has in fact discharged everything they said they would do. They have added to the equipment, try to run a quality operation, and have really done an excellent job. . . . I think they have done what they were asked to do and what they promised to do.

CHAPTER 4

Fast-tracking a Company:

The First Frenetic Year ¶ No one at VIA Rail until now

had told the winning bidder (or, for that matter, even Charlie Armstrong) that about 400 members of the Pacific Asia Travel Association—a potent group of tourism industry representatives—had been booked for a promotional junket on the *Rocky Mountaineer* that was less than three weeks away. "A couple of days after we won the bid," Peter Armstrong recalls, "Charlie Armstrong phones up and says, 'I'm very sorry, I've got some interesting news for you—I just found out that on April 15

. . .

*Left: Onboards Ian Buchanan, Wendy Armstrong and Judy Thomson
with carman/mechanic Gary Gervais.*

you are going to be carrying people from the Pacific Asia Travel Association from Edmonton to Vancouver.' And I said, 'What? We don't even operate out of Edmonton!' 'Well,' he replies, 'that's what it says on the program.'" This was just the first of a couple of unnerving surprises that the people then running the Crown railway would spring on the new owners of the *Mountaineer*.

"I was absolutely outraged," recalls Jess Ketchum, Peter's communications consultant. "This was one of those situations that could make or break a company, and here you have a brand-new one with no employees, no track record, and you're going to have a few hundred of the most influential tourism people in the world—surprise, surprise. It was a kind of 'By the way, did you know...? And you have to do this trip.' Well, of course, they didn't have to do the trip—I'm sure that Peter could have said that we are not going to do it and they are going to have to find other transport. But if we could pull it off, it made just a little sense."

Fortunately, Peter had already done some crucial recruiting: Rob Hamilton was his second-in-command, and Rick Antonson, general manager of the Edmonton Convention and Tourism Authority, was being courted to become the first vice-president of sales and marketing. Rick already had an impressive career in the British Columbia tourism industry, where he had been manager of the Southwestern B.C. Tourism Association.

'WHAT'S A PATA?'

RICK ANTONSON: A couple of years before, at the Singapore PATA conference, I saw a presentation on the *Orient Express*. I jotted notes to myself on what a great idea it would be to have a train in the Rockies. I can remember coming back and asking a lawyer buddy about registering names like *Rocky Mountain Express*. So I was predisposed; I'm a sucker for trains. My two sons and I have travelled from Moscow across Siberia into China by train. Janice and I got engaged on a train to New Orleans.

I've known Peter for a lot of years. In the '80s, I was managing director for a regional tourism organization and Peter was then president of Gray Line. When they were doing the bid, Peter and Mac Norris and I had dinner together in Edmonton. (I also met separately with Murray Jackson, who was looking for some support from Edmonton Tourism—

which I declined to give to either group.) The day after the announcement of the winning bid was made, Peter called and said, "So, when will you join us?" I said, "What are you talking about?" He said, "What do you think about joining us to head up our marketing?" It was totally out of the blue. Peter and I talked a few more times and he said, "You haven't said anything that scared me so far, so why don't you begin?"

That was April of 1990. I had just turned 40. He was hoping I would begin immediately working part-time, which to Peter is 40 hours a week. He wanted to get me a cellphone, but I was a non-cellphone guy in those days. He phoned one night at 3 in the morning because I was so busy I was never home, and it was the time he knew he could get me. Shameless.

I remember Peter phoning me and saying, "What's a PATA?" It was the first time that the Pacific Asia Travel Association had ever had its Travel Mart in North America, only the second time it had ever had its

Peter and Rick Antonson, the first vice-president of sales and marketing.

Flash forward: Eric Belanger and Scott Remillard help Arnold Sturgeon celebrate his half-century rail career.

conference in North America. The conference was in Vancouver, the Travel Mart the week before in Edmonton. VIA Rail had already promised to run the train—[but] not much work at all had been done to organize the train trip. Peter phoned and said—this is like a week out—that they were running it.

ARNOLD STURGEON, who became vice-president of operations (Dick O'Rourke and Howard Lyttle did not go on staff, as Sturgeon and Mac Norris did): The biggest headache was getting the cars for this special train from where Peter had purchased them in eastern Canada. Never mind the *Rocky Mountaineer* that was going to start in May. I hired a fellow from VIA, Gary Gervais, as a mechanical guy; he used to be a train rider, fixing anything on board that could be fixed. Then we had to get these cars serviceable for the operation of the *Rocky Mountaineer*. Nobody ever does anything with a train that you take out of service; it just sits. The biggest problem was getting the VIA people to do the work and get it ready so that we could take the train to Edmonton. I think we were working right up to the last minute before that train left.

PETER: We had no cars, no employees, no offices—we had nothing. I moved into George Hungerford's office and did nothing for two weeks but leases on offices, union contracts, five agreements with VIA, agreements with CN and CP. We had to get our insurance in place. We had to get some employees. The union [then the Canadian Brotherhood of Railway Workers] offered us 10 employees plus a manager—unemployed people who had been laid off from VIA. While the union had never done this before, it acted as an employment agency.

Mountain Vistas Railtour Services set up offices on the third floor of 625 Howe Street in downtown Vancouver. Among the first people Peter hired was Judy Thomson, a high-energy, vivacious chartered accountant who'd been in charge of recruitment, training and general office administration in the Vancouver office of Arthur Andersen. Rob Hamilton had approached her to join the company as director of customer services in April. Her first challenge, starting on Good Friday, was to staff the train and get it primed for the PATA trip.

JUDY THOMSON: The union provided us with people who were either laid off or going to be laid off because they were making all those cutbacks. Including Bill Romaniuk, Christine Murphy, Mark McChesney and Henry Newman [the first two still work on the *Mountaineer* a decade later]. When we did the PATA train, we took some of the VIA people and then everybody's relative: Peter's wife, Wendy, was on board [see *Side Trip: The Party on Wheels,* page 95]; Wendy's sister, Kelly; Peter's sister, Joy; Rob's brother, Doug; and Rob's sister-in-law, who was a flight attendant for Canadian Airlines—it was just a mishmash of people. We had tuxes for uniforms. I think it was Peter's idea: he said go down and rent tuxedos for everybody, including the women. It was actually very practical because they were dark. We had to fit people like Henry Newman, who's about six foot three, and little Chris Murphy, who is way down there.

BILL ROMANIUK, who had begun working on the trains with CP Rail in 1975 and had been a dining-car steward and train-service manager for VIA Rail before being laid off in 1990: We were all dudded up in our formal attire with the bow tie and cummerbund. For the work we did on board, like making coffee and handling trash, we were some of the most well dressed car attendants in the world. We almost looked like we worked at one of the five-star hotels on Park Avenue.

JUDY THOMSON: For food service, we had the caterers that VIA had used. We did stock a lot of booze. Peter and Rob said, "Look, no matter what, we are going to have enough liquor." And we had so much complimentary liquor that it was ridiculous (but we didn't use it all, thank God).

PETER: There was a case and a half of beer, a half-sack of cider, a couple of bottles of wine for each person—and some hard stuff. . . . We rushed down to the station to get our staff on board. VIA had said that they would undertake to load the train with all the supplies. Fine—we had 10 or 11 cars, and they put them all in the last car. So from Vancouver to Kamloops, our staff worked to sort it all out. It was a sign as to what was to come.

CHRISTINE MURPHY, who before being laid off by VIA Rail had worked for the Crown railway as an onboard attendant and porter for nine years—including two trips on the *Rocky Mountaineer*—was on the PATA trip: Peter's people had no experience. Judy and I were walking through the train car and saw some people and she said, "Who are they?" And I said, "That's the train crew—they run the train." I guess I was a little leery as to whether this was really going to fly or not. A few times I rolled my eyes back in my head so far, I'm sure I could feel my heels. One time on that trip was when Peter came out with an artist's rendition of [proposed] dome cars. It was incredible to have that vision, but at that time it seemed outrageous, because I didn't know him from Adam.

BILL ROMANIUK: I thought this guy had bitten off more than he could chew. He must have very deep pockets. VIA had the backing of the federal government and they were drawing $650 million from the government in subsidies.

RICK ANTONSON: It was really, really short notice, but boy, it was a stellar trip. You would not have known it was their first trip. The interior upholstery design was a touch bizarre. It withstood the test of time, if not the test of taste. Box lunches, but this is a very well travelled group. These people were marketers from 20 different countries and had lots of ideas: "This is how to sell to us in Australia"; people from the U.S. saying, "Here's how your car should look in the future." It was a million-dollar focus group that we could never have afforded to do. I left there with reams of notes; we were working off those notes for years.

And we had bags of fun on the train. One of them was when Joe Clark, external affairs minister at the time, was going through the coaches. I was introducing him when someone said, "This is the most spectacular train trip in the world." Then we went into the first coach and sat quietly down and introduced Mr. Clark to a few people. He stood at the front and said, "I'd just like to tell you this is the most spectacu-lar train trip in the world." We put it in quotes and it has been on everything of ours since then.

HENRY NEWMAN had begun working as a sleeping-car porter for CN in 1975 before mov-ing to VIA Rail, where he was sales and service manager (servicing the VIA version of the *Rocky Mountaineer*) at the time of the general layoffs in 1990: Joe Clark was handing out little contain-ers of maple syrup to everyone. He would start at one end of the train and shake hands and pass out these samples as a souvenir of Canada. He went through a milk crate full of syrup.

PETER: Tom Hockin, the federal minister of tourism, got on board in Kamloops to go to Vancouver. His aides were there and I was so busy, I said, "Tom, you're in the last car there. I'll take your bags and meet you there, but excuse me, I have to go move some beer to all the cars."

Joe Clark on board the Mountaineer.

And an aide who was a government lawyer said, "Do you know who this is? You should spend some time with him."

"I know exactly who he is. I will spend time with him, but it's more important for the minister that I deal with the 400 travel and tourism people we'll be boarding soon. . . ."

The manager the union had given us appeared to be a womanizer and had no managerial abilities at all. Judy Thomson was having problems with him, and I said I'd be happy to deal with this guy. We just kept him in the baggage car. We were running out of Creamos for the coffee, and he then tells us it's too expensive to get Creamos, we don't really need them. I said, "Look, I'm not going to tell 400 people that they have to drink black coffee."

JESS KETCHUM: My claim to fame was when we ran out of Creamos and I jumped off the train at Blue River as we came idling along and ran to the little corner store with the train rumbling behind me. There is this little grey-haired lady behind the counter and I said, "Do you have Creamos?" and she said, "Yes," and I said, "Do you have 2,000 single servings?" I bought milk and everything we could in Blue River, got back on the train, and then we had to call ahead to Kamloops to make sure that they had a couple of thousand Creamos waiting for us.

KELLY ROBINSON (later McKenzie), Wendy's sister, who had worked for Peter at his Spotlight Tours, Trailways and Gray Line tour-bus operations: The Creamos wouldn't have impacted on me. Nobody was doing the coffee thing in my car. I was paired up with a VIA guy. Our car turned into the bar car, the party car. I had no idea that this was not going on in other cars. As the day went on, we were opening up the beer and anything you wanted. The car got more and more crowded. People were hanging off the luggage racks; seats for two had about six in them. Because I'd worked with Peter, he knew how I was socially. He came through with Joe Clark handing out bottles of maple syrup, and Peter just grinned when he saw how many people were in the car, rolled his eyes and said, "There's a God after all." Kelly finally gets her comeuppance.

I was so busy; it was nuts. I ran out of something and had to go to Wendy's car, right beside me, and she's pouring tea to about six people: "Would you like a little lemon with that?" I thought all the cars were like mine. I had to go to another car and there was Henry [Newman], who was delightful. He had a map on his wall and with a felt pen was showing the route to these sedate, lovely little old ladies, maybe eight of them, all very sober. I go back to my car and I've got the yahoos. We stopped in Jasper and several of them got off, walking around with mugfuls of Grand Marnier. I said to one fellow, "I'm awfully sorry, we're out of light beer." He said, "That's all right; it's cat piss." Lovely—thank you, sir, for giving me that image.

JESS KETCHUM: Because the people on board knew that there had just been this transition, and Peter was anxious and had told them the story of what he wanted to do with the *Rocky Mountaineer* in the future—and that his wife and his friends were there working on the train with him—the trip was more successful than you could ever imagine. You know, we didn't have any absolute disasters. There were some air-conditioning problems.

BILL ROMANIUK: It was pretty toasty in some of those cars. Not only the air conditioning, but of course the brakes would be sticking and the brake shoes would be burning up and setting off hot-box alarms. . . . It was terrifying yet exhilarating because you're into a different avenue of employment. You are not just transportation, you are tourism.

JUDY THOMSON: You were mentally and physically exhausted—absolutely, totally—but you were also extremely exuberant because it has happened, it was successful, and you think, *Okay, we can do this.*

PICKING THE PEOPLE

BILL ROMANIUK, one of a handful of VIA employees hired for the first season after the PATA trip: I wondered, *What have I got myself into?* And I continued to look for other work.

HENRY NEWMAN: There were something like 11 laid-off VIA employees manning the PATA trip, but they hired only four of us.

JUDY THOMSON: We had a lot to do—we had about two weeks max—and had to determine which of the VIA people who'd worked on

Bill Romaniuk (right) with John McLaren of Argentina.

the train with us we actually were going to hire. Then I had to interview to the outside world, because we were looking for a mixture of people. You see, we weren't just looking for people who were involved in the train industry. We weren't trying to create a passenger service—we were trying to create an *experience*. People who were good with the public, could speak different languages, and even had some kind of entertainment experience, who were comfortable entertaining their guests for two long days. And had good stamina, because it's a physically exhausting job for them and they give a million percent.

CHRIS MURPHY: I asked Judy who the train managers were and she said, "Well, I am." And I thought, *Oh, my God, you're going to be a basket case.* But she did it by herself every single trip—and a good job, too. I mean, she was very stressed and completely out of her element: her background was numbers, not people. I asked about the scheduling. Because when VIA ran it, you left on a Sunday morning, arrived at your layover destination—Calgary or Jasper—on Monday night, and then you stayed there until Thursday morning and arrived back home on Saturday morning. Then you were off for an entire week. It turned out that [the new owners] wanted you to do three trips like that in a month and then work one week in the office, so I thought, *You guys are out of your minds.*

JUDY THOMSON: When we advertised for people, we did it in local newspapers like the *North Shore News*. And we *got* a real mixture—people like Chris Murphy and Mark McChesney, who unfortunately died not long ago. Henry Newman is just a walking encyclopedia about trains and the route, and when we put together the training program, we got him to teach. We had people with no train experience but maybe they spoke French fluently. And everybody had to have food and beverage experience. In the beginning, everybody did everything: you weren't just a train attendant, you did station services, you helped with baggage. Even though you think you're finished for the day, you can't say, "Talk to the baggage person."

ARNOLD STURGEON: Peter had the right idea when he started the *Rocky Mountaineer*. His philosophy was that we would do anything for the customer. It doesn't matter what they want or whether they are mad, happy, indifferent, we will do whatever they ask. And that was a philosophy that he embedded in all the staff on the train. If there was a complaint, it was looked after. It was really what brought this company along, because there was nobody who ever went away unhappy.

RICK BROWNING, who became chairman of Mountain Vistas: Peter is a great guy for getting you involved. If you've got a minute, he'll take five hours. All of a sudden, I'm doing this railroad thing. I always thought that the development industry had a lot of characters, but the travel business has some of the wackiest people that I have ever met. But the advisory rail committee were giving great direction. You have got to give Peter lots of marks for putting that team together, because these are all senior guys and they must have been somewhat reluctant to get back into the fold with someone who was not one of them. Even though the rolling stock was junk, those guys did a fabulous job getting everybody on side in terms of safety issues, the insurance and labour issues.

ARNOLD STURGEON: Of course, the unions came in and organized the onboard staff, and Peter had a pretty good contract. His first contract gave him a lot of leniency, and the guy who was the union rep from the railway just kind of let it run by itself the first year. The staff were well paid and got a lot of tips and bonuses.

CHRIS MURPHY: The three-year contract had been signed before we even were employed. Then it was renegotiated and it got a little bit better for the employees. We got more job security and more comprehensive rates of pay, and as the company has grown, the union has grown [the attendants are now part of the Canadian Auto Workers Union]. The relations actually have been very good.

THE ADVENTURE BEGINS

The first scheduled trip of the *Rocky Mountaineer* under the new owners began in Vancouver on May 27, 1990, with the former VIA Daynighter coaches, baggage car and steam generator cars pulled by a Santa Fe B36-7 locomotive leased from Canadian General Electric in Montreal. That season it made one return trip a week to Jasper and Calgary; the one-way fare was $350. When the train pulled into the Banff station, the *Banff Crag & Canyon* newspaper reported that "one person was overhead to say, 'Well, you know it's not a VIA train ... it's only nine minutes late.'"

RICK ANTONSON: I remember a staff meeting six weeks into it and Peter saying, "We've all got to do what we got to do." And he said, "I will do anything for this company, whether it's loading baggage onto the train or cleaning out the toilets." At which point, I stood up and offered 50 bucks to the first person who comes up with a picture of Peter cleaning the toilets. Rob Hamilton said, "I'm in"—another 50 bucks. We are talking about a 7-at-night meeting, and the next morning at 7 on our desks was a picture of Peter cleaning the toilet—with a note from Peter that Rob and I owed him 50 bucks. Peter, every single day for three months, asked me for that 50 bucks. After about 50 days, Rob came into my office one day and sat down and said, "I paid him."

"Why did you do that?"

"I can't stand it any more. I can't take it. Every day he asked me for it, so I paid it."

I said, "I'm not paying him." We had a picture of Marilyn Monroe in Jasper in front of a train, and I gave Peter a stale-dated cheque for 50 bucks and this picture with a little ditty that I wrote about "Some smiles can stop trains/You can train some people to smile." Peter continued to hound me that I owed him cash. Several years later I told this story at a roast for Peter and he got up at the end and said, "You still owe me 50 dollars." I took money out of my wallet and threw it on the podium: "Enough."

JUDY THOMSON became the principal director on train, or DOT (now called the train manager): In the first year, when we stopped the train [along the route, to unload garbage, for instance], we let everybody off and they would scatter. And then it was like rounding them up. Every attendant would have to make sure that they got all their people back on the train. Luckily we never lost anybody, but one time in Revelstoke, a beautiful little railway town, I checked with all the attendants and yes, they had all their people on board. Then I looked out the vestibule window and there was this older gentleman sitting on the chair outside the train station. He was waving to me, so I waved back. I thought he was just a local, because people often came down to see the train. Then we are just creeping away and the attendant comes in: "I'm missing Mr. So-and-so." And I am thinking: *Damn.* Because we didn't have radio contact on the train in those days, I had to run back to the conductor and tell him to stop the train. Well, we couldn't stop. They radioed the guys in the station, who got in a truck and drove this man to the crossing, where the train was stopped and we boarded him—with all his fellow passengers cheering him. I wondered what was he thinking of.

CHRIS MURPHY: Judy hired these two girls from the carnivals. We called them the carny chicks: Erin Manahan and Kiersten Enemark. When we stopped in Field, we used to tell people that they could get off and stretch their legs for a few minutes and then get back on. Erin, who was trying to get 10 things done at once, came out one day and said, "You're welcome to get off in Field and spread your legs for a while." And this was with a tour of really proper British people. "What did she say?"

Erin realized what she'd said and started laughing. That was the joke for the entire season: "Can we get off and spread our legs here, Erin?"

JUDY THOMSON: In retrospect, our first uniforms were not the best for that business; they were really more like flight-attendant uniforms. Karen Holms, who ran the office, and I—we were like glue, we did so much together—ended up going to Mr. Jax in downtown Vancouver, which made the Canadian Airlines uniform. Whatever they had, we bought, and our women staff went down and picked up a jacket and a skirt—all navy—and then blouses and ties from other places. We were running from supplier to supplier because we had only a few weeks. It's typical that though a man could get a suit made, the women had to buy off the rack. And the skirts were too long. The train business is not like the airline business; you have to climb around and you get dirty. The next year we asked the women what they wanted, and they wanted pants.

I had a little office on the train and would work non-stop. I walked through the train at 6:30 in the morning and heard something from everyone: "Look, this meal isn't very good . . . I have no beer . . . The person who stocked the fridge before didn't do a very good job. This galley is filthy." An attendant would tell me not to go into a car because she was so mad at the attendant from the last trip who didn't clean the supper up properly. But when the passengers showed up, the attendants would be smiling and no one would know that a total disaster had happened. I probably lost 20 pounds in that job. It was a great exercise program. (One year the staff even brought an odometer thing to attach to me because I put in so many miles in a day.) Wendy Armstrong relieved me on certain trips; she was my spare in the first year.

WENDY ARMSTRONG: Judy was becoming quite exhausted because she was doing the train all the time; she felt she had to be there. Peter asked me if I would do it. It wasn't like I was the boss's wife at that point, it was more like I was just part of a new team. It was perfect for me, because it had been difficult leaving the excellent job I had. Over the summer of '90 I did five back-and-forth one-week trips. Judy would travel for three weeks, and then I would do it for one week. Then she'd be in Vancouver and have some time off but also do all her office work. There were times when we overlapped, overnighting in Calgary together, and I'd find out what was going on.

We had this house there; that was quite an experience, bunking in with people from all different walks and all different ages. It was kind of weird for me because [aged 35] I wasn't part of that young set, going off to Electric Avenue in Calgary; I had kids at home. That was still fun. Judy and I would sleep in the basement.

JUDY THOMSON: It was a nice house in a nice neighbourhood of southwest Calgary with lots of bedrooms and a big backyard. We learned that people wanted their own space, but we didn't have a lot of money in those first few years, and it was cheaper to rent the house and have two people sleeping in the same room. There was a fax machine in the basement and it used to be so depressing: we would come in and there would be reams of paper on the floor—the manifest for the return trip. Everything was done manually in those days, and there would be the ticket packages for the trip with all these changes. We all sat in the kitchen making these packages, stuffing hotel vouchers in them—it was nonstop work.

HENRY NEWMAN: We had one of those huge, late-'70s, beast-style station wagons—the Wally Wagon [named for Rob Hamilton's brother, Jim—nicknamed Wally—who had originally bought it for $2,000].

WENDY ARMSTRONG: On Saturday morning I would drive the Wally Wagon to the liquor store with some of the other people and would literally fill it to the brim with liquor and then drive alongside the tracks in Calgary (which you would never do now) on the platform behind the Palliser Hotel and deliver liquor to each car.

HENRY NEWMAN: That first year there were six of us who went camping and Wendy came along. We drove in the Wally Wagon, with a lot of sleeping bags and four tents, to a campground just east of Banff, almost in downtown Banff. We had a campfire and made some spaghetti sauce—Wendy said it was like soup because it had such a thin consistency—and had quite a bit of wine. Wendy was sitting in a box when it was raining and somebody took a picture. When Peter saw it, he just shook his head and said, "Here's a picture of my wife camping, sitting in a box in the rain." That was quite the time there.

WENDY ARMSTRONG: On the train I'd have a clipboard and go from car to car asking the car attendants if everything was okay, if they needed anything, if there were any problems with any of the passengers. In those

Bill Romaniuk (left) and Henry Newman load the famous Wally Wagon.

days the baggage was on the baggage car, and somebody would have for-gotten their medication in their luggage. And Gary Gervais [a car-man/maintenance mechanic who rode the train] and I would go up to the baggage car to look for this one little piece of luggage in this huge car. Eventually I got relaxed and would talk to the passengers in every car and ask how they were enjoying the trip. I would spell off the attendants if they wanted smoke or lunch breaks.

A. E. SIMONS, a guest from Hertfordshire, England, who had a heart condition, was travelling on the *Mountaineer* with his wife while Wendy Armstrong was train manager—and later wrote to Peter: By the time we reached Kamloops I was sufficiently uncomfortable to visit the hospital, where the doctor in charge, after an examination, wrote me a prescription. For some reason I failed to grasp the fact that I would be unable to get the prescription filled before the journey started again the next morning, and so I set off without the medicine.

As the day progressed I felt rather worse and happened to mention the circumstance to the stewardess. She immediately informed the lady in charge [Wendy Armstrong], and between them they arranged to ring a pharmacy in Banff from the next halt, which was at Field. They somehow managed to interpret the doctor's illegible writing, with the result that the train was met at Banff by the pharmacist in a taxi with my medicine. Your staff refused to accept any payment for all this, and all I had to settle was the pharmacist's bill.

Such a cheerful and helpful service was beyond anything I had a right to expect, and, although I thanked all concerned at the time, I would be very grateful if you would be kind enough to let them know how very much I appreciated their help.

By the time we reached Calgary, the medicine had started to take effect and I was already beginning to feel better. I am now completely recovered.

JUDY THOMSON: You would see people get on our train with oxygen tanks. It was amazing that people have always wanted to do this trip—and they insist on coming.

CHRIS MURPHY: One time I had a gentleman in his late 60s in my car who got on in Calgary. He didn't feel well and was kind of faint. My first instinct was that he shouldn't be on the train, but he was so insistent that he had to get to the West Coast to see a relative and he'd never been there. I don't mean to be flippant, but I didn't want someone dying on my coach—he looked that bad to me. Throughout the course of the day, we had to ask if there were doctors on board. One of the attendants who had been an RN sat with him for hours administering oxygen, checking his heart rate, and as we were climbing an elevation he was getting worse and worse. They took him to the hospital in Kamloops and I said my goodbyes to him and wished him all the best. Who comes to my train car the next morning but this fellow again. "I have to get there; I'm a little bit better." He would have moments of extreme clarity and would be enjoying the trip and then be in terrible shape again. Three weeks later, I got a phone call from the relative: he had passed away two days after he had gotten there. But he made it out there and got his feet in the Pacific Ocean.

RICK ANTONSON: Peter's commitment was that the onboard experience would parallel the outdoor experience. We were struggling to make that happen. There were lots of things that went wrong. I can remember I was walking through the coaches and saw four couples in their 50s, all from California, heading into Calgary. In Calgary, I'd gone down to the hotel bar and in walks one of these guys. We were at the Palliser Hotel and I had a gorgeous suite: two bedrooms, seating for a dozen, big couch. This guy comes over to me and says, "Rick, we got a problem. The hotel doesn't have our reservation. And I want you to know that I'm a lawyer, two others are lawyers, and the other one, he's a judge."

I said, "Well, I got to tell you: you've got two problems. One of which I can help you with." (Of course, I know I can go sleep somewhere else and they can split up my big room.)

"What do you mean?" he asks.

"Well, I can get you rooms. It's no problem. In five minutes you will have rooms. But unfortunately, you'll still just be lawyers."

WENDY ARMSTRONG: At that point there was one VIA person on each car, just gradually training the other young people who were brand-new on the train. We had to start teaching the VIA people more about one-on-one service. Well, Henry Newman was fabulous; everybody loved him; he knew everything we passed by. Bill Romaniuk was very personable and in tune with the passengers. But there were some to whom it was just a job. Trying to get them to do all the little extra things was a bit more of a struggle. This isn't VIA; we want to make this a really special train trip for each individual person on each car. And some people would be too fast in tallying up the bills at the end of the last day; you're in Hope, but the attendants have to work right till they get into the yard in Vancouver, because the passengers have paid all the way. Or the attendants shouldn't be drinking anything in front of them. Little touches that make a big difference.

'DON'T WORRY ABOUT IT, HONEY'
JUDY THOMSON: We would often go out on Friday night but work on Saturday, and get up really early Sunday; we had to be at the train at 5 in the morning. And people would show up at the train station who you didn't even have on the list, because people had already booked months

and months in advance [of Mountain Vistas' taking over] and we had never been told about them during the change-over from VIA. So we would end up with all these people and had to assign them to a car and cram them in. (We allowed smoking in the cars in the beginning, and some of these unexpected people were smokers. Shortly thereafter we invented the smoking car. But in the beginning we allowed them to smoke in their car, which was awful.)

We always left the four seats in the front of a car empty, and we'd have seats in the back available for crew, so we had some playing room. But they weren't the greatest seats, and people would be upset and would come early the second day to try and take another set of seats—and then they'd have fights and our car attendants would have to pacify people.

That first year we had such a learning curve when it was cold, and we didn't have steam-generating units on some of those trips to create heat, so we would be freezing to death. We had blankets and pillows, airline-style. Or we would have extreme heat and the air conditioning on the cars wouldn't work. One trip we were making cold compresses for people and I can remember passengers from Texas who were having a great time. It was boiling hot in the car, and they were standing in the vestibule area and the wind was blowing and they were enjoying the scenery: "Don't worry about it, honey; it's fine, we live with this all the time." Passengers like that would make it all worthwhile, and their spirit would infect everybody else. But man, it would get hot—it was like a tin can with the boiling heat.

ARNOLD STURGEON: The biggest problems were that those cars were old. You couldn't get enough power for the coffee makers. They used converters to change the voltage from 32 volts DC to 110 volts AC. The generator underneath is a DC generator and it produces voltage in DC. Well, to run any appliance you need AC, so they had to have these converters put in and of course they were inadequate. We had a lot of problems with air conditioning. In the five years from 1990 until I left, the biggest problem was trying to maintain the equipment. You would just tear your hair out after a while because of the failures of the air conditioning: these DC generators wouldn't produce enough power and your battery systems would go down and then, of course, the air conditioning would go down.

The operation of the train by CN and CP was 90 percent of the problem—you couldn't maintain the speed to keep the batteries fully charged for the generators. Once the train drops below 15 or 18 miles an hour, the generator stops producing power, so your car lives off the battery power. We were stuck many, many times for long periods of time on sidings waiting for freight trains and other trains to pass us. All of the time that we are sitting we're draining those batteries, and when you get going, especially going up the [Fraser] canyon, you're not generating power. After I left, when they had the generator cars producing electricity, they weren't reliant on the DC generators, which are turned by a belt from the movement of the wheels.

JUDY THOMSON: Poor Gary Gervais, I think he worked every single train the first year. We would be running to get him and he would be exhausted. "Can you fix the air conditioning in this car?" And sometimes he would get it to come back on and everybody loved him. As I said, there was no money in the beginning, and the cars were very tired-looking and weren't reupholstered, and to jazz them up, we put up pictures of the Rockies.

RICK BROWNING, the chairman: I can remember the first time I was on the train, eating breakfast and thinking, *This is awful.* It was cold and ugly. The railcars were about 30, 40 years old. I was sitting there on the train and the *Canadian* [the VIA passenger train] was next door and it had just been refurbished. I thought, *That's a great piece of Canadiana.*

JUDY THOMSON: The first year, all the food was cold and served in huge plastic containers with hinged lids which weren't recyclable. They take up a ton of room and you end up with bags and bags of garbage, which we used to drop at Boston Bar and other stops, and all the passengers could see all this garbage. A couple of times, the garbage man hadn't come and the garbage would still be there from the day before and, even worse, animals had gotten into it. So we decided to invest in blue trays, because at least we could reuse them and it was better environmentally and also cheaper. You had to count the trays, otherwise the caterer would phone up and say they'd run out and you'd be running around to find out who had some.

The staff thought this was very funny, but it really wasn't. I became obsessed with this. One day in the office, I got a letter from this "concerned citizen" who had seen one of the staff throw this blue tray off the train and was very upset because it was such an environmentally beautiful area and why were they destroying it? Well, I never said anything to anybody, I just stored it away, and then I started getting other little jokes played on me about these blue trays. I wasn't biting, and finally it all came out that the staff had been torturing me about the trays. And that sort of thing built the camaraderie and the teamwork.

In the first year, people would show up at the train station and think that they could bring all their luggage on board and put it in their car. But it all went to the baggage car and they didn't have carry-on bags, so we invented these little blue nylon bags. And you would see people in the train station in Vancouver or Calgary re-packing their luggage, opening everything up and taking out what they needed overnight in Kamloops—it was chaos.

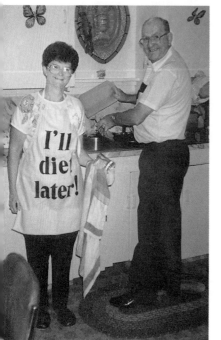

Flo and Doug Smith

DOUG AND FLO

In Kamloops the guests and onboard atten-dants arrived to the warm, welcoming arms of Doug and Florence Smith. Doug had started on the railroad as a dishwasher with CN out of Halifax in 1943, working his way up to dining-car steward in Vancouver, conductor and fi-nally service manager for the newly created VIA Rail. After he retired in 1982, he and his wife, Flo, opened a 40-seat café in Kamloops. Six years later, when VIA inaugu-rated its Canadian Rockies by Daylight service, the couple oversaw the train's overnight stop in the city. ("I knew that one person couldn't do what was expected," says Flo, who went on the VIA payroll in the second year.) They thought they were out of a job when Peter took over the service in 1990—and then they got a call from Arnold Sturgeon.

FLO SMITH: We never dreamed that they would want us, but Arnold phoned Dougie and Dougie accepted. Anyway, I was thinking about it all that evening and we got in bed and I said, "You know, I think we're really foolish to accept that job. All that work that we do . . ." You had to get up at 4 o'clock in the morning to get down to the station by 5, there's not much money for us, and it takes away your summer. And VIA had told us that we were going to be getting a nice increase. "All right," he said, "I'll phone him." But he got me to phone Arnold. (That's a common thing in this family.) Peter was quite uptight and phoned and wanted to know why we didn't want to work for him. He has never let me forget it. We didn't get an increase, but Peter said he would give us each a bonus at the end of the season. They had a rough first year and it took some time to get our bonus, but we got it.

DOUG SMITH: It's one of the best things that ever happened to us. . . . Our son was the first engineer to bring the *Rocky Mountaineer* into Kamloops. Peter and Greg were on the engine; Greg got on at Boston Bar.

FLO: This was just like another family to us. We have eight children of our own and we call the people from the train our extended family, because they treated us like parents. We had a little house on Battle Street and a beautiful yard.

JUDY THOMSON: Every year they would throw two parties—for the two crews—with the barbecue in their nice big backyard, and we'd sit down and have a real home-cooked meal. It was just so relaxing; there was no one else around. Doug would collect all the empty pop cans off the train and take them back to get money for our party fund.

SUE VELASQUEZ, one of the Smiths' children, who would go on to work with her parents: My dad was famous with the crew for his cabbage rolls and my mom for her Sex in the Pan dessert: it's a pudding/whipping cream/marshmallows sweet dessert.

FLO: One time I made 10 different Chinese-food dishes. They were always so appreciative, and after we finished eating, we had more fun standing in line to take turns to do the dishes in our little kitchen because I didn't have a dishwasher. . . . A number of times we had to take one of the crew to the hospital and then bring them back home here. And even passengers: I've spent lots of hours in the hospital with them for emergencies when they got hurt or took sick on the train.

DOUG: Or took them to the dentist. Got prescriptions filled.

FLO: Sent their false teeth to them when they forgot them at the hotel.

DOUG: And one August day when it was hot—106 [Fahrenheit] up here—Peter phoned and said, "Doug, can you get 400 ice-cream bars and take them to Savona, between Kamloops and Merritt?" I got them there with dry ice.

JUDY THOMSON: Guests would get to their hotel in Kamloops and ask when their luggage was coming and we'd tell them it *wasn't* coming [it was kept on board the train overnight]. "Well, I have nothing to wear and nothing to use—no one told me I wasn't getting my luggage." So taking a little baggage tag with a number on it, we'd have to go back to the train. Doug and Flo and Gary [Gervais] did this a lot: search through all the luggage and find the passenger's bag and take it to the hotel.

DOUG: One time a guy was standing around in Kamloops and was told three times that the train was going to go without him. He said, "Oh, they'll wait." He missed the train and then demanded that a helicopter fly him to Jasper. I said, "We're not flying no helicopter to Jasper"—but in the end they flew him to Blue River to meet the train. Then we had a writer from Australia we couldn't get out of bed, and I had to drive her an hour and a half to Salmon Arm to catch the train.

The Smiths soon were overseeing everything to do with the *Mountaineer* in Kamloops, from cleaning it to storing and distributing souvenirs to stocking the train with liquor.

DOUG: I had the liquor in our house—$6,000 worth of liquor under our roof.

FLO: We had no storeroom. We couldn't sleep some nights, we were so scared with all this liquor in our closet.

DOUG: I went to work and barred up that there room where I had all this liquor with four-by-eights.

FLO: The second year, Rob [Hamilton] says, "You guys, I'm not going to put you through that again," so they got a room in the station for the liquor. . . .

If we did something special, then the next trip I would get a bouquet of flowers. One time Rob and Judy phoned and said, "That was a rough trip. We want to take you out for dinner." We said we weren't really restaurant-type people, but . . . Rob used to come up and use my fax machine, and when the train came in this day, he said, "Can I go and do that now? You go and meet Judy at the hotel." Doug and I were sitting in our car waiting for her and she was being so slow. Finally she came out and said, "Rob is ready—we can go and get him now." We come back to our house and he has it all decorated: the table set for a meal, he has gone out and bought wine glasses, and it was another celebration. Everything we did, we got treated royally.

MARKETING THE MOUNTAINEER—GUERRILLA-STYLE
From the start, the new company had a minimum of funds to market the *Rocky Mountaineer*. Back in April 1990, Rick Antonson had still been in Edmonton, winding up his work with the Tourism Authority, when he began making plans to promote the newly privatized rail service.

RICK ANTONSON: I asked Peter, "Can you fax me up a list of the operators from the previous owners?" He sent it. So I phoned Peter back and said, "Can you refax it? Only one page came through."

He said, "You got the list." It had maybe a dozen names on it.

Within a year, we had set up 150 tour operators around the world that we were dealing with, going into our second season. General sales agents around the world. We had to track down agents, go and research all of that or find it in brochures. None of it was provided to us. We had to literally build that without any guidance as to VIA's contacts.

When I moved into Vancouver in July, they didn't have enough room downtown at the corner of Hornby and Pender. Peter had an office, there was a boardroom, Rob Hamilton was there, Judy and a few others. So CP Hotels had regional sales offices right across the street and we moved in there. First day in the office, I've got a pile about 16 inches high, no exaggeration—correspondence, everything—and there's a note on top from Peter: "Would you please phone Thomas Cook, the major British tour operator, and talk to them about selling us?" Thirty minutes later and I'm still rifling through stuff and making piles and trying to make phone calls. I'm down about six inches and there's another note in the pile that says, "Have you called Thomas Cook yet?" And then I get down about another six inches and it's an hour later and there's another note: "What did Thomas Cook say?" That's Peter.

I can remember Peter meeting me outside one day and he asked me, "What do we know about such-and-such a tour?"

I said, "Nothing, as far as I know. Why do you ask?"

He said, "I found this yesterday morning when the train left," and he pulls out of his pocket—and it's still wet because it was a rainy day and he'd been carrying it around now for 24 hours—this crumpled, wet baggage tag that has the name of a tour operator.

I said, "Where did you find that?"

"Well, I found it at the train station after VIA's train left. I was just walking over there along the tracks. Do we deal with these people? Could you phone them and find out?"

So we phoned them—they were from Ireland or somewhere, currently riding with VIA Rail—and they booked with us the next year. The tag just happened to blow off somebody's baggage, but Peter found it walking along the train tracks—pushing back the frontiers of market research, picking through the garbage. It was a lead. . . .

I would say the atmosphere was one of rapidly falling expectations—in terms of what would come from existing sources. So the atmosphere quickly went from one of concentrating on operating an efficient service to one of "we are in peril because the numbers aren't going to be there." It was the equivalent of climbing the mountain by day, sleeping on the mountain at night, waking up and looking down and saying, "Oh my goodness, I'm up here!" and climbing the next day and sleeping again. That was the learning curve. It was vertical—straight up. We were trying to patch it together. We'd put together terms and conditions for the tour operators, what were we offering, contracts—which of course were quite different in different European and Southeast Asian countries.

We were well into the first fall before we knew what the actual schedule was going to be for the next year, which would then complicate things because we needed that to go out with our contracts, with our tour operators. In September Doug Fyfe of Tourism Canada wanted somebody from the private sector to go along for a week in London and a week in Paris with the media. I walked into Thomas Cook in Peterborough, England, for a presentation, and they were livid with a guy named Sam Blyth, who had offered this luxury train trip across Canada and had just cancelled it. Thomas Cook had a two-page spread in their publications on the Sam Blyth thing. It was at press when we went in to talk to them. The first copies actually got brought into the meeting we were in; they'd found out too late to cancel. I said, "Well, what if we do something now?" So we got

No job too small: President Peter humps baggage for Rob Hamilton's parents.

talking about a two-page piece, inserted while the magazines were being printed. We got a deal, right there and then, for $10,000. I phoned Cathy Hann in our office, who got the graphics from our next available brochure. Got it all done and hot-couriered it over to them on an overnight to Peterborough. They stopped the shrink-wrapping of the publication, put the insert on the press, and printed about 100,000 of these; inserted them, and then shrink-wrapped the magazines and sent them out. They agreed to do what became a seven- or eight-page feature in the Thomas Cook travel magazine. All out of this one meeting—literally, in 15 minutes.

I also went to Saga Holidays, a big company in Folkestone, southern England, and they were very interested in the trip. This is now fall and all their literature has to be out, because the Brits get this stuff over the Christmas holidays and then start booking. I talked about getting someone to get on the phone to all these people, and Peter's suggestion was Murray Atherton. I just wonder where the company would have been without Murray. I mean, he would wake up at 4 a.m. and have a great time phoning a whole bunch of people in England. He cut a lot of contracts for the second year.

The enthusiastic, experienced Murray Atherton had been sales director for Delta Hotels when a much-younger Peter, then a Hotel Vancouver doorman, had his first business lunch to get Murray's advice about starting a tour-bus business. Murray later worked for Peter at Gray Line as manager of sightseeing sales. In 1990 he had his own hospitality consulting firm and taught hotel marketing and sales at Vancouver Community College.

MURRAY ATHERTON: I would get up at 2 in the morning and start phoning tour companies in the United Kingdom—nobody else was crazy enough to do this. The majority thought I was talking about VIA Rail; they had no idea if it was a two-hour dinner train or whatever. They would say, "It's just too expensive. It would make so much of a difference to our package price, we can't afford to." Or "A train? What a concept! Wow! The train tracks were there first, before the highway—maybe we should try that." Over the telephone, you just paint the dream, paint the picture with the quality of service and the fact that it would give their tour escorts an opportunity to sit down with the clients for two days. They wouldn't have to worry about commentary or anything else. It really worked.

RICK ANTONSON: The other thing was that the Tourism Canada folks had been doing videos of the PATA Travel Mart and the PATA conferences and had a lot of video footage of the train trip, which they'd used as a three-minute clip at the closing banquet. We must have had about 200 copies of that into distribution. We hit the ground running with modest literature, very strong media attention and a first-rate video we could use. It was door-knocking, shoe leather, phone calls. And an unnoticed weapon—because she left after a couple of years—was Cathy Holler (Cathy Hann then). She had tremendous experience and wonderful contacts for her work on tourism marketing. She helped us to set up some direct links into the marketing. Helped us set up with some airline promotions. Got us together with Canadian Airlines and shaped the agreement. She knew a lot of people in the U.S. and that market's huge now, but all the early spadework was Cathy's.

ONE DARN CRISIS AFTER ANOTHER

Cathy Hann had been one of the employees who came along with a travel agency that Peter bought, primarily to get its computerized reservation system for the *Rocky Mountaineer*. In scrambling to set up a company overnight, he had acquired Great Escape Vacations of Richmond, B.C., which had a hotel booking system called Resorts. Its inappropriateness for a rail service quickly became apparent.

RICK ANTONSON: Resorts was so terrible. Certain parts of it did not talk to others and, when they did, they seemed to send damaging pieces of information. You had to print out a two-hour report to get the last page of numbers—every night, somebody had to stay late to print them.

MICHELE DE RAPPARD, who had worked on the Calgary '88 Olympics for the Alberta government, was one of the employees who came along with the reservations system: It was very scary. There were times we were sitting in the computer room and had to run report after report on passenger volume within the next week and they never added up—the computer would double-count. We had groups show up at the train station that we didn't have on any manifest because the PNRS [passenger name records] from VIA wouldn't have them listed. It was a nightmare.

RICK ANTONSON: The first half-dozen departures, there was no seat assignment. Given the demographics of the market then, you can well appreciate that with a five-car train, you open the gates and it was like the Seniors' Olympics as they're going down there at varying speeds. [The company quickly learned its lesson and began preassigning specific seats in each coach.]

MICHELE DE RAPPARD soon left the reservations department to work as a coordinator of international sales, liaising with 10 general sales agents in other countries: I travelled in Canada, the U.S., and went to the World Travel Mart in England with Rick. People in the U.S., especially travel agents, would constantly walk up and say, "Oh, the *Colorado* Rockies?" In Canada, we did a show at the Calgary Corral. The reaction I got was either very bitter, from people whose fathers had worked on the railroad—and thought there was no real cross-Canada train travel any more—or people literally saying there are no passenger trains in Canada at all; they saw it on the news. And I'd say, "Yeah, we go right by the Calgary Tower." (Did they think I faked the picture of the train?) And that was in our own backyard, which has always been our toughest sell. Our "groups" then were basically 30 people who took two-day rail. Now we have a full customized group department that does seven- and 10-day tours, incentive tours with special dinners, the whole bit. At that time, if people asked for even a hotel outside the two days, we would refer them to somebody like Brewster's [the transportation and tour company based in Banff, Alberta] and give away the business. We had no computer or costing systems to deal with that package revenue.

RICK ANTONSON: In crisis management, make sure you have a crisis—and we had a crisis. The crisis was that there had been substantial media attention around the supposed demise of the train service from Vancouver to Toronto—based on a PBS show called *Last Train Across Canada*. It featured the last transcontinental on the southern route and talked as though train travel no longer existed. This wreaked havoc, both for us and for VIA Rail. There was just so much media attention around the lack of train travel. We did a lot of media trips, but we were also very aware that it was 100-and-some-odd bucks, net cost, to have people on the train—and that came out of the marketing budget. You could sit there and watch the budget evaporate. That said, Peter was very encouraging to get the media on board. At a trade show in the States, I can remember arguing with one woman travel agent who told me that the trains no longer travelled in Canada. Absolutely convinced because people had seen it on not just PBS, but Tom Brokaw on the evening news said, "Today is the day the last passenger train runs . . ."

Fortunately, the Rocky Mountaineer had a secret weapon in the American market to counter all the misleading information: Mike Leone, a public-relations specialist based in Los Angeles who had handled American media relations so well for the Vancouver world's fair, Expo 86.

RICK ANTONSON: Of course, you have to spend the money to advertise to the individual travellers who were going to come out of the U.S. But tapping into those markets required budget. Peter had an inspired idea. Just before I had arrived, a guy named Mike Leone walked in to see Peter through a mutual connection and talked about doing some public relations for him. This is Peter, the trusting; Peter, the immediate; Peter, the impatient. Peter gave Mike the business plan and said, "Go away and read this and come back." Mike came back after lunch and said, "I think we can work together." The amount of media exposure that his company, Leone and Leone, generated that first year in the American papers was probably the daily sliver of hope we had. And a huge contribution to the word of mouth—the buzz—that is the number one marketing vehicle. Leone just powered that stuff all across the U.S.

MURRAY ATHERTON: Mike has been part of the company since 1990 and has done an amazing job on showing us how to develop the press releases, how to get into the face of travel writers and editors. Every year, he and Peter go to New York and make personal sales calls and public-relations calls on the major magazines.

DERAILED

At 6:30 a.m. on Friday, September 21, 1990, a six-car CN freight train travelling at 17 miles an hour went through a switch that had been left open on the track in a Kamloops-area CN rail yard and collided with the stationary Rocky Mountaineer. It derailed two passenger coaches, causing an estimated $300,000 in damage. As the federal Transportation Safety Board noted, "13 minor injuries resulted from the collision, including 12 onboard service personnel on the passenger equipment and one to the yard helper on the yard assignment." But in human terms, the derailment was much more dramatic than the measured tone the "railway occurrence brief" suggested. Peter was at home in the shower when his wife, Wendy, handed him the phone. "I knew it was trouble," he recalls.

JUDY THOMSON: I was on the train. In fact, I don't think my back has ever been the same as a result of that. I was in the vestibule area and it was the strangest experience. One minute I was standing there talking to Gary Gervais, the onboard mechanical guy, and the next minute I was on my back upside down in total darkness. You think an earthquake had happened. And we didn't even get hit that hard. Everybody was stocking up and getting their fridges filled and unloading all their meals that had just been delivered. Just staff—no passengers, thank goodness. A fridge came down on Erin Manahan [she suffered a hip injury and minor burns from spilled coffee]. Things just came crashing down, there was food everywhere, and everything was smashed.

Kamloops, B.C., the overnight stop for the Mountaineer, *is set amid arid, rolling hills between the Rockies and the Coast Mountains.*

HENRY NEWMAN: Erin got blocked in her galley because the door fell off its track and she couldn't open it. Tracey Whiting, her aunt (she was just a couple of years older), came running back to my car. I had just opened my fridge door and all the cans of pop had come out and hit me in the face. My glasses fell down and one lens popped out. It's dark now because all of the power is out, and I'm looking for my lens, and Tracy was nearly frantic. I was able to grab hold of the door and move it out of the way and get Erin out. Then she just kind of collapsed in fear.

CHRIS MURPHY: I was sitting having coffee with Mark McChesney right behind the engine. There was a seat in front of us and when the train hit, I went over the seat. I saw what I thought to be smoke coming out of the electrical panel (it turned out it was dust). I thought the world was coming to an end and ran off the train screaming. I am so embarrassed, to this day. Mark ran up behind me and grabbed me by the waist and my legs were still going; I was Coquihalla-bound. It took a long time to finally settle down and figure out, but the attendants started coming off slowly after that. Some were pinned, and one fellow, Ian Buchanan, had some type of first-aid training and had the sense to get back and look for people. But we were very ill equipped. Now we receive incredible first-aid training.

After it happened, we were all sitting on the platform with our legs right on the curb of the platform and then the Scotch started coming off, which now we know is the worst thing you can do when people are in shock. We were all drinking Scotch, wrapped in blankets, and of course the reporters were there within seconds. So Judy had to deal with that and it was horrific—but a real wake-up call.

FLO SMITH: I was walking through the train to give Judy some information and when it hit, I was thrown—my glasses went and I was all bruised on my left arm and the back of my head. I was quite shook up and, of course, scared to death that somebody else was going to be hurt.

JUDY THOMSON: Everybody went to the hospital, but no one was seriously injured. More than anything, we were just so shaken up. So then the fun began, going around to all the hotels to pick up all 320 passengers as Doug and Flo and various other people reorganized and got buses to take them down to Vancouver.

CHRIS MURPHY: Then we were all taken to Doug and Flo's home, one of those tiny wartime houses with little fruit trees in the backyard.

We all piled in there, and Doug and Flo were amazing. It was all pampering, and Doug was very comfortable and very charismatic with the crew. Rob [Hamilton] flew in and was so shook up when he saw all of us that there were tears in his eyes. I remember being so moved; I knew he cared, but he took it seriously. We were in such a state of shock, I think that all of us got drunk and sober and drunk and sober and ate and slept three or four times that day. And then we flew home the same day and about eight or nine o'clock at night, there's a knock on my door and it's Peter Armstrong. "Are you okay?" I had worked for VIA, which is like some ominous grey cloud, and here I know Peter's wife, his kids, his best friend and Judy, there's this huge undertaking and then this big disaster—and all of this heartfelt stuff going around. It was really amazing.

The derailment was a warning bell to the company. In the following years, Great Canadian would focus on training staff for such eventualities, making safety a top priority in its extensive annual training program for new and returning employees.

THE SEPTEMBER SURPRISE

Come September 1990, any cash flow had ended, and there were heavy losses showing on the bottom line. "We needed something like 19,000 or 20,000 passengers," Peter says. "VIA had committed to turn over about 16,800 and we thought we could easily sell 2,000 on our own. They actually turned over 7,800 and we sold another 3,520—for a total of a little over 11,320 passengers." After the unexpected PATA trip, this was the second of the surprises with which the Crown railway had ambushed its rival. During the bidding process the year before, Peter's colleagues—communications consultant Jess Ketchum and lawyer George Hungerford—had warned him about depending on VIA's promise of passenger bookings.

JESS KETCHUM: Peter was accepting the numbers given to us by the government and VIA Rail on the previous operation of the *Rocky Mountaineer*. But all sales and revenue had been suspended [as VIA turned over the railway service to the private sector]. And George and I were nervous about that and raised the validity of the numbers with Peter. Peter's attitude was: "This is our government we're dealing with—and if we can't trust the government, who can we trust?" Basically he assumed everyone was dealing with the same information—if you had confidence that the internal [Jackson] group didn't have the advantage in that respect. Which I always thought they did have.

CHRISTENA KEON-SIRSLY, VIA's director of marketing planning at the same time she was a member of Murray Jackson's investment group, remembers how she had warned her colleagues to heavily book the *Rocky Mountaineer* for the first season under private ownership: I did get involved when they were discussing how they were going to handle the inventory for the next year. I said to them, "You guys have to *overbook* because this is very important." That's part of the first-year problems of Peter. The service should have been overbooked and it wasn't.

The depressingly low passenger numbers left the new company in the financially embarrassing position of not being able to pay its suppliers, particularly all the hoteliers in Kamloops. Yet these were the very people with whom it had to negotiate the next season's accommodation rates. In corporate memory, this period is always referred to as "the September Surprise."

RICK ANTONSON: Now, Peter dealt with Michael Lambert at the Hotel Vancouver, the regional vice-president of CP Hotels, who believed from the start and showed it. Peter has a huge loyalty to CP Hotels, and a lot of people think it's the product, but much of it goes back to Michael Lambert believing and telling Calgary hotels, like the Palliser, and the ones in Banff and Jasper, that he trusted this would work out. In the fall, I went up to Kamloops just to explain how we wanted to work through the payment terms. The first season was over and we were trying to get all the hotel space booked for the coming year. At the same time, the hotels are saying, "Well, we'd like to do that, but by the way, you owe us— you're over the limit here." That complicated the discussions.

DAVE MORRISON, president and CEO of Brewster Transportation and Tours, based in Banff, which has been selling tour packages to the *Rocky Mountaineer* since its days as a VIA service: They took Rick Antonson on board and he was probably the prime mover in making it into a real marketing organization. Peter was running around worrying about the cash, but it was Rick who smoothed things over when they were slow paying their bills. Rick is a very good facilitator. When they weren't paying their bills, he'd come out and talk to the people and try to work out something that was reasonable. We did get paid, eventually—before December 31 that first year. Quite frankly, we always owed them money, too. We learned very quickly that because we would owe them more money than they owed us, that would keep them honest. . . . So we were a priority at that time.

AND BACK AT HOME . . .

Near the end of 1990, Mountain Vistas Railtour Services changed its corporate name to Great Canadian Railtour Company and then christened its western Canadian tour service Rocky Mountaineer Railtours. There was another change: Wendy Armstrong decided to retreat from the railway and, while Peter bulled on to solve the financial mess the company faced, his wife stayed at home to care for their three children.

GEORGE HUNGERFORD: Wendy did not have an awful lot of Peter's time. She just had to look after the home front. Peter was really under a lot of stress. But Peter is always going to be stressed, because that's the way he is. If there's a mountain, he will climb it, and if there's a swamp out there, then he will somehow find his way in and wade through it and come out the other side. This was a big unknown swamp. This had mine fields and, quite frankly, a lot of the first two years that I spent with Peter working on the *Rocky Mountaineer* was not law in the strictest sense—it was really political advice and just common sense.

WENDY ARMSTRONG: So the season ended and there was a huge party that Judy and I organized down at Granville Island. By that time I realized I was Mrs. Armstrong; I wasn't Wendy any more, and it was time for me to move on, because I had to be more the boss's wife than one of the gang. I did get involved one more time. Working from home, I helped coordinate the first-aid and emergency procedures for the train in the second season. After that I wasn't involved any more.

And now I ride on the dome service and it's really neat to know how it started, to appreciate all that's happened from then until now. I can relate to what the car attendants are going through, and I like keeping abreast of what's going on in the company. But I realized at the end of the first year that one Armstrong was enough. The party was over.

SIDE TRIP: THE PARTY ON WHEELS

THE FORMER WENDY ROBINSON had no idea what she was getting into when she married Peter Armstrong in 1979. During his decade with the Gray Line tour-bus company, she was busy teaching high school. But on April 16, 1990, she began a one-year career with the *Rocky Mountaineer* on the inaugural run, packed with the party-loving tourism officials of the Pacific Asia Travel Association.

WENDY ARMSTRONG: None of us [outside of the former VIA employees] had ever done this kind of work before, never even been a waitress. We met all these new people in this little office downtown and then went down to Black & Lee to rent tuxedos. They deadheaded the train and a car full of supplies to Edmonton. We did a little bit of training on the way up, so that's how we knew what a coffee maker looked like, this is a galley, this is where passengers sit, here's how you serve them, and a bit of history of the route. My sister and I would just look at each other and say, "This is neat—yeah, we're doing this all the time."

We stayed at the Hilton in Edmonton, where a professional hockey team was staying, and had a fancy dinner that night for all the people working on the train as well as those supporting Peter in the city. The next morning we had to get up at 4 and meet down in the lobby. We're all getting that early coffee, wearing our tuxedos with our little bags, totally exhausted but excited about the adventure ahead of us. And at that time, Peter was quite relaxed and fun about it all.

BILL ROMANIUK, the VIA veteran, worked the PATA trip on the same car as Wendy: For someone who was a schoolteacher, she did quite well. She was a little wary when the train moved around curves and applied the brakes. She was a bit bruised and beat up, because you lose your balance on a moving train.

WENDY: It takes a while to get your train legs, and we just worked our feet off. We all had stupid dress shoes on, not comfortable ones for walking all day on those lurching trains. We'd be stopped somewhere and all of a sudden Rob Hamilton's brother, Doug, would bring a part from under the train on a white-linen cloth, as if he was serving wine, and show us, "Yes, this is what's wrong with the train." And if the air conditioning wasn't working, the carman would open up the panel and tinker with it with a fork and we'd pretend it was working again.

PETER: We found out that the air-conditioning units hadn't been converted from winter to summer operation and all the switches were outside, so we had to fix them at Blue River. Doug Hamilton— who is an engineer and went on to be a finalist as a Canadian astronaut—had never seen a railcar in his life. But he brought along a few basic tools and a voltmeter in his briefcase. He was testing and repairing things as we went on.

WENDY: It was so bizarre—like a party on wheels. The passengers were drinking like fish, and we're going up and down the aisle with garbage bags collecting cans. You just don't do that, but in the end, who cared? These guys weren't going to remember anything about this trip.

In Kamloops there were a bunch of cowboys on horses with flags who met the train. One of the horses sprayed stuff from its nose all over Peter ["*slimed* him," as her sister, Kelly Robinson, reports]. It was just hilarious. Sometimes when Peter is totally relaxed, he'll get into a laughing fit and he won't stop—that was one of the times. In Kamloops that night, [onboard attendant] Liz Coppens was soaking her feet in a bucket of water, she was so exhausted. I think she was studying for accounting exams; she had her textbook with her, so she couldn't relax and get into it the way the rest of us did.

Sisters Kelly Robinson (left) and Wendy Armstrong all dressed up and with somewhere to go—"it was like a party on wheels."

KELLY ROBINSON was working in the adjoining car: The next morning, we knew enough not to serve so much coffee. They wanted their eye-openers right away. At the end of that day, some passengers got very angry because we had to close the bar half an hour out of Vancouver. The car was just jam-packed with upset people. We said they'd have little bars in their hotel rooms; they'd be able to carry on.

WENDY: The trip was a great success. We were all on the same level as the former VIA people—it wasn't them and us, more of a united front. It didn't matter that I was Peter's wife.

Working on the Railroad:

The Adventure of It All ¶ Chris Murphy, the young

veteran of VIA Rail, had found a happy new home as an onboard atten-

dant in the first season of the reborn *Rocky Mountaineer*. "Everyone who

worked at that time had a lot of heart and were trying very hard to

be very professional and very proud of what we were showing people,"

she says now. "The standard of service was developed in those early days

through such adversity. At first the food was not that great. The train

was quite often late. There was no heat. The air conditioning seldom

. . .

Left: The Mountaineer *carves its way through such dramatically named places as Suicide Gulch and Hell's Gate Canyon.*

worked—it was a nightmare a lot of the time. But the people who were attracted to this sort of job took a lot of pride in what they did and wanted guests to be happy and really extended themselves over very long days." Reflecting on what's kept her coming back year after year, she explains: "Nowhere else in my life can I meet people from everywhere and get the type of adulation I do. People absolutely adore you at the end of two days, and it's really, really fun. I imagine it's like being an actor on stage—it's that same exchange, that same dynamic."

During the first three years, a half-dozen vital figures appeared in the annals of Great Canadian Railtour, people who would still be linked with it at the end of the decade. They all have stories to tell about the camaraderie of what was still a small company. Yet few of the employees then knew the pitiful financial condition the railway was suffering. Thinking back, Peter Armstrong says, "In that first summer, we lost just shy of a million bucks. I was pretty scared. We knew we were in trouble and we immediately approached Glenn Munro to go out and raise money for us."

A CAPITAL VENTURE

Glenn Munro, who became a good friend of Peter's as well as an ongoing financial consultant, was then a partner in Canadian Western Capital of Vancouver. Within a couple of years he would form his own firm, CapitaLink. The train-loving grandson of former CN president Gordon Smith, Munro had ridden as a child with his grandfather in the cigar-and-Scotch ambience of a private railway car.

GLENN MUNRO: Bev Armstrong introduced Great Canadian Railtour to our firm. Peter was in big trouble; even he didn't understand how big. We were approached to raise $2.5 million of equity for the company. The challenge, of course, was to find someone out there who was more than just a custodian of dollars but also shared the romance, the vision. That was not easy. At the end of the day, we had only one potential investor, Vencap Equities of Edmonton. [Listed on the Alberta Stock Exchange, it was then Canada's largest venture-capital company, which the Alberta government had launched with a $200-million loan.] I was dealing with the president, Sandy Slator, but more specifically with Mike Phillips, an investment officer. They actually had another investment in a

Glenn Munro and his wife, Margaret.

railway, a guy that bought about 50 kilometres of track and was running grain down this spur line in the middle of the Prairies—as it turned out, a great success story, which recently sold for a huge profit. So Mike shared the vision.

Mike Phillips had been a partner in a company offering management and financial advice to about 70 retail petroleum businesses on Vancouver Island. He had later joined the venture-capital division of the Federal Business Development Bank in Vancouver and then Montreal. In 1984 he'd returned to the West to join Vencap as an investment manager in Edmonton and Calgary.

MIKE PHILLIPS: I had always loved trains. You know, you start with a Lionel set and then you grow out of it, but for the rest of your life you regret it. So there was I, the only venture capitalist in western Canada who loved trains as a kid and was looking for a serious upgrade opportunity. . . . Peter is not a train guy. It wasn't a fool and a fanatic who likes trains running this company; it was a guy who saw a train as a means to a tourism end.

Mike Phillips

PETER: And we were able to raise $2.5 million from Vencap. We started negotiating with them in the fall that year and continued right up to the following March. We were in pretty tough shape. We were hobbling through to the next winter and went to our creditors and negotiated terms to pay them off by next spring and, as cash came in, we paid them off and just eked forward.

TRYING TO TAKE CONTROL

Perry Panchmatia was the company's first controller. Kenya-born, a graduate of the University of British Columbia, the thirtyish chartered accountant had worked at Gray Line Tours after Peter's time there. He came to Great Canadian Railtours in January 1991 when Rob Hamilton was "stretched between operations and a bit of finance." Panchmatia soon found that the whole company was stretched.

PERRY PANCHMATIA: Peter is now pushing everybody to get the passenger counts up to 23,000. We're closer to about 16,500. It's an absolute disaster, an almost $3-million loss that second year—worse than the first. The money from the venture capitalists has all been eaten up. You have great plans to put the money in capital improvements. There's no more money. You have a further problem: you also owe suppliers some money. This is the October Surprise in 1991. It fell upon me, being the finance chair, to go to all the suppliers and basically negotiate a payment schedule. All the hoteliers in Vancouver, Kamloops and the Rocky Mountains—Banff, Jasper. I would come back from lunch and there'd be slips of 20 telephone calls to return. You definitely learned very quickly not to take things personally. I've heard almost all kinds of language, but one bus-company fellow was on for about 10, 15 minutes. I realized that it was important for him to keep on going on—not to hang up on him. I was proposing: "Look, I owe you the money, but I want to pay you when I can pay you." At first I think most of them fell off their chair. One hung up; a lot of them actually screamed and shouted. Some of them just couldn't believe it. What I had to do was stretch a month to almost the next season, almost May. We called them the Schedule C Bankers.

DAVE DEOL, who was then general manager of the Dome Motor Inn in Kamloops (now GM and a shareholder in the nearby Sundance Lodge): It hadn't been so bad the first year because it wasn't a huge amount. They gave us postdated cheques, dated monthly, in small amounts. The next year, it was everyone in the city, over $1.5 million outstanding. In the second year, Peter came to me and said he couldn't pay. We were owned by a corporation in Calgary and my guys there just flipped. I'd known Rick Antonson at Edmonton Tourism, and now I got on the phone to him: "This is BS, man. I'm going to get my head strung up here. We're a little hotel and we can't afford to finance."

I called a meeting at my hotel and said, "Number one, guys: we've got to keep this out of the media. We're all upset, we've all got owners to answer to, and no doubt we're going to get hung. But the other thing is: are we all believers in *Rocky Mountaineer*?" And everyone said yeah. I said, "Well, it's going to grow. (I don't think anybody thought it was going to grow this fast.) I've talked to Rick Antonson, who's definitely a little upset too, but he gave us his word that this isn't going to bounce on us. I talked to Peter and Perry several times. Let me negotiate with Peter to get interest paid." I came back from negotiating and the media had already started phoning. Those guys drank coffee in my coffee shop every morning. I told them, "It's just a rumour. We've all been paid." I lied to the media, because it would have crushed the *Rocky Mountaineer*. I had a lot of faith in the company.

PERRY PANCHMATIA: About the end of 1991, we were able to get CP to give us a loan. The most important commodity at that time was cash. It was like a Christmas gift from CP, as I call it: a commercial loan in January '92. We were not out of the woods. But once you get past the curve of January, February, money starts coming in.

Eric Belanger joined the company in spring 1992. Grandson of a CPR station master, he was raised in Montreal and kicked around as a ski guide in Switzerland and a tree planter on the West Coast before studying tourism management in Vancouver and badgering Rick Antonson and media manager Nora Weber for a job. He succeeded Nora the following year and would later become director of media and public relations.

ERIC BELANGER: We had a tiny office downtown, and when I joined I had no desk, no chair, no computer, nothing. I would set up in the mailroom or the lunchroom and carry all my files with me. Whenever someone was out of the office, I would slip in and take their chair and get my work done. They had me doing a lot of the clippings, returning calls from the media, sending out press kits. My second day on the job, this journalist shows up unannounced from a radio station up in the Fraser Valley, and it's lunchtime and everybody else is out of the office. He pulls me into a quiet room where we have a tape-recorded interview. He's all excited about the company and the fact that it's just privatized and starts asking me what my favourite part of the route was. I say, "Well, I really like the Jasper route"—and not having been on the train, I was sort of going out on a limb here.

Eric Belanger

He kind of stopped and said, "The *Jasper* route? You must be out of your mind. The most beautiful part is along the southern route, along the historical CP track."

The interview continued and he asks how long I've been with the company. "This is my second day." And that was the end of the interview; he pressed the stop button right away. Obviously he wanted to speak to someone a little bit more senior. . . .

One of the first things that I was asked to do as part of the launch of the season was to create a little fanfare at the station. It was always on a

Sunday morning, really early, and it's a struggle to get the media on a Sunday. So the idea was that I would dress up in an engineer's outfit and hand-deliver invitations to all of the local media to try to get them down here to see the train off. The little cap, the overalls—the Casey Jones look. Eventually I deliver one to Alan Daniels of the *Vancouver Sun*. Alan is a true journalist, a no-fuss, just-the-facts kind of guy. "Mr. Daniels, my name is Eric Belanger, and did you know that this Sunday is the launch of our third season and we would love to have you come down and visit us." And he stands up, towering over me, and says, "Do you know how much I have written about your goddamn train?"—and he walks away.

In the off-season of the third year, Judy Thomson arranged the move of Great Canadian Railtour from the crowded downtown Vancouver office to 6,500 square feet in a two-storey, flat-roof building across the street from the Park & Tilford mall, near the industrial area of North Vancouver. Owned by Rick Browning, Jim Houston and Bev Armstrong, the structure had been a warehouse as well as office space. As Rick Antonson remembers, "Nobody walked anywhere in those offices. You'd get run down in the reception area. A lot of decisions were hallway decisions. It was a terribly exciting time."

ERIC BELANGER: It had lots of room for expansion, but what first started out as our storage room became the mailroom and then somebody's office. My first office was in a former broom closet. There was so much development and we were adding people so quickly, by the end of our time there we were just sitting on top of each other. Rick would always get the Dickie Dee ice cream guys to come by, and he'd buy a round of ice creams for the shop—18 to 20 people—to celebrate things like surpassing the previous year's benchmark in passengers.

SERIOUS RESERVATIONS

Scott Remillard, a chartered accountant with an MBA, had started with Great Canadian on a temporary basis in June 1991 to reconcile bank statements. (As a student he'd sent his resumé to Sam Blyth of Toronto, whose company had hoped—fruitlessly, as it turned out—to run a luxury transcontinental train service.) Remillard was working with Liz Coppens, who after being one of the first onboard attendants was now in charge of the accounting department. ("She was working ridiculous hours," he says.) Their boss, Perry Panchmatia, was still wrestling with the Resorts computer program for booking reservations.

PERRY PANCHMATIA: It was a very, very unfriendly reservation system. Because our systems wouldn't work, we had to have highlighter parties—highlight certain colours for certain items for the passenger reservations. The whole reservations office would sit around the warehouse. We couldn't afford air conditioners, so we had fans with water coolers. It was phenomenally humid.

SCOTT REMILLARD: They couldn't get accurate reports out of the reservation system, just a big dump of information. It would be four or five people—including Michele de Rappard, Cathy Hann and Helen Cho, who's an important part of our history as manager of the reservations department for at least five years. They'd be yelling out passengers' names and using highlighters to mark them to make sure they didn't have duplicates. The computer was so unreliable. . . .

Sometimes there would be six people lined up outside Perry's office. He'd spend 45 minutes or so solving everybody's problems as they came in. Perry never lost his temper. He was a facilitator between all the departments—reservations, marketing, accounting and operations.

PERRY PANCHMATIA: In 1992 Rick, Christine Pfeiffer and I go to Oregon to see the Tech 7 reservations system, which was geared to tour companies as opposed to hotels. It was unanimous when the three of us came back that this is the one we should get. In November '92 I've got $4,000 sitting in our bank account, we're trying to make the payroll, I have a report about the new system, and Peter says, "Well, we might as well go for it." We were creative: we financed 100 percent of it.

THE EARL OF EVERYTHING

One of the early employees was Earl Simons, who had been with Delta Hotels for 17 years. Starting in Kamloops, he graduated from manning the front desk to accounting to the opening and renovating of hotels (including Winnipeg's Marlborough, where he worked with Murray Atherton). He was general manager of Vancouver's Hotel Georgia in 1983 when he met Peter, who was promoting Gray Line at the time. "There's Peter Armstrong giving a speech to all my staff about his business and how they could win an ounce of gold if they sold his packages," Simons recalls. "I threw him out of there. But that was how he was successful: he was just everywhere, all the time." In 1992 Peter asked him to do a consulting job for the *Rocky Mountaineer*.

EARL SIMONS: I came in for about a six-week project with him, figuring out some of the VIA bills. They were just raking him. One season, for example, they charged him $10,000 to change light bulbs. So I asked him, "How did you get into this?"

He said, "Well, we put the company together in seven weeks, you know."

"Well, there's your first mistake." The contracts that they signed were unbelievable—very onerous.

PETER: The first year, I'd gone to VIA Rail and told them about our problems and they gave me some modest concessions. They said, "This is it, this is all we're going to do for you. But as part of that, you have to remove your right to cherry-pick those things you buy from us; you just have to buy everything from us." Because on their schedule for maintenance services, the labour cost was very low but other parts were very high—and they had it blended, thinking that I would take everything. But I was getting to buy things a little cheaper elsewhere. And Jim Roche, who was the executive VP of VIA at the time, said, "It's basically this way or the highway."

EARL SIMONS: Peter and I started a very slow process of going through every single contract. We got a lot of support from CN and CP, but it was VIA that killed us. When I came in as vice-president of special projects in November of '92, one of my jobs was to get several cars fixed that had been hit when that freight train backed into the *Mountaineer* in Kamloops in September 1990. VIA still hadn't fixed them yet, so Peter was running short of cars. I found out what had to be done and we just got it rolling. I then realized from my previous study how much VIA was charging. I said, "Peter, you can't afford to do this. Let's move everything to Kamloops." We talked CN into letting us use the Lorne Street station there. We parked all the equipment there, and that's where I started the renovations to the equipment, the painting of the cars, the interior renovations. We didn't have a lot of money, so it was, "Okay, what looks worst?" and we would get that fixed. We didn't go into debt doing anything.

In Kamloops we hired some of the Indian band people on a training program at a cheaper rate because they were learning a craft. They were incredibly helpful and resourceful doing the renovations to the car over the winter period. That's when we hired Rick Magill as chief mechanical officer; he came from BC Rail and CN Rail. Rick is the kind of guy who wouldn't ask anybody else to do the job—to his own detriment, because he would get so exhausted. We'd have to chase him away for a few days.

The first year, we didn't have offices in Kamloops—we didn't have washrooms. We're working with these native people who have never done renovations to a car. It was fun, though, because everybody really wanted to do it. We had a baggage car that we'd use for an office because it was 30 below outside. It was snowing and it was miserable. Of course, I went up there from Vancouver and I had my boots and coat on and I was pretending that it's not cold at all—because if it's cold, I'd have to buy them an office. But they would run out for 20 minutes and do some work on the outside and then come back in to warm up. They absolutely loved it because there was that camaraderie. And if they needed a washroom, they had to walk across the CP tracks to one of the hotels. . . .

In the third season, when we first had the trains renovated in Kamloops, we brought them down to Vancouver and the VIA staff were there sweeping and cleaning. We'd bought pizza and everybody was cooperating and feeling really good. And then Peter decided he was going to give an interview to the *Vancouver Sun* about VIA's transcontinental route and VIA in general. Now, we had worked until four o'clock in the morning and were coming back at seven. Then the paper comes out that morning with a headline like "VIA OUT OF CONTROL." When we started to work again, we noticed that all the VIA people were very standoffish, and we couldn't figure out what the hell had happened. When I finally found out, I drove over to North Vancouver, just madder than hell. Peter and I were in my office and had a big shouting match. Peter is six foot four, almost twice my size. I had a washroom for an office and here is this big guy standing at the door and he is not going to let me get out and I'm saying, "*Let me out!*"

PETER: I admitted to him I'd screwed up. I had hampered his efforts to get the fleet ready—my comments to the press were definitely made at the wrong moment! He and I are both dynamic individuals and we shouldn't have been so upset, but the circumstances had pushed us there. In the end, we both went on to do some of our best work.

Earl Simons's duties in those hectic early years included working on the trains along with other staff when the company was short-handed. He would play many roles, from baggage handler to train manager. "We all had our full-time jobs," he remembers, "but then we had to rotate on the train for four days, and you don't get any sleep when you're managing it."

SIMONS: I was exhausted after six back-to-back trips to Jasper. I got in to Kamloops, where the train joins to Vancouver. Judy had been on the Calgary portion, so she was in charge of the train. When we got to Boston Bar, to wake myself up a bit I got off the train and was just walking around by the locomotive. Then I turned around and everybody was on board and the conductor was way down at the other end waving. I waved back and he thought I was in charge of the train and just decided to let it go. Meanwhile, Judy was on the phone in the station phoning information in to Vancouver. A guy said, "Hey, your train is leaving!" She said, "No, it can't—I'm in charge of it." Then she started yelling on the radio: *Stop the train!* And I couldn't figure out why they had stopped the train, because I was back in my baggage car. She was madder than hell

Peter and Earl Simons in a less-than-sylvan setting.

and the CN conductor radioed ahead: "Tell Earl to go hide." So I went up and sat in the locomotive for a good hour and, when I figured she had calmed down enough, came back and took my medicine. . . .

We would get a little goofy because we were so tired. To make things interesting, we had a Stoney Creek Bridge contest. When we were overnighting in Calgary, I would pick up a bunch of balsa wood planes at a hobby shop. On the trip back to the Stoney Creek Bridge, which is a thousand-foot gap that we go over, all the guys on the train would make these planes, write their names on them, and hurl them out of the baggage car to see who could make it furthest down the valley. You could see for miles. We were doing this on a regular basis. (It was all biodegradable.) One weekend I picked up a red kite as well and we were off the back end of the train flying it. We were having a ball before it hit a tree just before the Stoney Creek Bridge—and then the conductors were upset: "Oh, we have to stop and get that kite." When I said to leave it, they said, "No, you don't understand: it's a red flag" [which can be interpreted as a train signal along the track]. So we stopped the train, got off, ran back, and got it real quick.

THE TRIP FROM HELL

EARL SIMONS: A man named John Kirkwood had a private car down in San Francisco. It took us months to negotiate with the railways to get it into Canada and hook it onto the back of ours for a trip. Peter was on board with me and so was a reporter. Whatever could go wrong on that trip did go wrong. We'd just pulled out of the VIA station when we had an electrical fire. (One of the VIA guys didn't hook the electrical properly and it sparked up to the diaphragm, which was just smouldering but looked like a fire.) I had just got word when Vicki's on the phone: "I hear you have a fire on board." Somebody had seen it and phoned her.

As we get to Boston Bar, I'm having lunch with Peter and the Kirkwood family in their gorgeous private car, all mahogany, and I'm wondering why we're sitting there so long. Rick Magill [the chief mechanical officer] said an undercutter—a piece of equipment that undercuts the track and then balances it—was stuck. We pulled out a little later but got about only 15 minutes down the track when we're stopped again. The undercutter is still stuck, so it was decided that we should back into

Boston Bar and let the passengers off. We told them we could be there from 15 minutes to three hours so please stay within earshot of the train. Boston Bar thought this was great because all of a sudden they've got 500 passengers in town—the ice cream man was going crazy and asking if we could do this all the time. Finally I'd herded everybody back on the train when I heard that a woman passenger had gone to a garage sale in Boston Bar and a black dog had bitten her in the butt. And now she wants us to find the dog and make sure that it doesn't have rabies. We had to phone the Boston Bar police, and it turned out the dog was okay. But of course this lady can't sit down and they've got ice on her butt.

Boston Bar, a stop on the Trip from Hell.

We keep moving, but we are now really late and Peter is getting a little antsy, because we had him on a flight back from Kamloops at 7 o'clock. He decided, "Well, I'm the president and I'm going to go around and talk to people."

PETER: It was the end of the season and I was concerned about the condition of the coaches (and I had lots of nervous energy), so I grabbed a cloth and a bottle of Windex—trying to demonstrate to the employees that there's no job beneath the president.

SIMONS: Every car that he goes in, he sprays the walls, then turns around and introduces himself: "I am Peter Armstrong, president of the company." All of a sudden, he's buying drinks for everybody because they've got to be happy. Meanwhile, we had this reporter on board who wanted to interview Peter. She was going to stay with the top tourism person in Kamloops, Lee Morris, but our train is late. She was getting a little ticked because she didn't know where she was staying. We finally got in and it was pitch-black and there were no lights, and these old buses with the old drivers were just screaming down to the train station to pick up the passengers. Peter was trying to organize all these people he'd bought drinks for on the train (so they're all loaded), and all they wanted to do is get to their hotel and get showered.

I dragged Peter away because he wanted to control everything: "No, we've got to get you to the airport." I didn't want him on the train the second day. In the cab to the airport, he called the tourist person on his cellphone to pick up the reporter, who was very upset with us and knew about the dog bite and everything else that was going on. She took the reporter to her place for the night. The next morning, we heard that the reporter arrived at her house and after she went into the kitchen to make some tea to calm her down, she came back and the reporter was naked. And the woman said, "I hope you don't mind me interviewing you in the nude; I normally do it this way." Lee has never forgiven us for that one!

Then the next morning we had a foreign photographer in jail and had to hold the train for him.

ERIC BELANGER: I used to spend the month of May on the train with journalists. This one foreign photographer was travelling with a writer and didn't understand English. In Kamloops he decided that he would go out drinking. I make sure all the journalists are put to bed, and then I go home and can sleep safely. The next morning I call a cab to go to the train station early, and when the driver finally shows up, I say, "How come you're so late?"

"Well, we had a bit of a problem with this fellow from on board the train who is down at the police station."

It was the photographer. He'd started waking up everybody in the hotel and tried to get his friends out of bed to go drinking with him. The police were called to the hotel and put him into the drunk tank because he was so obliterated. Nobody is aware of him being there except for me. We've got about 30 minutes to get on the train and they're saying, "Eric, if you can't control your journalists and they end up in the drunk tank, then we're not going to hold up the train for you."

I get on my horn to my assistant to get to the hotel, pack the photographer's clothes, bring all his stuff down to the police station. He was so totally drunk and didn't understand English. Here he is surrounded by these huge RCMP guys yelling at him—they think he's deaf—and the guy doesn't want to leave his cell because he doesn't know where he's going. Coming from where he lives, sometimes being behind bars is a safe place. So here they were pulling him by the legs and the waist and he was holding onto the bars. He had demanded that we contact his embassy, so I'm talking to the embassy, trying to get them to tell him to come with me. Meanwhile, the clock is ticking and I'm just starting to panic—and we get him on the train just in the nick of time.

Throughout the trials of the first three unprofitable years, a remarkable variety of people laboured long and hard to keep the *Rocky Mountaineer* on the rails—ranging from teenaged boys to single moms, from self-taught historians to accountants-turned-train managers. Even corporate presidents. Scott Remillard recalls: "One weekend I was working in the warehouse and Peter and his family showed up. His wife and kids came in and cleaned the office with him—*on the weekend*." Collectively, the anecdotes form a crazy quilt of memorable moments from the company's adolescence.

GAIL HEEZEN, who had worked at Gray Line Tours when Peter was a partner, joined Great Canadian Railtour in 1992 on a six-month contract and stayed for seven seasons, the first year in the sales department working with Rick Antonson: We loved Rick. He could start his own company and have instant staff. He's a real diplomat, sees the best in people, and encourages you with gentle nudging to do your best. Next to Peter, he is the second-biggest influence in my life in how to deal with people, personally and professionally. I used to have a picture of him on my desk when I moved to Res. People asked if my husband was jealous and I said, "No, my husband likes him as much as I do."

When I started, Rick sent me a letter saying, "It's really nice to have you here. We have no idea what you're going to do, but we'll deal with this on a weekly basis." The first thing I had to do was write down a list of every single place I could think of where a tourist would go in any of our destinations. I did presentations to tourism associations and hotels, seniors and trade shows for agents—even model-railway shows—in B.C. and Alberta. I learned a lot of Rick-isms, like "It's better to beg forgiveness than to ask for permission."

CHRIS MURPHY: We had a stowaway who got on in Kamloops one morning. He was going through the coaches and asking the attendants if he could buy a drink. And he would be told, "No, you have to go back to your own coach to buy a drink." Finally it started clicking with somebody: who is this guy and why is he walking around? He went into the galley and stole mickeys of rye and drank it in the bathroom. It took maybe two hours before we finally sorted it all out and found all the empty booze in the washroom.

(*Left to right*) *Lori Biglow, Petra Wagner, Judy Thomson, Christine Rowley, Tom Ballantyne, Christina Smith, Henry Newman, Tasha Enemark, Tracey Whiting, Bill Romaniuk, Anita Martin, Fawn Foster, Sandee Karbovszky, Tina Thomas, and Lina Nichol.*

GARY GERVAIS, the Kamloops-based carman: The worst thing that happened? At the beginning of the third season, we had to get all these different things done. We had to test all the compressors for the air conditioners and then they tell us, by the way, there are these five cars that they need up and running. We had to rip apart two bathrooms to put fridges and galleys in them, and they also wanted all the cars painted. It ended up that we were about a month and a half into the season and still painting certain cars. We found a place on Annacis Island [in Greater Vancouver] in a little gully between two buildings; one happened to be for Simmons Mattress. We had tarps up to stop the wind, but as soon as we started painting, the people in the buildings would smell it, so we had to go in at about 9 o'clock at night and work until about 6 in the morning, before they showed up. Then we had to keep all the fans going to blow all the smell out and we never had any power. They hired three guys to work on the train—none of them had ever done bodywork or painting. We spent a week showing them how. And I'm still trying to get all the other stuff done.

GEORGE HUNGERFORD: Our son Michael started working for the company as a jack of all trades. A problem developed because the luggage would go with the passengers on the train and then hopefully in Kamloops it would be available for overnighting there. But the VIA employees had to load it under the union contract onto the trains, and it was causing delays in departure time. Peter knew that the VIA brass were doing everything they could to sabotage. And if you miss your time slot on the rails, then your train arrives two to three hours late. Peter wanted his service to be something special and said, "This is not going to work—what we had better do is put all the baggage on a truck here in Vancouver at the train station, and the truck will then race up the valley and arrive at Kamloops before the train." Which is still being done today. But Peter had no one to drive his truck, and so the decision was taken at the executive level (such as it was) to rent this huge truck.

And I suppose they looked around the office to see who was available and our son Michael, who was 18, says, "Sure, that's fine." Rob Hamilton never asked if he had ever driven a truck; he just assumed he had. So Michael's mother goes crazy, especially when he comes home to pick up some overnight gear and she sees the truck parked in front of our house. She's on the phone to Peter, saying, "What are you doing with my son? You're putting him into this huge truck—he's never driven anything like this before in his life." His father was under a lot of pressure to intervene. But I didn't.

JUDY THOMSON: [In the second year] Lori Biglow, who worked in the office and eventually became an attendant, did a lot of research and writing for the onboard newspaper. We went to the archives and looked for pictures. And Henry [Newman] was involved making sure the details were right.

HENRY NEWMAN: One thing would always irk me. They would say, "Henry is our railway expert." Actually my main interest is history. I have about $150,000 worth of books—over 10,000 books. Even the book-cases in my bedroom are stacked two deep; there would probably be a good 500 right there. I used to take up to five crates of books on the trains with me: history guides, field guides to flowers, railway books. I have a photographic memory, so I could tell passengers: "Within the next eight miles we will be going through the Spiral Tunnels, of which the lower one is 3,255 feet in length. There's a 288-degree curve inside Cathedral Mountain, which is 10,464 feet high . . ."

JUDY THOMSON: We'd inherited golf shirts from VIA the first year. We knew nothing about the souvenir business but thought baseball caps would probably sell, and we tried sweatshirts one year and train whistles. We came up with about 15 souvenirs and then had to get our staff to sell them on board. Initially they weren't too keen, but we gave them commissions, and then they were eager to sell. We then got into selling bus transportation on board the train so that when people arrived in Vancouver, they could board a bus to their hotel. . . . The attendants hated cashing out as a group when they came in to the station. They would have their money everywhere—four of them huddled over, trying to reconcile one person's books. (They weren't accountants.) They sat on the steps of an ATCO trailer because they couldn't leave until they had handed in their cash.

MICHELE DE RAPPARD: In 1991 we had a fam [familiarization] tour for travel agents from Hong Kong. The worst thing was that we didn't have hot food then. At one point when we were boarding in Kamloops, they said they wanted to run across to a store to buy gum. "Wait a minute—we have to get on the buses" (the rickety old school buses that we had back then). But they all just deserted me and showed up with instant cup-a-soups and, on board, were asking for hot water.

HENRY NEWMAN: One of the carmen would smoke up in the baggage car, and on one trip he had a cigarette there and put it into a bucket. The bucket started on fire, and he threw it out of the baggage door and started a fire on the side of the tracks. The train stopped and Rob Hamilton—he was being our DOT [director of train]—and a bunch of us were grabbing water and fire extinguishers to put the fire out. We were frantic. Some of us were using bar glasses of water. We had tubs to carry pop that probably held a gallon of water, and Rob finally used that to put it out. All the passengers saw it and they were clapping their hands. Everybody thought we were great heroes for fighting this fire that we'd noticed on the side of the tracks. No one ever realized that it was set by our maintenance man in the baggage car.

GARY GERVAIS: We had a gentleman on one trip and his luggage was missing. So we went through the baggage car trying to find it, but it was gone and he was staying overnight in Kamloops. There are probably 500 people on the train with all their luggage, and we're going through every single bag trying to find this man's. It turns out that he is a retired Supreme Court judge—oh no, we have to find his luggage! He doesn't even have a toothbrush and he's going to Banff. The next day, we're still ripping out the baggage car and we can't find it anywhere. It's not in Vancouver and it never got sent to Jasper. And then Judy gets a phone call: the judge's son is looking for him—he just went missing.

"Well, what do you mean he went missing?"

"He just disappeared."

Apparently he was starting to suffer from Alzheimer's and was downtown by the Vancouver train station, saw the train, and decided he wanted to go on a train trip (with no luggage). He just walked into the station, bought a ticket, and got on. The son got thinking his dad liked trains and maybe he took a trip. And we were all panicky for two days trying to find this guy's luggage.

CHRIS MURPHY: One woman really pulled my heartstrings so badly that I was crying. She had MS [multiple sclerosis] and had a gentleman companion travelling with her who also had MS. She was so demanding of my time, and even the people around her were starting to notice that I couldn't get my work done. She was constantly asking me to sit with her and listen. She was quite articulate and interesting but completely unaware that I had 40 other guests to look after. I would go back to the smoking lounge and break down and cry because I didn't know how to make her aware of that. The only thing I could do was just try, and hope that everyone else around me understood. And they did—but she had that whole car in the palm of her hand. Even right at the end, she had the train manager, Gordon Sim, crying. She hugged him and said this was one of the most incredible things that had ever happened to her in her life—and so there we were, both bawling.

Seeing Light at Tunnel's End: The Big Breakthrough of '93

Approaching 1993, Great Canadian Railtour faced financial ruin. In rail-

road terms, the company was running out of steam as it chugged

through a long, dark, spiralling tunnel that seemed to have no end in

sight. After its third season of operation, the *Rocky Mountaineer* had lost a

further $2.4 million, following losses of about $2.9 million and $1 million

in the first two years. Perry Panchmatia sets the scene: "1992 was another

year of phenomenal disaster. Everybody is tapped out. The shareholders

. . .

Left: Engine 803 rounds into the Lower Spiral Tunnel.

are not willing to put in any more money." Peter Armstrong had to continue to deal with VIA Rail, paying for its expensive station services and train maintenance. He tried to win some concessions from the Crown railway, but it was playing hardball with him.

Meanwhile, Holland America's Westours division was talking with an American rail-tour operator about getting into the Rockies market with a rival daylight train service on the CP line, and the Toronto travel entrepreneur Sam Blyth was again actively promoting the idea of a luxury transcontinental train that would mean more competition for the *Mountaineer*. Although neither competitor would ultimately follow through, at the time they represented a real threat. Through 1992 and into the next year, Great Canadian Railtour could see no light at the end of the financial tunnel in which it was trapped.

OVERDUE BILLS AND BAILIFFS

SCOTT REMILLARD: We owed creditors over $800,000. I did a schedule where next year we could make $125,000 profit. Peter asked me, "Scott, would you invest in this company? Do you think we can turn around? Do you think we can make the $125,000?" and I said, "Yes, I think we can." Even before that, the bailiff was coming to take our leased phones, and Peter got so mad he slammed the door on our accounts payable person. Suddenly the bailiff got to the top of the list of the people we're going to pay. There was a time when Liz Coppens and I were phoning the government to see what priority wages had in bankruptcies. Every day we'd leave wondering if when we came in tomorrow there were going to be locks on the door. It's the biggest secret we ever kept; here we are talking to everyone else in the company as if things are normal. We never told a single soul.

PERRY PANCHMATIA: We were running out of money in September. We realize very quickly that if we don't start putting a game plan together, then we're going to lose whatever credibility we had. A telephone call wasn't going to be enough. We literally had to make a road trip to Kamloops, to Banff and Jasper. Christine Pfeiffer and I went out there to negotiate the payment schedule [with the hoteliers]. What was interesting is they had all met just before we got into the field and understood exactly who we were seeing and at what times. They'd already talked and wanted to have a concerted effort. They made some very strict requirements of us.

PREVIOUS PAGE: *The Mountaineer's westbound journey begins beneath the downtown Calgary Tower.*

INSET, PREVIOUS PAGE: *Banff National Park.*

RIGHT: *The Three Sisters—so-named because they look like a trio of nuns—rise almost 10,000 feet outside of Canmore, Alberta.*

Outbound on the Jasper
leg of the journey, guests
can view Mount Robson,
at almost 13,000 feet,
the highest peak in the
Canadian Rockies.

ABOVE: *Muleshoe lake near the Banff resort town.*
RIGHT: *The bi-level GoldLeaf Dome Coach offers a unique vantage point.*
OVERLEAF: *Crossing the 484-foot-wide, 325-foot-high Stoney Creek Bridge amid B.C.'s Selkirk Mountains.*

RIGHT: *The Thompson River runs through sagebrush country near Kamloops, B.C.*

ABOVE: *The Fraser River Canyon is famed for its plunging gorges and terrific rapids.*
LEFT: *Ottertail Creek, near Field, B.C.*

RIGHT: *The Mountaineer winds through the lush beauty of the Coast Mountains of B.C.*

OVERLEAF: *Journey's end, the port city of Vancouver, B.C., stunningly situated between the mountains and the Pacific Ocean.*

SCOTT REMILLARD: We dealt with seven, eight hotels in Kamloops and owed them hundreds of thousands of dollars. They knew Perry's itinerary ahead of time because they all got together and decided that they were going to be a force. [They knew] as soon as he booked a meeting and when. Poor guy. He'd tell them: "Hey, we're not paying you any more." The good part was that he'd say, "Okay, I'm going to pay interest and I'm giving you these postdated cheques." We never bounced a single cheque.

PERRY PANCHMATIA: If you talked to some people, they'd say my character was as hard as Teflon Plus in dealing with these situations. They thought I had two horns on my head because first, I had the gall to say that they are not going to get paid, and the second thing was I wanted to sit down and talk about next year's rates. They really thought I'd lost it.

DAVE DEOL, the Kamloops hotelier: Now, I've got to sell this to my owners' group in Calgary—who aren't happy. This is May and we still haven't got paid for last year. When I had to tell them on the phone, they just went nuts on me, screamed and hollered, flew me to Calgary to see what's going on. Then Peter actually met my group at Rendezvous Canada, the big travel trade show, in Calgary. Our CEO is Ed Holt, of Ormskirk Investments Limited, a branch of United Management, which is huge in Alberta. Ed says he's got to meet this guy from *Rocky Mountaineer*. I forewarned Peter that the CEO of my company would be there and "he sure as hell wants to meet you." Peter was cool, all charisma: "I want to thank you very much for your support. We know you're behind David in all of this." He sold it to my guys, who knew about the loan from Vencap. They started talking finance and I left the conversation—and they hit it off. The thing is, we all got paid, no matter what. It just took longer.

GETTING ON THE RADAR SCREEN

Two possible solutions presented themselves: to find more equity financing, which would be difficult to attract to a failing company, and to try to renegotiate the original agreement with VIA, an equally tricky ploy considering the political clout of that railway in Ottawa. Peter Armstrong decided to pursue both options.

RICK BROWNING, who rode shotgun for Peter on some of his visits to VIA Rail's headquarters in Montreal: Peter is not only figuring out how to run the company on vapours but also to get the national profile up and to fight the fight of all times. It was a business world that I didn't really understand. VIA was the most feudal example of Canadian business that I had ever come across. Peter never went with cap in hand and he treated all these guys as equals—which drove them nuts. This is not the Montreal that we know, Ste.-Catherine's in the pub. This is downtown Montreal, very establishment, there is lots of security, and we get ushered up to the executive vice-president's floor. We sit there cooling our heels for a while to show respect. Then we get ushered into this mammoth office and a valet comes out and offers us coffee and out comes our pal, Jim Roche. His office was half the floor. He has got access to a private railcar and travel in limousines and we're thinking, *This is taxpayers' money that supports this.*

Jim Roche would say something that was very inflammatory and Peter was right back at him. He didn't show the kind of deference that you would have typically thought from someone in his 30s in talking to a guy who obviously has some real power over him. And you see this guy doing the slow burn. I didn't think that this was the approach. It's fine to be a tough guy when you've got some of the cards in your hand, but we were trying to figure out how we were going to survive. I don't think any of those meetings did anything. I came out of that meeting with Jim Roche absolutely shaking my head and disgusted with the way that Canada worked.

GEORGE HUNGERFORD, Peter's legal counsel: In the first three years, I went to Ottawa with Peter a number of times. We communicated with all the parties—not just the government side. For the most part, it was an awareness campaign we conducted, trying to establish a comfort level so that all the politicians and the bureaucrats knew what this great initiative in the West was all about. Our motto was "Anybody who will listen to us, we'll tell the story."

JESS KETCHUM: The problem was the federal government, and the solution had to be the government. I engaged Jerry Lampert, who had been a friend of mine for years. We'd worked together when I was in Victoria and he was executive director of the Social Credit Party. He went back to Ottawa to be executive director of the Conservative Party, and now he was back in Vancouver with his own consulting firm. He had very solid connections in Ottawa and knowledge of the process. We went to Ottawa and created the recognition that there had been a mistake made—that for the *Rocky Mountaineer* to fail would be a serious failure for government, because this was the first privatization. And to have it fail because of misinformation provided to the buyer would have been catastrophic for the government. We had to get Ottawa to accept the case so they would move it forward to mediation.

PERRY PANCHMATIA: Signing those cheques for the consultants in Ottawa were the best dollars we ever paid.

PETER: Ramsey Withers at Industry-Government Relations, the former chief of the Canadian defence staff and a former deputy minister of transport under four ministers, was our political advisor in Ottawa.

GENERAL RAMSEY WITHERS: We were government-relations lobbyists. I suppose Peter was our smallest client. All the people that I reported to said, "How come you're putting so much effort into that for that fee?" It wasn't much of a fee. But it was good public policy. Now, people criticize lobbyists, saying that they are special-interest people. If you examine public policy, you'll find that almost every piece of legislation that has ended up as good public policy started as a special interest. We could see there was the possibility that a little guy like Peter would get marched over by the giant—namely VIA Rail. The thing is, it would be clearly good public policy to achieve some kind of privatization within the rail-passenger sector and have it be successful in the hope that it would promote others.

What we did was prepare a strategy, prepare an action plan for him. Obtain information, intelligence. Review his submissions, maybe do a little bit of writing for him. My rule always is the person that I want to put in front of ministers and officials is the CEO of the company, not a lobbyist. Peter presented well.

The most important person in Ottawa is the desk officer—you're now down about five levels from the top. That individual's mission is to know everything that he or she can possibly know about the policy area in which they are working. That person is the one who drafts briefing notes to everybody. That official, whose name will never be seen, passes it up the line to a director, director general, assistant deputy minister, deputy minister, the minister's office, into the minister's briefing book, answer in the House. That person has to be enormously accurate. I always say the best thing is write the briefing note for him.

Peter did the slogging. He was down here all the time. We would confer by telephone, almost on a daily basis. The thing is, quite frankly, officials like that kind of contact. They want to be kept informed, too. The other thing is that officials don't like a pest. It's very much a balancing act.

MAC NORRIS, who accompanied Peter on many of his trips east: This is where almost all of my time was spent in the next few years. We wanted to get some redress from VIA or get before a third party. We were not about to have a lawsuit. We would probably shoot ourselves if we did. We were meeting with [CN and VIA chairman Ron] Lawless all the time—and, of course, I had a real insight into Lawless. He would say that between companies there's nothing wrong with a lawsuit—you know, the courts can address that. And, of course, that was part of the scheme.

Now the thing that we had going for us was the fact that the Conservative government wanted the railway to succeed. It looked ideal for privatization. I guess over that period of time we must have seen almost every minister in Ottawa and the executive assistants of any importance.

David Aftergood of Calgary had worked for Prime Minister Brian Mulroney's office as the liaison with western Canada before becoming Transport Minister Benoit Bouchard's executive assistant. He was now assisting Charlie Mayer, the minister responsible for Western Economic Diversification, in Edmonton, where in 1989 he had met both Peter and Hugh Horner, the former Alberta deputy premier, who'd been lobbying for Murray Jackson during the bidding for the *Mountaineer*. Aftergood proved a sympathetic listener to Peter's current plight, taking Great Canadian's case to his minister and to Don Mazankowski, the former transport minister, who was then the deputy prime minister.

DAVID AFTERGOOD: I told Peter, "You didn't come into this business thinking it was political, that you'd have to deal at a politician's level. But that's what you're going to have to do. At this point now, you're dealing with competing interests that are much bigger than whether or not a train goes from Calgary to Vancouver. You're dealing with the very heart of whether VIA Rail stays in existence—at least, that's what *they* believe. If you're there to show them that you can run a profitable part of their network, then why in the world would the government continue to subsidize them? We're paying VIA $600 million [in subsidy] and they want to get back up to a billion and the good old days, and we want to get rid of them. And you've got good right-wing ministers in there." . . . This now becomes a wonderful western issue. We started introducing him to Maz, all the guys in Ottawa. Dave Allin was very helpful.

DAVE ALLIN, the Saskatchewan-born executive assistant to Don Mazankowski, recalls Peter coming to him with a sheaf of invoices from VIA that gave no detailed accounting of the high-priced services the Crown railway was providing the *Mountaineer*: I do recall having quite a heated discussion with Ron [Lawless] over the *Rocky Mountaineer*. I said in quite a loud voice: "Ron, if a mechanic gave me a bill like this for my car, I wouldn't pay the damn thing. You can't send out these empty invoices and just call it $40,000 for maintenance. First of all, Peter thinks the cost is atrocious, but you at least have to justify the work that was done." And in their minds, they didn't have to do that. . . .

It was a very arrogant attitude and I don't know if it was Lawless himself or another official who said, "It doesn't matter. They are not going to make it. You cannot run a profitable private-sector rail line in Canada— you cannot do it."

Before one meeting, I said to Mazankowski, "We need to straighten out this *Rocky Mountaineer* thing. I want to raise that with Ron after the meeting." As the meeting broke up, Maz turned to me and said, "Oh, Dave, is there something you wanted to raise with these guys?"

I said, "Well, it's the *Rocky Mountaineer*."

And Lawless said, "Oh, no, it's all worked out."

That's when Maz said, "I heard that and I will hold you to that."

Obviously, it was not all worked out.

MAC NORRIS: Peter and I couldn't accomplish it. Jim Houston had to go down, because Lawless did not want to give in to a 35-year-old lad. So Jim went down and Lawless said, "At last I have got a businessman here. We can make a deal." So I said to Jim, "Jeez, did you go to bed with him?"

JIM HOUSTON: Lawless couldn't quite handle Peter, because he was so young. And Lawless, of course, was the ultimate politician. . . . He was the president and CEO for eight or nine years and, several years into it, they did an internal management study which acknowledged that among the nine or 10 major railroads in North America, they were eighth or ninth in terms of almost every category of being badly managed. And his comment was, "Well, now that we know what's wrong, we are going to get things fixed."

RON LAWLESS, now the 75-year-old president of Bishop's University, reflects on his involvement in the process: Usually it was after Peter and [Jim] Roche couldn't agree on something. Peter had a contract with CN for track usage and a contract with VIA for services and other things. There seemed to be a constant battle with no clear understanding what the intent was, and unfortunately those battles went back and forth and usually they escalated. I found myself trying to defend VIA, of course, but trying to understand what the basic problem was. Several times it was a senior partner, Jim Houston, I met with, and we came to some agreements and settled some things. Sometimes the issues seemed trivial; other times it seemed Armstrong is going to go out of business unless— I was never sure whether he was playing trains or that he really was going to be able to make any commercial financial success of it. That comes back to my background, looking at passenger service, saying you can't make money in this business. . . .

Now have in mind that he was fighting an uphill battle with people inside the VIA organization. They lost their beautiful service. We made them give it away to Armstrong. So he was having a hell of a time with these guys.

MAC NORRIS: Here is the thing that we were up against: Lawless had been around Ottawa for so bloody long and nobody ever thought that there was anything wrong with him. He was absolutely confident that he could win in Ottawa any time—and for a long time this succeeded. But fortunately we had impressed this fellow with the minister of transport by the name of Greg McLean. He was the executive assistant to Jean Corbeil.

DAVID AFTERGOOD: I brought Greg in because the other people in Corbeil's office were [uninterested]. VIA Rail is a very powerful organization in Ottawa—maybe nowhere else on the friggin' globe. From that moment on, it was funny as heck because they're not as sophisticated as they like to think they are. You knew what moves VIA were going to take. They were so blatant about the fact that they hated Peter and it was just in their interest to get rid of him. So every move that they would pull was telegraphed. Roche made sure that [the issue] would keep coming back, wonderful guy that he is. That's why Peter needed to have constant attention. Ministers go from issue to issue; they need assistants who will follow up on the file. That's where Greg McLean became helpful.

MAC NORRIS: Somehow Greg McLean began to believe that we were sane. He helped like you would not believe and has all the guts in the world, because he had a very junior position and the political [assistant] was really pissed off at Greg. Now the political guy normally has the politician's ear more than the technical guy . . . so, anyway, Greg persevered.

Greg McLean of Edmonton, who had worked for federal Conservative minister Harvey André for several years, joined Jean Corbeil's office when the labour minister moved to transport. McLean coordinated three policy assistants specializing in marine, air and surface transportation. He had met Peter and believed his story about VIA's mishandling of the *Mountaineer*: As he recalled thinking, *I can see he is an honest man and I can see he is having difficulty now.*

Greg McLean

GREG MCLEAN: The new surface assistant in the office was a guy named Gerard McDonald. A good man, Gerard, but hired from within Transport and as a result had a different bent on a lot of issues than we had as a political office. So Gerard and I clashed conceptually on what should be done with this issue. I kept the issue alive at that point. There were some heated moments in our office, actually. . . .

There was a lot of double-billing going on. That was a main issue. Peter provided copies of the bills where he would get charged twice for the same section, and at one point VIA said, "If you don't pay the bills, you are shut down." That was when we said, "Ron Lawless will not shut this company down"— because the bills were in dispute.

"Well, they owe us X hundred thousand dollars."

"They dispute that amount. So let's see it through as opposed to shutting them down."

I told Hugh Porteous, their government-relations person, my main contact and always a gentleman: "I am telling you from this office that my boss does not want it done. My boss will call Ron Lawless tonight if you want, but I am telling you that you better plan to deliver those services tomorrow morning."

MAC NORRIS: There was one meeting in Montreal in particular when Peter got really angry and said something that he shouldn't have and I saw Lawless's eyes light up. So I said to Peter, "Come on outside. I want to talk to you." And I told him, "That's what he wanted you to say, and he's going to report back to Ottawa that you said that. Now go back in and get back to your original position." So he did, and we went back to Ottawa right away and said to McLean, "Here's the meeting we had, here's what was said, here's what Lawless is going to say." Just as night follows day, that is exactly what happened. Lawless walked in and didn't really tell what had gone on at the meeting. So they began to have some doubts about Mr. Lawless.

RON LAWLESS: I had a lot of sympathy for Peter because he was swimming upstream. I was constantly trying to mediate between my own guys and him. My own guys were right a lot of the times, but sometimes they weren't so right. It was a difficult chore. [But] when Peter decides to go around the process—the end run with the politicians—that's when he lost me.

GETTING TO YES, PART 1

During the ensuing negotiations, Greg McLean and surface-transportation assistant Gerard McDonald flew out to Vancouver one day in a bid to resolve the issue in a meeting with Peter and VIA officials, including Jean Patineaude, the Crown railway's legal counsel.

GREG MCLEAN: Jean Patineaude had explicitly laid out the VIA position—what was the truth and what wasn't the truth—and he was briefing the minister's office. Peter said something at one point when it didn't seem like we were getting anywhere: "Well, that's because of this." All of a sudden, Jean said something that directly contradicted what he had briefed us on, and I looked at Gerard and said, "We need to caucus right now." Gerard and I caucused and he said, "Yeah, I heard what you heard." It was the deciding moment in who was telling me the truth there and who was not telling the truth. That meeting where Jean Patineaude got caught offside provided us with the opportunity to push the issue to mediation—with no ifs, buts and maybes. Minister Corbeil had a meeting with Ron Lawless and told him that he would go to mediation.

PETER: And this was the most critical moment of our company.

First off, we had trouble even getting VIA to agree with the questions we were going to mediate. Finally we got our questions on the agenda. In July the mediation began at the International Commercial Arbitration Centre in Vancouver. The mediator, a lawyer named Donald Munroe, asks both sides if they have the authority to mediate. Both sides agree. Based on a Price Waterhouse impact study, we knew that to get out of the hole was going to take many years or a lot of money. We wanted a multi-million-dollar settlement for the misrepresentation [the fact that VIA Rail had turned over only 7,800 passengers to Peter Armstrong's company in the first season instead of the 16,800 the Crown railway had promised]. Being behind so dramatically in the number of passengers promised put the viability of the whole venture totally at risk. It would take over four to five years to correct the problem created by this shortfall. Each one of those years would have a huge loss while we built up the volume to a break-even point.

The fundamental issue was they did not provide the business that they said they were going to provide. Then VIA lied to the mediator in saying they had the authority to settle. They knew going in I was looking for $16.5 million. The mediator then said, "Peter, $16.5 million won't go—what's your best absolute price?" So we worked with our controller, all of our accounting staff, we did models, I got on the phone to my board. We were there for about 10 hours, and at the end of the day I said, "The best number I can give you is $10 million." And he said, "Oh, my God!" He told the VIA guys and they said, "We don't even have the authority to go to anywhere near that level." So he was, all of a sudden, very angry and told them to go away and think about it till the next morning.

VIA was still adamant—no way. We told the mediator we were ready to present. We understood that if he wasn't able to mediate, he had been asked by the federal minister, Jean Corbeil, to present him with a report on all the issues, and we are ready to present our position. "Well, why don't we take a five-minute break and then get together?" he says.

Canada Place, former home of the B.C. International Commercial Arbitration Centre.

Stephen Gill was our lawyer, from Edwards Kenny & Bray, working with Bob Ward and Sue Fraser. He starts presenting our case in minute detail. They were somewhat blown away by this, and by the end of the day we got a sense from the mediator that he was getting a flavour of the issues and unless there were good counter-arguments, he was not going to be too impressed [by VIA].

The following week, VIA present their case and what they don't know—and what I've been working on for months—is a piece of paper I found in the public domain from a hearing done by [member of Parliament] Erik Nielsen in Mulroney's government. He has done this study and VIA submitted some financials and I got a copy. It says that they spent $2.7 million in marketing in the previous year [1988] for the

Rocky Mountaineer, but for 1989 they only did $132,000. Now, after they presented, we got to do a rebuttal. Our lawyer has set them up: they're saying they did all the required marketing for us, and he asks if the marketing is the same from one year to the next—$132,000? "Absolutely," they say. And then he pulls out this piece of paper and they knew they were sunk. Caught them out in a big lie after a lot of little lies. The mediator presented his report at the end of August.

DONALD MUNROE, in his mediator's report: As regards the main issues, I believe that GCRC (Great Canadian Railtour Company) has a strong case that it was misled by VIA Rail; and that GCRC suffered financially as the result.

JIM ROCHE, who today is a partner with the Ottawa lobbying firm Secor, where he still consults to VIA Rail: After the mediation, there was argument about what the mediator had said. . . . I am no particular fan of Mr. Armstrong, not because he bought our train, but because I felt most of his complaints were unjustified. I find him smarmy and unctuous. . . . So he kept coming back: he didn't want to pay for the equipment, although he was supposed to pay for the equipment, he kept whining about the order book, about how we sold him short on it or something, or no one had shown up, or that there was bad faith, we weren't making any of the equipment right, or that we were charging too much for this or we shouldn't charge him for that, and he would only pay us after the season. And it would go on and on.

RANDY PETTIPAS, who became the Alberta-reared advisor on western Canada to Prime Minister Jean Chrétien: Peter gets a fair hearing in Ottawa, number one because he makes a point of staying in touch with people, not coming just when he has a problem. He has never, ever come whining. He's approached it very professionally, he keeps people up to speed regularly, he always presents his case in a logical fashion and is respectful of other views although he forcefully expresses his own. His work over a number of years, in not only regularly talking to people in Ottawa but in the way he does it, has built an extremely high level of trust in Ottawa for Peter Armstrong's views.

PETER: In September [1992] we were corresponding with the minister, who was encouraging VIA to settle. The magnitude of the settlement was only about $3.5 million. We had mediated on five issues, but we went to the ministry and said, "It's not enough, we need to mediate on the other 10 issues." We wanted about $7.5 million—what we'd lost in the first three years.

The man who was helping us politically, Ramsey Withers, had said, "Peter, accept the mediator's report of $3.5 million. It's fabulous. You've had a clear victory." He even used Biblical terms to describe it.

RAMSEY WITHERS: It might have been Ecclesiastes: "There is a time for all things. There is a time to live, a time to die, a time to love, a time to hate."

PETER: And I said, "This is a great victory, but I have run the numbers and I know that it's not enough. We should have been given some kind of compensation, because we went through three years of absolute hell." I knew that without a complete recovery, we'd be so far in the glue that we'd never be able to get out. We needed to do a lot to turn ourselves around, and while this broke the back of it, it still wasn't enough. But if we got about $3 million more, it was enough.

RAMSEY WITHERS: I always thought this young man would have made a good infantry officer. Because the first principle of war is selection and maintenance of the aim. Peter was unwavering in all his efforts to achieve that singular aim. He had good discrimination about his actions. Took advice well. Always listened very carefully and attentively to what was said. Made his own judgements. In my battalion, he would have been one of my company commanders.

STARVED FOR CASH

PETER: This is the most courageous moment, because in September we're going into another winter and I still had the cash flow problems, and until I got this thing signed, I had nothing. And VIA didn't want to settle. I believe they wanted to take as long as possible. They knew I was starved for cash and couldn't hold on forever unless more money came in. And, frankly, my partners were financially exhausted. Jim Houston, Rick Browning and Bev were willing to step down from their investment for a dollar. So it took a lot of time and effort, and as we approached November 12, 1992, I was running out of cash. I had $4,000 in the bank, $1 million payable and a payroll coming up. I was facing bankruptcy. My own personal lines of credit were drawn. I went to a number of people—

including friends of mine in the bus industry—and asked them to participate but unfortunately was never able to convince them. I can remember that November consistently, every morning and every night, looking over the debt.

JIM HOUSTON: I mean, the idea of pumping a lot more money into the thing at that point wasn't very exciting. It was difficult to see how long it was going to go on before it turned around—*if* it would turn around.

GLENN MUNRO: Rick Browning approached me on behalf of the board of directors, of which he was chairman. We looked at various scenarios. One was raising some more equity; another was selling the company. The directors were ready to walk. The best scenario was that they might get their money back—and even then they would take it over time. So I did a big canvass, contacting companies around the world that I thought might be interested. The Rank Corporation, in the movie and entertainment business in the U.K. And Tag Heuer, a company in Switzerland that makes watches and provides the timing mechanisms for sporting events. I felt they had the resources and were crazy enough to do something involved in a company like this. Just two names on a long list. I basically got no response or polite responses saying, "Thank you, but this is not the kind of thing that we have any interest in."

RICK BROWNING: Glenn and I became very good pals. I always regarded him as our financial consultant. While he wasn't a board member, he was at most board meetings and had a different perspective on what went on. He used to chuckle about all the infighting between different members.

The president and his board decided to approach Vencap Equities for further financing. Peter staged initial discussions in his office, with director Jim Houston and chairman Rick Browning facing off against Vencap's Mike Phillips and a colleague in what turned out to be a tense meeting.

RICK BROWNING: Mike Phillips and this guy from Calgary [Rick Harland] were really using the old high-handed financier approach: "What are you guys going to contribute?" Of course, this is where Jim is at his best, because he would sit there and be expressionless. They would go through their spiel and burn themselves out and Jim would not say a word. He was just staring at them, and you could see them start to melt down and get very uncomfortable, because this wasn't going to work.

Then this one chap got up and made a speech about how difficult he was going to make everything. And Jim came out with some comment about how there isn't any blood on the ground yet, some real tough-guy speech. Phillips turned white and I thought, *Poor old Mike, you don't know Jim well enough. You'll live to get on the plane and go home.*

Then all the feedback came from the meeting. Mike Phillips and this other chap were totally incensed at what they thought of as being physically threatened—this comment about blood and knives coming out—and they went and complained to [Vencap president Sandy] Slator. Peter phoned me to say Jim had gone too far and Peter was going back with cap in hand to smooth the waters and to ask for more money at the same time (while Jim is threatening to slice people up). I said, "You know, Peter, Jim's preamble to 'the blood on the floor' was a really good speech. He talked about the strength of entrepreneurialism and [said] 'We are

Brothers Bev and Peter Armstrong.

not asking you to do our job for us. What we come to you for is money and then we pay you for the money. And you are not here to give us a lecture on ethics.'"

MIKE PHILLIPS: Jim Houston didn't want to put any more money in. As it turns out, I discovered about a year ago that at that meeting he thought we were bluffing and I thought he was bluffing. I said, "Jim, if you don't put more money in, we're not going to put more money in"—or words to that effect, because I thought Jim had a bundle, but it turned out that he wasn't on a roll and didn't have any money available. But I guess he had faith in Peter too, because he did come up with some money—not a lot—and the deal got done.

BEV ARMSTRONG: By then we had suffered through the first year and a couple more years and then it got worse, it escalated. Peter had $7 million in losses, so that more than ate up the initial equity that we put in the business and the additional equity that Vencap put in. The company had tremendous negative working-capital deficiencies. . . . But it wasn't any more or less than I was prepared to lose or had lost or had made on other deals, so it went with the territory. Jim or Rick would have been quite happy to be out of the business, and they had sort of given up on it. Then Peter phoned Mike Phillips at Vencap to appeal to them to put some more money in the business and he said, "Don't bother." But Peter and I flew up to Edmonton one afternoon [November 11], and we had to meet him the next morning. And the first thing when we walk into the meeting, they say, "Well, we told you not to come."

PETER: We met again with Sandy Slator and Mike Phillips. Sandy was wonderful: "Peter, you get into any other deal and we will support you, but if it has anything to do with VIA or the government, we want to stay a hundred miles away from it."

I said, "Well, thank you very much, but what would it take?"

"No, Peter, you don't seem to understand: we are not going down that path."

"I heard you, I understand that, but still, you have $2.5 million [invested] here. What will it take to convince you to give me another million to get me through the next season to right the situation?"

And he said, "Oh, gee, I don't know"—and that's when I knew I had a chance. He recognized that he still had $2.5 million on the table. It wasn't yet lost—was there a way to save it? So he went away with Mike Phillips and his group of advisors and came back a while later and said, "We need concessions from CP and CN. They need to buy in. You need to get the deal done with VIA Rail. That's going to be a little bit tougher, but you need to get the full settlement from VIA Rail."

I said, "Seven days from now, I've got a payroll. If I get some movement, will you support this?"

"I'll think about it carefully," he said.

BEV ARMSTRONG: Even at 10:30 it wasn't looking very good, and when Sandy Slator came back into the room and laid these conditions on us, I think he thought that he had met any obligations that he had. I don't think they ever really expected us to deliver on it. I can distinctly remember leaving their office and going down in the elevator and not knowing whether we should congratulate ourselves or be saying, "Well, now what do we do? How are we going to deal with all these issues?" Peter asked me to drive the rental car, and I assumed we are going to talk about this on the way back to the airport. But Peter is going through his Rolodex—and Peter has the most incredible Rolodex—and he's immediately got CP on the phone, the direct line of the most senior-level guy, and it's explained that he needs to meet with him. Peter has gone to work.

PETER: As Bev and I are driving out of the parking lot, I'm on the phone to Rob Ritchie, the president of CP Rail. He had once made the comment that if I really get into trouble, give them a call. I said, "Rob, this is the call. I'm in trouble." CP and CN are great partners. We told them we couldn't pay them today what we owed, but if they helped us, we'd make sure we paid them back. And on that basis, both—with slight variations—gave us concessions. CN and CP both deferred some of the past season's trackage fee. They said, "We will lend you money back from 1992." We always had to pay interest, but they gave us time to pay all the trackage rates. Because we never argued and lived up to all the terms of our contracts, both railroads cut us some slack. But all loans were on commercial terms—with everything spelled out. CP and CN gave us the breathing room to get back on our feet, while ensuring they earned a fair rate for the use of their trackage.

GLENN MUNRO: So Peter was able to resolve many of those problems, and Sandy Slator put up $1.1 million. That got us through the year.

MIKE PHILLIPS: Sandy and I were not prepared to let the company die because of a shareholder squabble, so we put the money in on a debt basis with the final terms and conditions all unresolved—but at least the company got the money.

GETTING TO YES, PART 2

PETER: But then VIA dicked around until March of '93 to actually sign the damage settlement agreement.

GREG MCLEAN: Lawless came to Minister Corbeil and said, "The mediator missed everything, and so we are not going to honour the terms of the mediation." And the minister said, "Yes, you are." That was actually after some input from the Prime Minister's Office. We kept the issue alive in our office but Hugh Segal—chief of staff to Brian Mulroney—actually pushed Lawless to get this settled. The mediation had happened and VIA was going to waffle on it. It was a key point in my relationship with Corbeil. I walked into his office and he says, "I have carried this ball long enough for these guys. They can figure it out themselves now. I am dropping the ball."

I had no idea what I was saying. "Minister, I cannot accept that." The chief of staff was there and he said, "Okay, what do I do then?" It was an absolute job-defining moment; the words are coming out of your mouth and you can't pull them back. You realize that you are actually putting your job on the line with your boss because you feel so strongly. I think the issue was actually solved when Jerry Lampert and Jess Ketchum went to Ottawa and got Hugh Segal involved and provided him with the background and he went to bat for it.

PETER: Finally we got everything back the way we wanted it. We got $100,000 in cash, an extension on the contract, an arbitration clause, debt forgiveness of $1,969,243 (that's pretty good) and service credits of $3 million. We said we didn't need cash today, we'd take service credits, which allowed us to use VIA's facilities, and when they invoiced us, they applied it against our credit. . . .

We will forever be in the debt of those who stood by us in the toughest of times: the shareholders, the suppliers, the railroads and the politicians (including Don Mazankowski and Jean Corbeil)—and especially Greg McLean—who believed in a private-sector solution for passenger rail.

That year we made the small profit predicted by Scott Remillard.

By 1993, several key people had left Great Canadian Railtour. Rob Hamilton had departed at the end of '92 after a falling-out with his old friend Peter; he is now a principal in a hot-food service business and a holding company for high-tech investments. (As Kamloops hotelier Dave Deol said later: "Rob Hamilton was a tough negotiator; he was a grinder. He was very bullheaded and kind of rubbed the hoteliers the wrong way.") Judy Thomson moved to Hong Kong to work for her alma mater, Arthur Andersen Inc. Perry Panchmatia went into the high-tech sector before becoming controller of the B.C. Legal Services Society. And Rick Antonson took on the fresh challenge of running Tourism Vancouver, where he still was in 2000. It was almost as if, having pulled the train through the worst years, they could leave with a clear conscience as it picked up speed toward success.

MARKETING—CASEY JONES-STYLE

MIKE PHILLIPS: Things gradually started to get better and the company made a little bit of money, although it took years to come out of a deficit retained-earnings position. But every year the customer accounts got better and every year, a piece at a time, it started to happen—mechanically, and Earl Simons with his great depth, and Murray Atherton, the optimistic generic marketer.

MURRAY ATHERTON, who came aboard full-time when Rick Antonson left in 1993: When we decided that we were going to get into packaged tours [the same year], I was talking to one of the hotel managers in Banff, who said, "Murray, don't even think about getting into that side of the business. You've got such a terrible reputation for paying bills. You'll never get any hotel rooms; nobody will do business with you." I said, "Well, give us a chance." So he did, and two years later this particular gentleman said, "I don't know what you guys do. I know that we have your people coming into our hotel, but we never talk about you. You always pay the bills within two weeks, so you never make a payable statement. You're never a topic of discussion. It's unbelievable."

The department was myself and Jane Tom; Michele de Rappard (who was on maternity leave); Marg Fartaczek, who was our tour sales coordinator in North America; and Helen Cho, who was doing Europe. We were working with a company called Canadian Travel Specialists, a

Stuart Ellis-Myers hams it up as Casey Jones.

Gail Heezen (left), Helen Cho and Murray Atherton with the Reservations crew.

division of Canadian Airlines. We had reps in the U.S., a brochure distribution company down in California. It was costing just a fortune. So I went through and made a couple of changes in our brochure distribution, trying to cut as many of the costs as we could.

Then I just hit the road. I went to London for the first time to attend the World Travel Mart. Rick had loved this little hotel called the Fielding. The bedroom that I got, you could not open the door into the bathroom, and you had to sort of squeeze past the toilet to close the door. There was a sleeping platform, not a bed. The lobby was about six feet by six feet. It had a little breakfast room downstairs that was right below the sleeping platform. So the guys at 5 in the morning would be in there banging all their pots and pans. It was just the worst hotel I've ever stayed in. And this was Rick's favourite in London. I thanked him very much and moved over to another hotel, so I could at least have a mattress.

Working on such limited budgets, the only place you could get major distribution without spending any money was with tour operators. The next challenge was to build the travel-agency business, to get them knowledgeable. We spent a lot of time developing what's called "preferred supplier status" with a lot of the major agency groups to make sure that our brochure would get distributed in the agencies, that we could attend their regional meetings, that we could do training sessions in their agencies—get people on the train. The biggest seller that we have is not the brochure, it's not ads, it's people. Once people get on that train and experience it, they'll sell it.

I developed the first "preferred supplier status" with Marlin Travel while I was still a consultant, then with GEM Travel (Go Earn More), which was an association at that time of 250 agencies in Canada—it's now up to about 650, part of a group with over 6,000 agencies around North America. We became preferred supplier with GIANTS, which is another group of independent travel agents; we did Thomas Cook; and now we're a preferred supplier with a number of organizations around North America, including some of the major AAA [American Automobile Association] groups.

We needed to develop our own group of independent representatives. I had known Stuart Ellis-Myers for years; he was in incentive sales down at the Bayshore [Hotel in Vancouver]. "Stuart, I have the perfect job for you: director of travel-agency sales."

He said, "I've never sold to travel agents."

"Stuart, you're the best salesman that I know. I'll give you a product that you can be proud of. I'll give you a costume, I'll give you a stage—go for it."

GAIL HEEZEN recalls how she had pioneered the female version of an engineer's costume during her first season with the company as a salesperson: We'd had a hard time even getting people to come to our trade show booth. I wanted to liven it up, but we had no money. I had this idea about wearing an engineer's cap and those striped, blue-and-white engineer's overalls—$49 at Mark's Work Wearhouse. Rick said, "Go try it." So I'd go up the aisle of the trade show dressed in overalls and cap and blow the train whistle. There were some people in the industry who thought it was a bit tacky—and it was, but our whole point was to get attention.

MURRAY ATHERTON: Stuart [who succeeded Gail Heezen in sales] was an actor, and he became Casey Jones personified—he was actually considering changing his name to Stuart Casey Jones. At the trade shows of all of the major travel-agency groups around North America, there'd be 400 booths and everybody was wearing suits—and then there was Stuart, blowing his train whistle. He developed a sales seminar and became a presenter at these shows, dressed up as Casey Jones and using *Rocky Mountaineer* as the product to teach them how to sell.

I gave him the two challenges. One, to develop the preferred supplier status around North America, get the travel agents to know us, then to develop 13 independent sales reps around North America. He actually worked himself out of a job. We took Stuart's position and divided it into two because he had done such a good job. Larisa Zenjin became manager, travel-agency sales. Stuart also got 26 agreements from travel-agency groups around North America. Each one of these needs individual marketing plans, special programs, incentive programs, follow-up, and [in recent years] we have a new position: manager, national accounts.

ERIC BELANGER: In '93 we started marketing the train with package tours. When we recognized that people came for more than just the train trip, that really changed the focus of the company and our position within the travel industry. We became a much bigger player overnight, and all of a sudden we were open to a lot more business. What really took it to the next level of package tours was when we brought in Fiona Barclay from Brewster Transportation and Tours. She was responsible for producing similar extended-tour packages for Brewster, so she brought in key expertise. We didn't stretch too far: different combinations of the train with Vancouver, Victoria, and the Rockies and Banff/Lake Louise and Jasper and then Calgary—a selection of packages of different lengths which would cover the highlights like the Columbia Icefield, the canyon walks and Lake Louise. Then that evolved to include Whistler and winery tours in the Okanagan and some tours up to Tofino. We had some packages that have been with us for a long time, including a rail circle tour with BC Rail.

Ann Coombs, a futurist and service-excellence consultant based in Vancouver and Toronto, was introduced to Peter in 1993. Her clients included major companies in the retail, tourism and financial-services industries, among them the Body Shop and the Ritz-Carlton Hotel.

ANN COOMBS: I met Peter in his old office in North Vancouver. It was a very hot day and the office was not air-conditioned. He was surrounded in a small office with train memorabilia, and I can remember making this proposal for a considerably large amount of money for the company's first secret service-excellence surveys. I was very, very apprehensive, and as I broke out into a menopausal flush, I was concerned that Peter would consider that maybe I was somehow trying to put something over on him. I decided that the best thing to do was address it. I said to him—as I was turning purple and perspiration is dripping down my forehead—"I'm really very sorry, but I'm sort of at that certain age and I get these all the time." And he said, "Well, so do I." He made me feel very at ease.

I realized that when I met Peter he was not an easy man to read, and I was at that point always aware of my client base: I knew a lot about the person I would be meeting with. This was a first-time meeting with a president and making the pitch all at the same time. I found the meeting certainly memorable. But he gave immediate approval to the project in the last five minutes—and he never showed his hand until then. He did a lot of listening.

The contract was to conduct three customer-service excellence surveys on the train— measurement standards on commentary, food

Ann Coombs

service, car interiors, reservations department, the actual onboard experience from a consumer's perspective. I had professional teams of two go on board—no one knew who or when, not even Peter. At the beginning, the "opportunities" were pretty extensive—

a polite way of saying it. The company was still in a start-up stage; they had no official training for the onboard teams other than just product knowledge and systems and operations. The washrooms were appalling, the food service was disappointing, half their cars weren't air-conditioned.

And I was on the train when it hit somebody. It was a very tragic moment. The other team member was actually out in the vestibule and saw the accident. The engineer had no hope of stopping the train; it was a suicide near Mission in a truck. The driver just pulled right in front of him. The crew handled it as best as they could—remembering that they had no training. And they were upset. The senior train management handled it as best as anyone would have imagined, because they were train officials. The onboard team itself were devastated but still did an admirable job under the circumstances. They're now better prepared for something like this.

The first year, the key management were upset with me—demoralized. Peter hadn't discussed it with them. So that when I came in with the results, it was like me throwing cold water on all of them. And I can tell you that if I thought the first meeting with Peter was difficult, it palled by comparison with what happened at this meeting. I had to be sensitive to the fact that these people had not been informed. It changed the way I do business: now everybody has to have seen the reports before I go in to do a debrief. I liken it to a situation where the devil has arrived, because I'm bringing them not a lot of good news.

PETER: She gave us the reports back and I was crushed. I asked her, "How do we rate?" She said, "Peter, I am your paid critic. I have to find everything wrong or you wouldn't pay me. Second, compared to any other company I would give you a B+."

"Based on your report, I would have thought that you would have given me an E."

"No," she said, "you're doing really well."

Then I had her address my whole management team, and they were depressed like I was.

ANN COOMBS: The fact that I went on to have a relationship with those people was a miracle. But [among other improvements] the breakfast service changed immediately from plastic containers with a cold breakfast to an interesting basket presentation and warm muffins. And the interiors of the cars were changed, with posters being placed in washrooms and the cars themselves. Peter always said the reason I was around was to be his critic, not to tell him good things.

The whole point of Ann Coombs's surveys was to improve service to the *Mountaineer*'s guests—often a very unpredictable lot. Sometimes, as the following stories from one turbulent year suggest, the passengers can be a complete mystery to everybody else on the train.

JUDY THOMSON: In 1993 we stopped for the opening of the Revelstoke [railway] museum. We have a little celebration, and now we have to get all these people back on the train. As we're starting to pull away, an attendant tells me she's got a man in her car she doesn't recognize. We're thinking he's from another car. I say, "Sorry, sir, which train car are you in?"

"Well, I don't know," he says. "I just got on in Revelstoke." He thought the train was just going for a little short jaunt down the track. So we had to stop the train partway to Calgary, let him off, and radio to Revelstoke to come and get him. Oh, we always have problems in Revelstoke.

GAIL HEEZEN: In 1993 I was called by a lawyer in Calgary. At first I thought it was a bit of a crank call. He had somebody very special to put on the train, but we wouldn't be able to know the person's name. He said there would be about five people travelling and they wanted the whole car, exclusively, and nobody could have access to it. I thought it was odd, but being a salesperson, I didn't want to say anything other than "Oh, okay—fine." He gave me his name and phone number and I phoned directory assistance; the number was real. I went to Scott [Remillard, the controller], who figured out our first rate for a whole car, additional tours and other extras—I think it was about $70,000. We had to get a limo for the group in Kamloops (we didn't know if they even had limos in Kamloops). Starting to think of this as real, I phoned the lawyer's secretary, who knew nothing about what I'm talking about—he had told me to talk only to him. He called me back and asked what accommodations we had in Kamloops. The next year we were going to use a new guest ranch there, with a big family home and a guest suite. The beautiful ranch house was ready now.

Then the lawyer said, "Now, you have to rendezvous with the RCMP."
Me.

"So can I know the name of this person?" I asked him. "Because my company has a policy of putting names on all of our documents."

"No, you can't. The RCMP will travel with this person. As a matter of fact, we don't want you telling anybody at your company."

At this point Scott and I were the only ones who knew about this. I had to liaise with the RCMP in Calgary, because they had to check out the tracks.

They asked me every possible thing that you can imagine: "This person has to be loaded before anybody comes in. What time do you load? Where are people going to walk in?" The RCMP had to follow him the whole time in Kamloops. And his private plane was flying in to Kamloops and landing there in case he only wanted to do one day on the train. I said, "We can't refund half the train trip."

The lawyer said, "Oh, no, that's not a problem. This man's a train buff and he's heard about your train."

So it all happened—boom, boom, boom! And every single person involved with the train had no idea who it was.

Chaim Herzog, former Israeli president— and mystery passenger.

He was the president of Israel, Chaim Herzog [who was travelling with several agents of Mossad, the Israeli secret service].

And, of course, Peter being a history buff was just so excited that he wanted to meet him, but we were to pretend that he wasn't even travelling with us. There were five of them—him, his wife, two bodyguards and an RCMP officer—and they had a whole train car's worth of food and three onboard attendants, who gave a little bit of commentary. The guest ranch had everything prepared for him: a beautiful outdoor barbecue, golfing in the evening, a formal dining room—but he sat down in the guest kitchen and ate dinner there. We were really excited the next morning when I found he got back on the train and hadn't flown out of Kamloops on his own private plane.

SIDE TRIP: 'CANADA IS GREAT TOO MUCH'

Sometimes it seemed like the whole world was getting aboard the *Mountaineer* in those early years as guests arrived from Europe and Asia—including a young Japanese man who afterwards wrote this enthusiastic letter to car attendant Anita Martin.

KOICHI OHNO: How are you getting along? First of all I thank you very much for your kind and heart-warm services in the Train on the 3rd and the 4th of June. It was nice for us to meet you! Time flies like an arrow! Two weeks have passed since we left Vancouver for Tokyo.

You have no idea how happy we were and enjoyed the two-day travel with you doing sights of beautiful Canada: Mountains, Lakes, Rivers, Forests, Fields and so on. We could see glaciers brightly reflect against the blue sunny skies. Really we spoke much of the Canada's beauty even when we were busy preparing for pack baggages in hotels. I'm happy to tell you that I could hear them speaking of how fine and beautiful You (Anita) were.

My Conclusion of our travel this time:

CANADA is great too much;

ANITA is splendid and More beautiful. . . .

Finally we wish to see you again anywhere in the Western Japan or Kansai area. I'll tell you that! And we hope we could have good time with you at my wife's Tea ceremony room.

Friendly yours . . .

C H A P T E R >

Picking Up Steam:

The Dome Era Begins ¶ With the

renegotiated VIA Rail settlement, Great Canadian Railtour was back on

track—or perhaps riding firmly on the rails for the very first time. Now

Peter Armstrong and his people were finally free to focus on broadening

the company's base. In January 1994 they introduced a dozen indepen-

dent package tours, ranging from three to 15 days, to complement the

two-day train journey, and in March a group-travel department began

offering customized itineraries for group, incentive and leisure travel.

. . .

Left: Dome chefs Ole Nichum, Phung Dang, Doug Workman and Allen Hall

As Scott Remillard recalls, "With the new computer system, we were able to handle the volume of package tours. We could not exist today if we didn't have them: the rail is a magnet to attract the volume, but the profit is in the private package tours."

The rising passenger volume meant much more work in Kamloops. In 1993 Doug Smith had retired from running the guest and station services with his wife in the layover city. Flo stayed on another year, until she turned 65. "The station platform is cement and you spend hours up and down it, and it was tough on us at our age," she says, almost apologetically. "I've said to Peter many times since that if I'd been younger, he never would have gotten rid of me." Fortunately there were many other family members to take over. Not only was their son Greg a CN engineer, *his* son, Greg Jr., began to help stock and clean the *Mountaineer* and their daughter Tanya handled souvenir orders. The couple continued to work for another daughter, Sue Velasquez, who inherited the servicing duties from her mother (although in 1999 Flo was still working from home to analyze the hotel manifests, order the passenger buses and do the Kamloops payroll). No wonder there's a painting at Doug and Flo's new home that portrays the train station as "Fort Smith" and a sign describing the station: "Population varies—all Smiths. Trespassers beware: guard Doug on duty."

With all this activity along the line, it was time to realize a dream the visionaries behind the revitalized *Rocky Mountaineer* had conjured up half a decade earlier and were finally in a position to pursue. The company began talking seriously with Rader Railcar, owned by American Tom Rader (who had been involved in the original discussions with Peter about the *Mountaineer*). The ambitious project: to build the rail service's first dome car. The multi-million-dollar bi-level dome coach with a state-of-the-art design would have panoramic windows on top and a dining lounge, fully equipped galley and observation platform on the lower level. It would be the first of its type ever to operate in Canada and the first new Canadian passenger-rail coach of any kind in 40 years. The luxury service, accommodating 72 guests, was to be called GoldLeaf, while the 21 regular coaches offered Signature service (today called RedLeaf).

By the end of '94, a Calgary research firm, the Strategy Group, estimated the annual economic impact of Great Canadian at $23.7 million, generating 492 person-years of employment based on the 110 personnel on staff during peak season. Among them were two people who remain key to the *Rocky Mountaineer*'s success to this day: Vicki Haller and Tony Pellegrino.

THE TASMANIAN DEVIL

Vicki Haller had joined the company as Peter's executive assistant in December 1993. She'd been doing public relations for the Vancouver Aquarium following a decade at the University of British Columbia, where she had wound up as assistant to John Brockington, head of the theatre department. (Her work there was probably good training for the dramatic characters she'd meet at the *Rocky Mountaineer.*)

MURRAY ATHERTON: Peter's assistant has to be a very special person, because he's got so many balls up in the air and needs somebody who is so committed to not only the company, but to Peter as a person—and Vicki is. She worships the man, she hates the man; she has a love-hate relationship because he's a very difficult person to deal with. I consider the secret to his success is that he has absolutely no idea what it takes to get the job done. He's a dog with a bone. He needs someone who can make sure that things happen. Vicki is that person.

VICKI HALLER: It's not just about the *Rocky Mountaineer,* it's how Peter is part of the community and how the community perceives what the *Rocky Mountaineer* is. He's on the board of directors for all these organizations—like Grace McCarthy's CHILD Foundation—and my job includes getting to know the executive assistants out in the community, like the mayor's assistant and the people at Tourism Vancouver and the Young Presidents' Organization. We've all become friends as well, so there's this network of women who all work together.

Vicki worked for more than a year in the North Vancouver offices. It was in those crowded quarters thate she came to know the larger-than-life personalities who populated the place—starting with Peter Armstrong.

VICKI HALLER: Peter is the first person to say that it's not him who built this company, it's all the people who have been connected to it from Day One. In the old days, he knew every single person, he knew their life history, he knew who their family members were. Now it's physically impossible and I think that bothers him a bit. . . .

We were in the old building in North Vancouver one night, Earl and Murray and I. It was 11:30 and we had all been there proofreading a brochure. We were all punchy and nobody could see straight when Earl came out of the back with a poster tube and smacked it on my desk. Of course, I jumped sky-high. Murray in the meantime went in and got a

Vicki Haller

poster tube so as not to be outdone. Soon we were all fighting with tubes—and then out came the squirt guns. When I went home I was soaking wet, and the next morning I had the biggest bruise on the side of my hip that I've ever had in my entire life. . . .

We were right opposite a Save-On-Foods store, and at 11:30 at night we'd run across before it closed to get something to eat back at the office. Somebody would come back with a big tray of doughnuts. We must have gained a ton of weight in that place until we put in a rule: No eating at desks.

Earl Simons used to call an irate Vicki "the Tasmanian Devil." She was in a good position to observe his own infrequent anger. Although Simons's detail-oriented personal style usually meshed perfectly with Peter's broad-strokes approach, occasionally the two men seemed to be working at cross purposes—as the following story so vividly illustrates.

EARL SIMONS: Peter and I were negotiating with executives from CN Rail on our annual contracts. We were getting nowhere and Peter got up out of his chair and went to his office to take a message. I was sitting there with the CN people and finally got through to them; they understood what we wanted and agreed to it. Then Peter came back and started off by giving away something to them so we could get what we wanted. I kicked him under the table and he said, "Who kicked me?"

VICKI HALLER, who witnessed the scene: And you could see the steam coming out of Earl because he was just furious and said, "You better follow me into this office." He slammed the door and said, "What's the matter with you, Peter? Why do you think I kicked you?"

"*You* kicked me?" Peter says. "Why did you kick me?"

MURRAY ATHERTON: Vicki takes the company and Peter so personally. When we introduced the first GoldLeaf dome President's Trip in 1997—for heads of major companies and government officials, a wonderful variety of people—Vicki actually wrote a poem where the initials of each line spell *Rocky Mountaineer*. Instead of just sending out an invitation, she sat down and wrote this poem:

Royal Service has always been our style
Our GoldLeaf Dome brings us another mile
Come join us on our inaugural run
Keep us on track and have some fun
Your presence we would appreciate for two days
Majestic beauty will capture your gaze
Our Two River Junction Dinner/Revue
Up in Kamloops is a must to do
Nothing compares to our Chef's daily creation
This inaugural run should also provide relaxation
A trip on our train through mountains by lakes and the sea
Is the chance to play tourist and travel worry free
No other experience we think can compare
Everyone wants you to be able to share
Each mile along the scenic route we proudly display
Ride with us and enjoy—the GoldLeaf way

TALES FROM TONY

Tony Pellegrino comes from a railway family and has been working with trains for a quarter-century. After attending Sir George Williams University in Montreal, he began his career with Canadian Pacific as an 18-year-old office boy in 1972, became a systems and procedures inspector with VIA, and oversaw the new systems for Canadian Rockies by Daylight when the Crown railway launched the service in 1988. Six years later he was intimately reconnected with what had become the *Mountaineer* when he joined the staff of Great Canadian Railtour. "It was so ironic," he recalls. "I was the one who closed the CP line in western Canada, station by station, the last person to lock the doors, from Calgary into Vancouver. It was sort of eerie when I came back with Rocky and pulled into the Calgary station for a new life, a new career. I was thrilled, like being reborn again." As operations manager for three years—and more recently deciding to be a train manager so he can be out on the road—he has gathered a wealth of well-told tales.

TONY PELLEGRINO: After I did all the closures for CP, I'd opened up a small import-distributing business. In 1993 I had some bad news, ended up having cancer of the kidney, and was very lucky because they got it early and I had my kidney removed. Since then, I've been clean. Then I got a chance to get back in railroading with Rocky Mountaineer. An old friend, Henry Newman, put in a good word with the director of customer services and operations at that time, John Matthews [who joined in 1993 for about a year]. In 1994, a year after I had cancer, I took over as operations manager from Henry.

In November that year, we had the great opportunity—and Peter grabbed hold of it—to bring the Grey Cup from Calgary to Vancouver. Canadian Pacific, Canadian Airlines and Rocky Mountaineer Railtours came together with the CFL to promote the 1944 Grey Cup champion team—Montreal Navy [which beat the Hamilton Wildcats 7 to 6]. We had old-time CFL all-stars on board, all kinds of CP officials, including their president, and Peter. And it was a dry train—no drinking—because we didn't want to have any mishaps. I was running the trip as train manager. It was sort of magical: you had all these legends on the train, including 14 players from 1944 in their 70s wearing their old jerseys, and they were so enthusiastic that we were doing something like this. We stayed over in Kamloops, where they had a special night at the Coliseum.

Fiona Barclay, our director of guest services then, was with me on the train. We got into Revelstoke, where they were changing our crew. One of the guests was Miles Gorrell, about 350 pounds, an all-star lineman for the Winnipeg Blue Bombers. Miles somehow jumped off the train at Revelstoke—the liquor store was very close to the train station— grabbed a case of beer and a couple of bottles, and jumped back on the train. Fiona saw him.

I said, "I don't know if he's going to take it too kindly when I ask him not to start drinking. This guy's six foot nine."

She said, "Don't worry, I'll handle it." I watched her go in the car. Miles was reclined in a seat and had a stash underneath it. He was trying to hide an open can of beer. Fiona just grabbed him by the shirt, pushed

The Canadian Football League's vice-commissioner, Larry Smith, boards the Rocky Mountaineer *with the Grey Cup.*

him down with all her weight—she's a whole 120 pounds, soaking wet—and said, "I told you, there's no drinking on this train." As she was choking him, Terry Evanshen [the Calgary Stampeders' pass-catcher] and Peter Dalla Riva [the Montreal Alouettes' receiver] were cracking up, laughing. "Now, do you want me to let you go? You give me all your stuff and you'll get it back tonight in Kamloops."

This giant agreed to the whole thing. I would have got punched in the head. . . .

That same year we had the Indian ambassador to Canada on the train on his way to see the Victoria Commonwealth Games. We had a lot of security. He smoked a pipe, and at that time we didn't have the dome cars; the tail car on the train was the 5749, the smoking car. We don't really allow people to smoke pipes in the train. So, making an exception for him, we had to get RCMP to surround him. He was smoking off the back of the vestibule so he wasn't in sight of anybody, with three Mounties blocking the view. . . .

Another time in '94 we were in Calgary during the Stampede. We have small wheelchairs so [disabled] people can go through the aisles and into the washrooms. We had one wheelchair for each train, but unfortunately somebody took my chair and put it on the consist to Jasper. Turning around on Sunday, we had this lady from England who was a paraplegic, and without that chair she couldn't go to the washroom. It was one of the most horrendous, touching things to see her. This was her life's trip, her husband was with her, and I couldn't board them because I had no wheelchair. She was crying, so I had to make a decision and phoned every airline. Finally I bought a chair from Canadian [Airlines] for $150. I sent our station manager down through Stampede traffic to get it, and I took a two-and-a-half-hour hit on the block [the steel shock absorber at the end of the rail line] waiting for that chair. I had talked to every guest on the train, and they were mostly understanding. Then we boarded the lady and she was ecstatic. CP punished us pretty badly because we missed our time slot, and we got into Kamloops at 9 o'clock at night. That was a tough day. . . .

I once got a call from train manager Gordon Sim in Hope telling me he was missing two guests. They'd been missing from Boston Bar, coming into Vancouver. Their wives were frantic. I'm beside myself. I thought maybe they fell off the train. I'm starting to report to all the police forces. I've got search parties out there with CN. In those days we brought our trains head-in to the block in Vancouver, and I always used to meet the train on the platform. As the train's pulling down track number 6, I look out and there's the two missing guests—standing on the locomotive, smoking big stogies. They had been travelling there from Boston Bar, where we change crews. They'd jumped off the train, got on the front end and rode it all the way to Vancouver. Well, I had a long talk with the crew, and it was not in the normal English language; it was more in the vernacular.

In 1994 Peter called for recommendations to improve the company, the best of which would be honoured by the first President's Awards. Brad Noyes, an onboard attendant for two years, suggested giving employees the option to work in each other's jobs briefly to increase the bond between the unionized attendants and the non-union office staff still housed in North Vancouver.

BRAD NOYES: Peter liked the idea and chose me to be the attendant he was going to follow, so he could actually see what an onboard attendant did for a couple of days. We got him a uniform, myself being five foot six and him being 20 feet tall. He had a name tag that said Pete— Chris Murphy called him Petey. We left Vancouver together on the train with about 40-odd guests in our coach who had no idea who he was. We explained that Peter was a trainee, he was the one who had to do the job, and we were hoping that he would have a good future with the company. We got him doing breakfast service, serving coffee, a bit of commentary and cleaning the coach up. Did very well; the guests were happy. Good conversationalist.

The deal was, I had to follow him around as president for a couple of days as well. That night we had a cocktail party to go to in Kamloops, being put on by the chamber of commerce. I cut a little earlier since I had to be fresh the next day, and he stayed a bit longer. I was identified as the "acting" president and learned what it means to schmooze with people; you definitely need to be a master of small talk. He made sure he spent enough time with each individual so they felt they had his attention. Next morning he was on the crew bus with us and we got down to the train and he set up the coach: set up the carts, made coffee and tea, got the juices prepared, the breakfast ready, did muffins and bagels. He did well—at that stage. He's a trooper. We got the guests on board and greeted them again; they're a lot warmer to you the second day, because they've gone through their comfort-zone change.

He did the breakfast service by himself that day. The funny thing, the cart probably comes up to his waist, where it at least comes up to my chest, and he was bending over the whole time. It was like a big guy pushing a little wheelbarrow down the aisle. He did more commentary—it was weak. There were [only] a few things he knew. He learned how im-

Gerard Burke (right) reacts as Peter goes overboard on his disguise.

portant it is to have all the tools that you need to work with. It was his job to run back and forth between lunch and dinner services to get a corkscrew for the wine. From that point on, we did have corkscrews in every car. He did the basics okay. He had done the lunch service, so I sent him off to have his lunch—just as we were about to enter the Mount Macdonald Tunnel. And he was sitting in a dark baggage car for about 20 minutes, unable to eat his lunch, unable to move because he couldn't see anything. (He still razzes me about that.) But he's a trooper.

On the second day, though, when it came time to cash the guests out, that's when it became a bit more obvious that he wasn't necessarily the man that we had portrayed him to be to the guests. He had a bit of a struggle using the Chargex machine, which was one of the first things that made the guests realize he was not who we said he was. When we did let them know later that he was the president of the company, they were all very impressed. A pilot and his wife, a stewardess, from American Airlines were just in awe and were going to tell their president he needed to do the same thing. We made a fair buck off that coach; they tipped us very well, and Peter was generous enough to hand all the money over to me, although I had promised him a beer—and I still owe it to him.

I came in to do a day with Peter, follow him around the office. It started early, about 6:30 in the morning at the Hyatt in Vancouver. We had breakfast with Jess Ketchum, a slight visit with Mark Andrew [then running the hotel], and covered what was going to happen during the day. There was lunch and various meetings. It was the day of Murray Atherton's 50th-birthday party, late that afternoon, and there were other things that needed to be tied up. So we were in Peter's office and he dropped me off about 9 o'clock. The thing that affected me the most was the amount of detail that has to be dealt with on a daily basis to make this company work. Peter has hired a lot of the right people to help him with that but at that point was still in charge of the company, overseeing everything, with a huge amount on his plate. I was very intrigued and impressed with how well things run—when you realize how many little things should not be presented to the guests in any way, shape or form.

That following season I stepped into the job as train manager because he coerced me into it by calling me a chicken. Then I became assistant director of train and station services. I still owe him a day as president. He keeps reminding me about that, but I just haven't had the time to do it.

THE BUYOUT

By late 1994 some of Peter Armstrong's partners were getting a little restless and talked of pulling out of Great Canadian Railtour. Among them were chairman Rick Browning, one of the original investors, and Vencap Equities, which had been the company's financial saviour on more than one occasion. Vencap was now largely controlled by Gerald Schwartz of Onex Corporation, the Toronto-based investment colossus (which in 1999 would make an unsuccessful bid to acquire Air Canada and combine it with Canadian Airlines International).

GLENN MUNRO: In fall 1993 I'd started beating the bushes looking for another investor. It was simply "Let's find a major investor and if they want to take us out, fine"—us being Rick Browning and Bev Armstrong. All we knew is that we needed more money.

RICK BROWNING: Glenn and I had a list of players: the *Orient Express* guy in England (who was always of the opinion that he could do it himself here), Holland America, Princess [the other major cruise line], a venture-capital group in Boston and a couple of private individuals in Canada. I mean, these were people who could quite easily put significant capital into the company, which would take us to the next level.

GLENN MUNRO: I was not getting anywhere and eventually we decided to go back to Mike Phillips.

RICK BROWNING: At this point I am still chairman of the board, but Michael Phillips has moved from Vencap to the Working Opportunity Fund [the Vancouver-based investment fund], and we are now having serious dialogue with him. It's reality time, because we haven't made any money yet and I haven't been paid a nickel for all the time I put in. So I threw my 8 percent or 9 percent shares into the ring. It was time for me to get out. I didn't make any money—well, I made some interest—but I got an unbelievable education, which I am going to use now.

PETER: It was an opportunity for me to buy some of Rick's and my brother's shares and bring in the Working Opportunity Fund.

MIKE PHILLIPS: This was my first day on the job. I was sitting in my office with my feet up on the desk, looking at the view of English Bay and counting the freighters and sipping on my Starbucks, and it was April and it was lovely—and the phone goes about 7:15 in the morning. My very first phone call, I reach for the phone, guess who? Peter. I said, "No, no more money. I am not giving you any more money until you get things straightened out." Well, you see, at that point it *was* straightening out, and it may not have been completely apparent to us all, but the ship was slowly turning around.

PETER: Mike Phillips and I had become friends, and he always accuses me of phoning him for money five minutes after he got to WOF. There's no question that did enter my mind, but the original thought was not to just bring him in for money. We had an opportunity to upgrade our service with GoldLeaf dome coaches, built by Tom Rader, but we needed to clean up our balance sheet first. At the end of the day I had a few more shares, and then we brought in the Working Opportunity Fund for $1.6 million of new equity to strengthen our balance sheet.

It was in '95 that we bought out Vencap. Gerald Schwartz of Onex had bought Vencap and then started to assess which companies he wanted to keep in their portfolio. We were one of the ones he wanted to dispose of. I negotiated with Frank Stack, a Great Canadian board member representing Vencap.

GEORGE HUNGERFORD: Gerry Schwartz, who was a very sharp operator, took advantage of the fact that Peter was doing better and extracted a settlement out of him. Peter didn't have a complete deal in writing. I remember sitting with him on the beach at Savary Island. The plane was coming in just as we were opening up this whole discussion on how to deal with Vencap. I said, "Peter, you have to get this in writing." He didn't get the contract in writing on the first go-round and so we had a tough time with the contract to take Vencap out. Peter wanted to do some deferred-payment plan and my advice was: "You don't want them around, just pay them out right now." In the end he paid much more for that. Peter had his mind made up on that one.

BEV ARMSTRONG: The other shareholders in the company were skeptical that we could buy Vencap out. And that's when I got involved with helping to restructure the financing, and once we had done that, Peter saw what he could do with creative and aggressive financing.

PETER: We had agreed on a price, Glenn Munro had written up an agreement, and all of a sudden we couldn't understand why things weren't going very well. Then we find out that Frank [Stack] had gone and shopped the deal. If he wanted to shop the deal, that's his right as a shareholder, but he should have told us going in. He went to David Morrison of Brewster Transportation and Tours, who are owned by a big American company. It came as no surprise to me that Brewster's would be interested in us. But we hadn't really seen it coming and needed to find some money to deal with it. All my dealings with Vencap in the past had been so above-board. Unfortunately, Sandy Slator, Mike and Lane Kranenberg were all gone.

MIKE PHILLIPS: When I was at Vencap, everything we did was so ethical, it was unbelievable. I would never, ever have shown private financial statements to somebody who was both a customer and a competitor [of the *Mountaineer*, as Brewster's was] and who we thought might be in league with VIA. I would never have shown them legal documentation. I would never have done anything like that without the permission of the company. So our confidential stuff that was given to Vencap in good faith was distributed. Individuals involved in Vencap at the time said, "We can do whatever we want. We see nothing wrong with this whatsoever." Legally maybe they could do what they wanted, but ethically I had a big problem with it and so did we all.

So first of all we went to provincial Supreme Court to stop them from releasing the information to Brewster's—and it was quite a muddle, actually. We are all trying to be reasonably polite to each other, and we find a judge who listens to us for a while. Then all of a sudden, this judge leans over his bench and looks at the whole courtroom with his glasses down on the end of his nose and says, "Tell me again: why are you all here?" This judge was a wise man, right? Everyone on both sides of the argument were aghast, the lawyers were aghast, and everybody thundered out onto the concourse to settle it.

BEV ARMSTRONG: We were sitting in the courtroom with our lawyer arguing the case, an experienced litigator. Once I was in the courtroom, I realized that this was a disaster and that we were not winning and he was not getting the message across to the judge. I took Mike and Peter out into the lobby and said, "We have got to settle this right now." I took the fellow from Vencap aside and we basically cut a deal right then that we would accept the higher price that they were going to get from Brewster's. *Let's just get on with it*—because everybody had lost sight of the fact the business was continuing to prosper. We were fighting over what was a relatively few dollars while the actual value of the business had increased by so much more than that. The best we could hope for was a deal with Brewster's, but we didn't have a deal with Vencap—we had a handshake with them, so we would have ended up having to renegotiate with them and they would have based it all on the new numbers.

DAVE MORRISON, president and CEO of Brewster Transportation and Tours: When we made an offer to Vencap, Peter tried to say it wasn't legit and the court threw it out and gave us $10,000 in damages. Vencap gave us a hundred-and-some-thousand bucks. Once Peter lost in court, he upped his offer and Vencap picked up a couple more million bucks than they thought.

PETER: We were hoping to be able to get an injunction to stop this process so that we could then raise the money. But while this was all going on, we went to the Royal Bank and they agreed to provide the leverage to buy out Vencap's position. With the strength of the Working Opportunity Fund and Jim Houston and most importantly my brother, we were able to accomplish that.

MIKE PHILLIPS: What Vencap didn't know was that Great Canadian had been running around scrounging up finances from the bank and had enough money to make good on the offer that Brewster's had made. So we said, "Here is the cheque; give us the shares back"—which they were then obliged to do.

OH, GIVE US A DOME...

GLENN MUNRO: The $1.6 million we got from the Working Opportunity Fund in early '95 was absolutely critical and, in my opinion, one of the most important turning points. The addition of the GoldLeaf dome coaches essentially put the company in a position where no one else could match our service.

EARL SIMONS: So Peter decided that we're going to go for a bi-level dome car. I remember Jim Houston didn't want the dome cars: "No, it's too risky." He was the last holdout. At the meeting I finally jumped in—I very rarely put my neck on the line—and said, "Jim, if we don't do this, you're not going to have any travel writers coming back to write about the company. The company will not grow. They've got to have something new to come and look at." He finally said, "Well, fine, you guys go do it. If it's wrong, it's your problem." But he was very supportive once we made the decision. So we went down to Denver and talked to Tom Rader. Of course, Peter, being Peter, wanted it done in less time than what Tom wanted to do it.

TOM RADER: Peter finally gets things healthy enough that he can come and talk to us in the summer of '94 about buying new cars. He wanted a price on building one of our double-decker cars. He also looked at the single-level car pricing, but he loved the double-decker from Alaska, because he understood what that car could do for him from a sales point of view. We screwed around and negotiated and finally signed this bloody agreement in January of '95 for delivery in May. It was more than fast track—we actually had been working on the car since November. He had the challenge of getting his financing together. In the meantime, he gave us cash to get started on the cars. We started without a firm contract, which

Peter and Murray Atherton with Terry Gainer, vice-president, international sales, look over the dome-car model.

is something I would normally never do. I knew Peter and knew he'd get there. He's a tough guy—nobody's going to get him down; he's going to succeed. So we started on that car and we were woefully behind. Earl Simons was the on-site guy; he'd be down here every couple of weeks.

MAC NORRIS: The key guy in getting those GoldLeaf dome coaches built was Earl Simons. Earl went down there and got the damn things built and nearly killed himself doing it.

PETER: We had to make miracles happen and Earl was fabulous. No other human being could have done what he did. He would work all night, all day, catch sleep on the train, and just keep going until he got all the bugs out.

TOM RADER: I had a mattress in my office—literally. I can remember getting an hour or two of sleep a night and being under that dome car: we had a brake leak and couldn't find the leak in the pipe to save our souls. We worked probably 19 hours, 24 hours a day for a week, getting all these brake leaks solved. It was the wildest thing I can ever remember being involved in. This was being done right in the middle of an 18-car train set we were building for Philip Morris. We had 325 employees and probably averaged between 20 and 45 on Peter's dome car. It was a major advancement in structural design—a more sophisticated, stronger structure and with different electrical systems. It was a coach-seating car instead of a table car and had a much narrower window, because Peter wanted one window for every seat. There were lots and lots of changes.

EARL SIMONS: We had only six months, but everybody was saying it could be done. It was an old commuter car they just stripped down. All they used was the centre beam out of it, then went and built all the structure in there. On May 17, we get the promotional pictures taken [of the exterior] and we're telling everybody, "Oh yeah, we'll get it there"— and on June 6 we're supposed to be running our first passenger. The car isn't anywhere near finished, but I wasn't about to tell anybody back home that. We had to make it work or else. The generators weren't even in yet. The electrical—all they had was wire strewn down there like spaghetti on the floor. They hadn't got the toilets in yet. The seats weren't even finished. On May 31, no carpets, no wall covering, no nothing— with a one-week deadline. We ended up cancelling the first trip for six people. (Later we gave them the option of a free round trip on the *Rocky*.) The next deadline was June 10. So we had about 40 people working on this thing, getting in the way of each other. I stayed down there for two weeks.

SCOTT REMILLARD: Earl went down there and hijacked it, basically. He said, "I don't care whether it's finished or not, it's leaving now."

TOM RADER: The time came to deliver the car and we weren't complete yet; we were working 24 hours a day. When the car got shipped, we had handrails that weren't in and wall fabric that was loose in the corners and seats that were being bolted down—all kinds of stuff. It was just a disaster. Earl was riding along with it and he was the greatest guy in the world—anybody else would have come totally unglued. He would check the contract progress plan and say, "Okay, where are we on this plan?" We had the car up there with a crew helping to finish it while they were putting the upstairs seats in.

EARL SIMONS: Tom said, "We'll put it on the back of the Amtrak [train], and we'll have guys on the back of the car, finishing as we're going up." We were all set to go. It was a monsoon the night we brought the car out of the shop to put it on the tracks. And we got it stuck in the mud. We had all been up 36 hours straight. Called in a couple more tow trucks; we had one push while the other one was pulling the 180,000-pound car and finally burned out the tow truck. This car was supposed to be taken down to the Union Pacific yard in Denver, to be picked up by Amtrak. Well, then Amtrak derailed on its way to us. It's not going anywhere for four days. I'm not cancelling another trip [for passengers who had booked to ride the dome car]. So Tom and I made a deal where we would rent a private locomotive for about $60,000 and take this one car all the way up to Vancouver from Denver.

We didn't get too far before a generator broke down and we had to go outside to fix it, maybe 50 miles out of Denver. Meanwhile we're welding on the back of the platform at 60 miles per hour. This thing was a moving billboard, that's what it was. It had *Rocky Mountaineer* on the outside, but the inside was totally unfinished. This one locomotive is pulling it down the track in the middle of the night. We're welding and we're cutting; there's sparks coming off the back of that thing. Of course there are phone calls right, left and centre that there's a fire on the back of the train.

Bearing in mind we worked with it for the following six weeks after we started running, I'd say we were somewhere between 80 percent and 100 percent finished. On the way up, I'm phoning Peter on a cellphone from the train saying, "Now we're 5 percent more finished than we were last time I phoned." I was leaving him voice-mail messages about the progress because he was really nervous. He thought we'd better cancel the next trip. "No, Peter, we're going to run it." We pulled into Vancouver, trying to trace all the electrical and get it wired up and running. We're trying to install all the lighting; we're doing the seats up top; I'm down on my hands and knees vacuuming while somebody else is coming behind me messing it up.

The GoldLeaf dome car leaves the factory en route to Vancouver.

We pulled into Vancouver about 4 in the morning. I promised Peter I would phone when it arrived, and he wanted to come down and see it. We're not quite finished, but we're finished enough. All the guys had been up for four days straight and just wanted to go to sleep. I said, "I'm sorry, guys, you can't go yet, we've got to take all this equipment off here. Our staff has got to come in here and stock this thing up and get it ready to go." So we had to spend the next three hours off-loading all our tools and parts. The guys hated me. Peter shows up and I haven't shaved because we had no water. When we went through the Cascade 10-mile tunnel, the back door was open because they were welding and a coal train went in front of us. We were just black. Anyway, I'm really proud of this car: "You should have seen it four days ago, Peter." And Peter is saying, "Oh, my

God." Fiona Barclay was Guest Services manager at the time, and when I saw the look in her eyes I said, "What's the matter, Fiona? We vacuumed."

I'd phoned ahead and asked Vicki to go out and buy plants. Herman Shadd used to run Sheraton hotels in Vancouver, and Peter brought him in to help Guest Services get this car going. I had a picture in my mind of what this car should look like with tablecloths on it, candles and everything. Then Herman came in and was very positive. I was just so tired, I had to go have a shower and grab a few hours' sleep. I came back six hours later and Herman had that whole car looking absolutely gorgeous.

VICKI HALLER: Peter phoned our house at 5:30 in the morning to say the dome was in. I threw my jeans on and told Roland [her husband] I had to go down to the station. I was so excited. I got there just as Peter was jumping on, and I was right behind him. After we were really excited, Earl gave me a list: "Okay, we need an ashtray for the vestibule, a plant for right here." Peter said, "We need a camera and a bunch of film and we need hotel rooms, we need air flights back, we need. . . ." And, of course, it's early in the morning and I said, "Fine. No problem." First I ran Earl out to the airport in Richmond because he'd left his car there. By 8 a.m. I was on the North Shore running around to get all of the odds and sods, including taps. And they had the car up and polished within the 24 hours—cleaned, the kitchen stocked, everything installed.

SCOTT REMILLARD: When I first went aboard, the freezer was warmer than the oven and the wiring was all mixed up. And we had to redesign the toilets: the train had to go a certain speed to make them flush. There was an awful smell for about three weeks.

In preparation for the dome car's arrival, the company hired Gerard Burke, who had managed 1066 Hastings, a restaurant in downtown Vancouver. He and Herman Shadd had designed the special GoldLeaf car service without ever seeing the dome coach until 4 p.m. on the day it arrived at the station.

GERARD BURKE: I hopped on and was just amazed—but there was no dining room, the seats and tables weren't in downstairs. I said to Peter, "Well, jeez, I guess we're not going out tomorrow then, are we?" And he said, "Gerard, you are going out tomorrow and it will be a trip that you will remember for the rest of your life." And it was. When we first got on, there were guys fastening the seats and the tables in the dining room. We went around them and stocked the dome with plates and spoons and china until about midnight and then went home to be back at about 5 in the morning.

EARL SIMONS was a wary observer on the first trip to Kamloops: I was in a three-piece suit because I'm representing the company. I'm on board, I'm tired. We carried a spare car in front, just in case. If the air conditioning broke down or the power went, we had to have someplace to put passengers. We only had to use it once in six weeks, which really amazed me. The air conditioning was touchy: if you didn't have somebody monitoring it all the time, it would either get too hot or too cold. Or it's too hot at the A end and too cold at B end. The kitchen would kick on all the equipment at once and blow everything, so we had to start again. Of course the toilets were physically blowing up. They had this plastic tube going down for the sewage and the water coming in. The air pressure somehow got doubled up and it blew the things up. The staff were phenomenal: they just pretended that nothing was wrong. "Oh, we're just having a little bit of problem with the washrooms, so you have to use that washroom up there."

GARY GERVAIS, the carman based in Kamloops who rides the train as a crack mechanic: The way the generators were designed for the dome car, the starter motor was turned, so to get at it you had to get under and try to reach up and use a mirror to see the one bolt at the top. It would take two days just to get that out. All they had to do was have the motor turned the other way.

EARL SIMONS: On the very first run of the first car, we learned that unless we had a filter in front of the radiator and changed that every night in Kamloops, all the dust from coal cars on the tracks would get in there, because it would pack up with fuzz from the cottonwood trees. And, of course, the radiator would overheat and shut down. I had a travel writer on that I was trying to impress. Fred was his name; he was looking for problems. The air conditioning conks out 10 minutes away from the station at Revelstoke. I grab a broom and go outside and lift up the side of the car. I've got a suit on and I'm in there just a-sweeping to clean up the radiator. As soon as I cleaned it up, we fired it back up again and it gets air flow through it, cooling it down. Everything is working fine. Well, unbeknownst to me, Fred was out there on the platform watching me do this. He showed me the story: " . . . and there was Earl Simons, quite a nice chap, but looking like a perfect idiot out there beating something underneath the car, but it worked."

On that first trip we almost derailed in Kamloops. We'd just off-loaded everybody. We're backing the car into the switch on our track and the switch failed—and we've got two wheels off the track. Luckily they were being so careful with this car, and when our carman stopped the train, we just sort of gradually pulled it back forward and onto the track. We checked the wheels and the bearings and everything was fine. We spiked down this track and away we went. Everybody was panicking and, of course, we're all smiling. We don't want anybody to see this.

The disability elevator wasn't wired yet, so it wasn't working. Of course, who do we have but a man who's got diabetes and who can't really walk that well. Well, jeez, I felt really bad now. So we did our usual safety walk with him, one guy behind and one in front of him, and got him up the stairs. At the end of that trip that guy was running, he was having such a good time.

PETER: I was pretty shaken up that first trip. I knew all the problems. The first hour out of Vancouver is not the most attractive and this man from Florida comes up and tells me, "I'm a psychiatrist and I travel first

Under glass: elegant dining and superb service.

class all over the world." He lists off the TGV, the *Orient Express*, the Concorde, the *Queen Elizabeth 2*. He's been everywhere with his wife and son, first class all the way. *Oh boy*, I think. And then he says, "This is the best thing I've ever been on—you're not charging enough." I knew we had a winner.

BABYSITTING

There were continuing challenges with the new GoldLeaf dome coach as the Mountaineers worked out the bugs, especially with the air conditioning. But in at least one case, the problem arose from an inexperienced carman's costly error.

TONY PELLEGRINO: I had finally got a couple of hours off in Vancouver one Friday night in '95 when I got a phone call on my cell. It's our train manager Gordon Sim. He's quite excited: in Field we used to take some water on, and this time the carman on duty put water into the diesel fuel for the generator—which shut down our new dome car. My heart just about came right out of my throat. I immediately got ahold of Rick Magill [chief mechanic in Kamloops] and said, "You're on a flight in two hours and I've ordered you all kinds of equipment." I'd talked to Earl Simons and then I had to break the news to Peter, one of the hardest things I had to do. Luckily, between Field and Calgary, we gave the guests service out of our other cars. Rick flew into Calgary and worked literally 24 straight hours to drain the tanks, put in special filters to gather any of the water in the system, and restarted those generators. He did the impossible. The next day, Sunday, guests came back on in Calgary and nobody missed a beat. It cost maybe in the $20,000 range because we had to redo the engines later. It still makes me cringe.

EARL SIMONS: Meanwhile, maintenance-wise, every single night we're still up working underneath the car. Rick Magill was with me for six weeks. We did nothing but babysit that car and make sure it worked. We had a problem with the holding-tank valve. Rick was so tired, he got under there and was fixing this thing and then we couldn't find him. We've been up all day and now it's the middle of the night and I'm looking for Rick, because I was buying everybody pizza. I found him sound asleep under the car, right in the middle of the track. He wouldn't have gotten hurt, as long as he stayed asleep.

TOM RADER: I fancied myself a pretty good marketer. But when Peter had told me what he was going to charge for this double-decker service—which was just about twice his normal price—I said, "Peter, I think you're crazy." And to this day I still laugh, because not only does he get the price, he sells out the car before the season even starts and calls

Tom Rader

me: "Can you get me some other dome cars?" I did—I had built a single-level dome car, very much like the original design we'd given him for his presentation to the government [in early 1990] and built that as a prototype for the Florida Fun Train. The Florida people were just in the process of raising money for a public offering and they didn't need the car that summer, so I got him together with them. They sent the car to us on lease to him, we repainted it in his colours in a week and a half, shipped it to Canada, and he used it for the next two summers. So that built the basis for him to have the cash to order more dome cars in 1996.

Tom Rader has now built a total of eight GoldLeaf dome coaches. As Mike Phillips of the Working Opportunity Fund points out, "Mechanically, the first one was the worst dome; the crew called it *Mir* [for the troubled Russian space station]. But it was an immediate success."

AN OLD RIVAL RETURNS

As the *Rocky Mountaineer* rolled towards increasing profit, a name from the past resurfaced: Murray Jackson. His lawyer accused Peter of having gone back on his word in 1989 not to break the confidentiality of Jackson's discussions with him about bidding for the rail service being privatized. "Once we'd put our own bid in," Peter remembers, "somebody told Murray Jackson, because I got a letter from his lawyer saying 'you committed to confidentiality'—which I never did. And that was the cause of the lawsuit which came much later. We never had another letter from him until three or four years later, when he finds out I am profitable. Then he tries to launch his lawsuit."

JIM HOUSTON: I wasn't emotionally involved, and my experience with lawsuits is that nobody wins and it was a cloud. It was taking up enormous amounts of Peter's time and the legal costs were ongoing.

BEV ARMSTRONG: Peter wanted to fight it. The board thought about where our time and Peter's time would be best spent. Is it fighting this lawsuit, which can eat up a lot of time and takes a lot of energy away from running the business? We had already proven at this point that the business was making money and it was an opportunity that had to be pursued. And this lawsuit had Peter gearing up for a turmoil and preparing like he prepares for everything, which would have taken him out of the picture for running anything. We didn't have a knockdown fight, but there were always Peter's objections—he had his own integrity and honour to prove as much as anything else. [In the end] he agreed that we should try and see if we could settle it.

I suggested that we had to have somebody other than Peter approach Murray Jackson—not thinking that it would be me, but that's ultimately what happened. Through the lawyers initially and then meeting directly with Jackson. It was interesting, because I wanted to see who this guy was. Meeting with him didn't change my opinion that we had a winnable case but that the solution was to get him out of there. Because we knew that Murray Jackson wasn't working at the time, our first offer of settlement was an offer of employment for him. The big premise of his own case was that he had this great approach to marketing and how he was going to do all these things. So we said, "Well, we will pay you to bring that expertise—we will employ you and pay you well with an incentive and everything else." It was basically a way of calling his bluff on that and to quantify a number.

He came back with a classic. He said, "I don't really want to work for you. I don't think I could work with Peter"—and we knew that anyway.

Peter was very skeptical when we suggested this strategy to him, but it was a way to put a quantity of dollars on the table—and that got us into settlement talks. We settled. And while we would have won that case, we had already spent a small fortune on legal costs and could have easily spent another fortune on top of what we'd already spent. Peter, to this day, still thinks that he shouldn't have settled, and I think he blames me for settling it. But we went on and had a good year.

SIDE TRIP: DELIGHTS OF THE DOME

FRED FRAILEY, deputy editor of *Kiplinger's Personal Finance* magazine and the author of books about trains, was among the first passengers to ride the new dome car that first year. In Calgary, he, his wife and their two children upgraded to the GoldLeaf service on the spur of the moment—and were delighted they did. He describes the tail-end of the trip in these excerpts from an article he wrote for *Trains Magazine*.

FRED FRAILEY: The scene is changing. The hills are becoming wooded on each side of the Fraser [River], and the canyon even deeper and more spectacular. Past Hope, B.C., CP rails go their separate ways in the widening valley. By then we're eating—yes, one last round of gluttony: chilled salmon, prawns, scallops, and mussels with a creamy raspberry vinaigrette, preceded by salad and followed by dessert and coffee, the whole event washed down by Australian wines.

Afternoon becomes a time to relax and talk to the people you've begun to get to know—a time to anticipate the end of a pleasurable experience. If this sounds like an anticlimax, I certainly didn't think so at the time. Plenty of things are happening. First, we lose our engineer, who becomes so sick that the train stops and we wait for a CN truck to pick the fellow up.

Receiving the statement for the upgrade to GoldLeaf service, Frailey reflects on what the extra money has bought him: "Playing railroad president in the front of the dome car and tycoon on the observation platform, plus four great meals . . . and better motel rooms."

FRED FRAILEY: And for the same amount of money, my trainophobic wife has had a great time, too—for me, an incalculable benefit. Our two youngest children have seen the most spectacular scenery in North America and had a railroad experience with their dad that they'll never forget. Without regrets, I sign the Visa slip. . . .

You have to wonder how much better business might be if people knew about the *Rocky Mountaineer*. Most people's knowledge of Canadian railroads is what they gleaned from the Public Broadcasting's feature *Last Train Across Canada*, narrated by a lovable old coot, Australian journalist Murray Sayle. But the faux-sentimental documentary is studded with inaccuracies, beginning with the title. . . . To the degree you could ever cross Canada by passenger train, you still can, on VIA's *Canadian* on CN. Again and again the point is made by *Last Train*: For travelers, the Canadian rail experience is over.

But it isn't. So weep not for the *Rocky Mountaineer*. It is finding the traveling public, if not yet the railfans.

C H A P T E R   8

Highballing: The Great Growth Years

¶ It was a richly symbolic move. As the

number of passengers and employees began multiplying with the intro-

duction of the first GoldLeaf dome coach, Great Canadian Railtour

decamped for greater if not greener pastures. In November 1995 it left the

cramped 6,500 square feet of its suburban North Vancouver offices for a

spacious 17,000 square feet downtown in the former CN Rail quarters at

Pacific Central Station. The 1919 Neoclassical Revival stone structure fac-

ing Vancouver's gritty Main Street had long ago housed the Canadian

.   .   .

Left: The cast of Two River Junction, *from left to right: Chris Doherty,
Tina Moore, Gary Nielsen, Gord Milne.*

177

Northern Railway, another private railroad launched in the West by bold entrepreneurs. The *Rocky Mountaineer* now shared the station with VIA Rail, its old antagonist, which would soon mount a new campaign to subvert the success of its private-sector competitor.

Fortunately Peter Armstrong had added some executive strength to allow him the time and energy to do battle with VIA. In July '95 he had hired a new director of guest services and operations, James Terry, and a year later hired his first senior vice-president and chief operating officer, Rosemary Pahl. "As each manager came along," recalls Vicki Haller, his executive assistant, "Peter had to give them a little bit more responsibility and then he became more comfortable. But in the beginning, it's kind of like taking a baby away from his mother to walk a few steps: gradually he can do a bit more and finally he can run. Rosemary was the first person in her position, so it was very difficult to relinquish the reins."

HOPPING ABOARD

British-born James Terry had been managing director of a Vancouver company that owns four high-end restaurants, including Seasons in the Park. He brought an elegant kind of ebullience to his position as overseer of the station, onboard staff and the *Mountaineer*'s guests. But his first meeting with Peter was less than auspicious.

JAMES TERRY: Peter says, "Well, I need a person who will schedule the staff and make sure the train is clean, make sure the guests are fed." I thought, *How uninspiring a job you've made it sound* (but I didn't say that to him). Peter suggested I spend a couple of hours with Murray—Murray Atherton waxes lyrical about how incredible the company is—and then Earl Simons was able to talk to me hotelier to hotelier. As much as I'm an Englishman who was brought up with trains, they don't do anything for me from a romantic point of view. I love being on the train, but it's not my passion. My passion is managing people, making guests wowed— that's where I get my high. The thing that really did it was when Peter suggested I fly out to Calgary and come back on the train. I spent one day on the Signature service and one on GoldLeaf and experienced unbelievably enthusiastic personalized service in an incredible setting. When I got back, he bought a hamburger for my three-year-old daughter and signed me up in the McDonald's in the station.

While James was being run ragged with his dual role in guest services and operations, Peter was still without a second-in-command to lighten the administrative baggage he was bearing as CEO. He turned again to Bob McMillin, director of executive search services for Price Waterhouse Management Consultants, to help run a high-level search for a chief operating officer. As it happened, the winning candidate was a wo-man Peter already knew who had a surprising lack of background in either tourism or trains. Rosemary Pahl was president of two Vancou-ver health-care groups that had merged the operations of four hospitals on eight sites, with 5,000 staff and a budget of $300 million.

James Terry

JIM HOUSTON, who was still a partner in Great Canadian: Let me tell you, it was a three-year battle to hire Rosemary Pahl. Peter needed help; he couldn't do it all. He was a control freak.

BOB MCMILLIN: Rosemary had been brought out here a couple of years earlier from Edmonton, where she was the president of Glenrose Rehabilitation Hospital [Canada's largest teaching-and-research rehab hospital]. It was questionable initially because her back-ground was health-care administration and management. A great deal had to do with the confidence that Peter had in seeing her in the Young Presidents' Organization, where they work in case-study groups and build a mentoring sort of relationship. Rosemary had listened to him make a presentation at YPO and had an inkling that she wanted to get into the private sector. She had a bachelor of science nursing degree and had come up through nursing management, did her MBA at West-ern, and then went to work for KPMG for four years in Edmonton in a health-care consulting practice—doing a lot of strategic planning and organizational design for hospitals. So she was an interesting, eclectic mix. Rosemary was up against some incredibly powerful competition, but Peter had faith in her.

ROSEMARY PAHL: I really do have a private-sector mentality and believe that you can get things done by motivating teams and that everybody really wants to do a good job. My job as a CEO of hospitals was to have a safe environment for the patients and the staff, so that at the end of the day the patients got service and quality and value for their money.

Rosemary Pahl

The Rocky Mountaineer is a company that provides a service, and as the train goes through the mountains, there's a safety component as well. Passengers pay a lot of money and want to be treated well and to have an experience. The basic principles were exactly the same.

VICKI HALLER: Rosemary was very good for Peter. She would listen and take it all in and then do it. If she disagreed, she would say, "Well, Peter, maybe if we tried it this way . . ." It was under Rosemary that we split up operations and guest services and put it under two vice-presidents.

BOB MCMILLIN: At the Rocky Mountaineer she brought the beginnings of infrastructure. She was a lovely complement to his dreaming. Rosemary was able to interpret what he wanted into operational plans, draw up a business plan for the business unit, draft out a proper organizational chart and actually look at where the growth was coming. She worked it all out and figured that if Murray was going to get double the seat sales, then James was going to be overwhelmed—because all of it would come down on guest services.

BLACK SUNDAY

It all came crashing down on both James Terry and Rosemary Pahl on July 26, 1996, just 10 days after she had joined the company. It was early morning on a Sunday, with the train scheduled to depart the Vancouver station for Kamloops. Peter, knowing he now had a COO in charge, had taken the rare opportunity to escape with his family to their place on Savary Island, three ferry rides and several hours up the coast.

ROSEMARY PAHL: It was the first weekend since I'd started work and I decided to get up at 5:30 and go down to the station. We had over 600 passengers that day, a brutally hot day, and by 7 in the morning the passengers were all loaded on the train. And the air conditioning wasn't working—it would start up and stop.

JAMES TERRY: The air conditioning is electrically run by power cars at the front of the train. Somebody had turned them off overnight, and even before we called the "All aboard!" we knew we couldn't get the power car started. Every time we connected it, the whole thing defused.

ROSEMARY PAHL: And we kept trying and trying and meanwhile the air conditioning was working on two dome cars with their own generators. Also at that time—which is not the case now—most of the Signature service cars didn't have holding tanks, so the washrooms were locked in the station. The people were served breakfast on the train but then obviously couldn't use the washrooms. The weather report said it was expected to be over 100 degrees in the Interior that day, and we knew it would be a health and safety risk to go. People were starting to get irate; what are we going to do? There was one school of thought to get them to a city hotel, feed everybody really well, and by later in the afternoon we would have the train fixed. But it's a 10-hour trip— and look at the average age here and these people have been up since 5 in the morning. If we keep them in Vancouver, then we have a problem, because if we get the train to Kamloops to get it fixed, and if everybody doesn't make Day Two [to reach their destinations], then they're going to miss their connections. James and I, through the process of elimination, figured that no solution to keep the people in Vancouver was a good one. So the next question was: how do we get 600 people to Kamloops (minus however many were on the dome cars, which did have generators)?

We had people on the phones, rounding up every bus they could. Well, it became obvious that we were only going to get about three buses. And there are seats for about 30 people in the station—nowhere to sit, nowhere to go. Finally I decided that maybe we should just hire taxis. Everybody thought I was crazy.

JAMES TERRY: We literally rented 100 taxis to Kamloops—*non*-air-conditioned taxis.

ROSEMARY PAHL: Grant Setter, the Vancouver station manager [who died in early 1999], was on the phone, and Yellow Cab wanted $700 per taxi. Grant just about had a heart attack. I got on the phone and negotiated it down to $500 per cab. We had an assembly line going, loading up the taxis, and told everybody to stop on the way to have lunch (and keep their receipt). I actually got a phone call later from Merritt from someone wanting to know what this fleet of Yellow taxis going down the highway was all about.

Other people were still working the phones to find buses. There were two or three passengers that you could not reason with—one of them named Armstrong, whom we always thought was Peter's cousin; we put him in a hotel. One guy got a limo because his rental car broke down. And when one fellow refused to go, one of the staff went in the baggage car—which must have been about 140 degrees—and found the man's baggage for him. The last person left Vancouver at 10 to 1. . . .

I figured I might have had the shortest career with the *Rocky Mountaineer*. James had tried to phone Peter, who was on his way back from Savary and got part of the message before his phone cut out. He was having a fit, not knowing what was going on. By the time he arrived, the passengers had left, and we had apology letters ready. He couldn't quite believe what had happened: that the train didn't go—that was a first ever—and then that we had hired a fleet of cabs. When he heard about the taxis, he wasn't happy. His first reaction was that we should have let the passengers stay in Vancouver and got buses later in the day. Within a couple of hours, Peter thought the taxis were a great idea. And for the rest of my time at the *Rocky Mountaineer*, every time he wanted to tell a positive story, he used the taxis: "Yes, these things happen, and the company would rather lose a few hundred thousand dollars than jeopardize somebody's health."

JAMES TERRY: We met in my office to decide what we would do to make these people happy. I said [a refund of] $400 per person—more than half their fare—because their holiday was ruined. And we gave them our *All Aboard!* gift books and free booze on board the next day. I flew immediately to Kamloops to meet and apologize to people and arranged free dinners, wine and beer for 600 guests. [Among many other volunteers from the community, the general manager of Kamloops's Coast Canadian Inn and his wife helped seat people, and their catering manager worked the bar.]

Some passengers had waited and stayed on board in the domes, because they have their own air conditioning. They got to Lillooet, the hottest 100 yards of track there is in the whole of Canada, when all the gas ran out and the generator packed up. It was just injury upon injury. We had to send out three buses from Kamloops to pick them up—*non*-air-conditioned buses. Then we were up all night in Kamloops trying to repair everything.

CHRIS MURPHY: This company on a couple of occasions has made me so proud that they've just given me goosebumps. One of them was that Black Sunday when the train never left. But they got the people to Kamloops, even in taxis if that's what it took, and the next day they had letters of apology and gifts for them. They made people feel really good about what they had gone through.

SARAH DARLING, a travel consultant with Ellison Travel & Tours in Exeter, Ontario, wrote a typical letter of thanks after Black Sunday: I have just received on my desk the letters of apology as well as the cheque for $400 from yourself to my clients . . . and even though they were disappointed about what had happened, they were very happy with the service they received from your company. They said that everything came across well organized even though I'm sure that staff were panicking since this has never happened. They still enjoyed the tour very much. . . . I would never hesitate to use your company and I know the client would love to travel with you again. This letter to my clients was among the nicest ones I have ever seen from a supplier.

ROSEMARY PAHL: After the Train That Didn't Go, I honestly believed that James Terry had a job that was beyond any human being's capacity, because the spread was the entire business—operations, all the mechanical, all the dealings with the railroad plus all the service side, the onboards, the food. James was working seven days a week, 16, 18 hours a day, and doing a fabulous job—but it was going to kill him. I felt that he was functioning at a vice-president level and that we could split his job in two and have someone handle the mechanical-operations side and interface on a daily basis with the railroad.

The Rocky Mountaineer's *22-hectare rail yard in Kamloops.*

UP IN KAMLOOPS

While James Terry became vice-president of guest and station services (which now encompassed reservations), the first-ever vice-president of operations was Doug Kelsey, whom Rosemary Pahl describes as "very dedicated, with an unbelievable work ethic." Kelsey, who had 15 years in the multi-unit retail, waste/recycling and petroleum industries, oversaw the relocation of staff, equipment and key suppliers to the company's new maintenance facility in Kamloops, where he was based for three years.

EARL SIMONS: In '96 we looked at going double frequency. That's when I bought a second fleet of cars from VIA—17 café cars and a couple of baggage cars—and had them all shipped to Kamloops. We were renting space; we knew we had to develop this yard up there. We were working on that with a company that was going to put a depot in for us adjacent to this land. When the company went broke, I had only three days to put the whole thing together. CN gave us an S track all through their yard and we worked out a deal on a handshake. We started building the yard on April 17 and had it open on July 18. That's three and a half miles of track and underground facilities—sewage and water, power, built a compound and opened her up. We tend to do things fairly quickly around here. . . .

One night we're up in Kamloops and had arranged the cleaning of our dome cars on the outside. Now, these cars are 17 feet tall, so they are difficult. Rick Magill [chief mechanical officer] had this idea to just climb on top of the dome car, walk down the centre and clean the windows that way. But it's a safety issue. Rick's old-time railway: "Ah, not a problem."

"You can't do that, Rick. We've rented you lifts and everything. You go up there and clean it properly." Rick was running behind schedule because the train came in late, so he decided that he was going to sneak up there this night and do it his way. He's walking on top of the cars and he's got a cellphone hanging down. Peter and I pull into the parking lot together. Rick has got his back to us so he doesn't know we're right down below him. Peter borrows my cellphone and calls him: "Hi, Rick, how are you? What are you doing?" "Oh, I'm just helping wash the dome car."

Peter: "Oh, how are you doing that?"

Rick: "With a squeegee."

Peter says, "Turn around, Rick, and wave at me." And Rick turns around and knows he's in trouble.

At budget meetings, Peter would always bring this up as a joke: "Rick, you didn't tell me the truth that time you were in Kamloops. How do I know that you're telling me everything this time?" Finally Rick said, "I made one mistake. Come on, give me a break." And Peter said, "Okay, you'll get 10 bucks from me every time I tell that story." Well, he can't resist telling that story, and he would come back and hand 10 bucks to me and I'd make him sign it and take it up to Rick on my trips to Kamloops. Rick got them all framed.

PETER: I started telling that story incessantly, and when Rick would hear it from people visiting in Kamloops, he'd want to tell his side. When we were running the Longest Train Ever (see page 193), I'd told him, "Rick, you run the train without any failures or delays and I'll pay you $10 for every time I tell that washing-the-dome story." I think I've paid him about $100. And Rick says the money would appear like manna from heaven.

In Kamloops, Doug Kelsey had strong support from contractor Sue Velasquez, Doug and Flo Smith's daughter, who had soon assumed masterful control of the task of servicing the trains and passengers there with her own company, under contract to Great Canadian. She had found her vocation in the astonishingly complex supervisory role, and eventually she would also find a new romance.

SUE VELASQUEZ: After my mom told Peter that it would be her last year, in the last couple of weeks of the season my daughter was in a serious car accident, and I didn't even think about taking over from Mom. It wasn't until January that things were settling down and I had to get my life together again because I needed income. I went to see Peter in Vancouver and he said, "Don't be afraid of making mistakes, because if you don't make mistakes, then I'll think that you're not learning"—and that made me feel better, because I was very nervous. He asked that I check into some courses on business and tourism, and I said I would. But I've been too busy.

My phone is on 24 hours a day. If I have a nap, I'll put my message machine on, but other than that, it's on all the time. On train arrival night, it's right beside the bed. Train arrival day starts between 6 and 7 in the morning. I have reservation and station reports that come in from every station, and they tell me hotel accommodation problems, people who "no-showed" on the train, people who arrived at the train station with no bookings. It's like a big jigsaw puzzle that I have to put together: place and switch people and book and cancel hotels. Then shipping companies phone and my assistant, Kyle Erickson, and I have orders to receive, including souvenirs.

We have a stock order that I have to get ready for the train cars: the food, liquor and all the other supplies that we replenish in Kamloops. The food for RedLeaf service is done by a separate contractor. We have our own executive chef for the dome cars, who looks after all the food that's cooked in the kitchen with about 21 staff. The food in my area is all the cookies, the chips-and-bites, sugar, tea, coffee, liquor, as well as the pillow slips, blankets, corkscrews, cutlery. Then I do up the car-cleaning checklist for my crew. I have two supervisors for the cleaning crew, because we have a staff of about 40 to clean and stock the coaches.

Now we have three arrivals a day, a large train from Vancouver and the others from Jasper and Calgary/Banff. The first one usually comes in about 3:45 in the afternoon and the last one is due around 6:20. Since we went into this double frequency, it's very seldom we have late trains. Once the people are in town, it's my responsibility to make sure they're happy in their accommodation.

On train departure day, I get up at 4:45 a.m., because the crew has to be down to the station by 5:30. (I've slept in once.) We have to communicate with the train managers who are looking for supplies or souvenir orders that may have gone to the wrong car or some that weren't filled. The buses start heading out to the hotels around 6, and I'm on the bus radio in contact with them at all times.

Among those Sue Velasquez would work closely with was Gerard Burke, the senior GoldLeaf service manager, based in Kamloops.

GERARD BURKE: From the beginning, when Sue and I started communicating, we have always been like best friends. Sue would tell me her problems and I would tell her mine—and it just went from there. It was in 1998 that Sue made her big move and became single again. It wasn't too much longer after that I said, "Hey, would you like to go out with me?"

SUE VELASQUEZ: Well, we used to hang out a little bit. It went from hang out to a real date and *Wow, this is really strange.* But because we knew each other so well, we just connected.

Sue Velasquez

GERARD BURKE: Then we had the concern of how we would work together after the relationship developed. We were discreet about it, but not as discreet as we thought we were. . . . But [looking at Sue] it is awesome, isn't it?

SUE VELASQUEZ: It's great, but you know there are times when we're overtired and we get a little cranky. I'm a contractor and he works directly for the company. I look after my staff, and he wants them to do extra duties on his dome car and I say, "Well, we don't get paid to do that." Those little things happen once in a while, but not very often. Gerard is an asset to my area and I am to his. We work very well together. . . . Sometimes we have to deal with people who take sick in Kamloops or they've fallen on the train.

GERARD BURKE: In 1998 one woman tripped on the stairs in the dome car, had a bad fall, and sprained her ankle, broke her wrist, and cracked her ribs—an older woman with her husband. They were in their late 70s and they were newlyweds. Sue got a cab for her on arrival and I went to the hospital with her. She was all concerned about not missing our dinner-theatre show, God bless her heart. I stayed with her as she got X-rays and they admitted her. They had to do surgery on her wrist because it was a bad break. Between Sue and me, we were there until 3 o'clock in the morning on and off. Then we had to get a prescription for her and picked up her husband, who was in the hotel. They ended up missing the train the next day—although even after surgery she was adamant to get on it. So in the morning after a couple of hours' sleep, we went to the hotel at 5:30 with the wheelchair ready to pick her up. But she was out of it from the medication. Sue looked after the couple for two days. The woman was released and we made arrangements for them to get on the next train to Banff, all propped up on pillows. But she never did get to the dinner theatre.

TWO RIVER ERUPTION

The evening show the injured woman missed had become one of Doug Kelsey's responsibilities as VP of operations in Kamloops. He collaborated with Rosemary Pahl on deciding the fate of this entertainment venture that Peter had commissioned for *Mountaineer* passengers who stayed overnight in the Interior city. As communications consultant Jess Ketchum recollects: "Peter let it be known that he thought that the business community should be developing an attraction of some sort that would take advantage of all these people he was bringing into town. When nothing happened, he offered $100,000 in seed money to anyone who could come up with a business plan for an attraction, and he'd be a partner." When nobody took the bait, he decided Great Canadian itself would produce a dinner theatre. An effervescent Albertan-reared arts promoter named Tracy Lakeman moved from Vancouver to Kamloops in early 1996 to create and manage what became known as *Two River Junction*—named for the conjunction of the North and South Thompson rivers, which would play an unexpected part in the theatre's history.

ERIC BELANGER: Tracy worked for Sam Feldman [the Vancouver talent agent] and Arts Umbrella [the performing- and visual-arts school for children on Vancouver's Granville Island]. Tracy's a jack of all trades: a promoter, a special-events coordinator—a multi-talented lady. She did a promotion that involved the train back in '93 called Bud Country *Rocky Mountaineer* Express. She had a bunch of musicians in Vancouver that she wanted to bring to Calgary for the Canadian Country Music Awards, and so she hooked up the *Mountaineer* with Budweiser. For the inauguration of our fifth season, I brought in Tracy and she put on a fabulous little special event.

Tracy Lakeman

TRACY LAKEMAN: I'd decided I wanted to live in Kamloops. Peter talked me out of buying the South Thompson Ranch near there as a small conference facility. But he seized the opportunity and sent me to Kamloops to look at different sites for a dinner theatre. We started working on it in October '95. I went full-time with the company in January and moved up here April 1, to be open May 5. Between January and April, we started to discover that the community was not thrilled with this idea, because they felt they would lose business because of *Two River Junction*. There was a letter to the editor saying "How dare *Rocky Mountaineer* do that to this community?" . . . But we have at our fingertips one of the best communicators I've ever come across, by the name of Jess Ketchum.

Jess and I started to build a campaign. We sent out invitations to all the restaurants to meet with myself, James Terry, the VP of guest services, and Jess. Some of the restaurateurs were hysterical—one gentleman was screaming at us. We said we were basing *Two River Junction*'s attendance on only 30 percent of the train, which still left 70 percent going out into the community. I was hiring 30 people during the summer season and a local caterer to handle all the food, who in turn was hiring all kinds of people to prepare it. And we were bringing an attraction to the city that hopefully would encourage other tours to come to Kamloops.

JESS KETCHUM: Some of the restaurateurs were agitating with city hall. It was explained to them that these were, first and foremost, *our* guests, and we were bringing them to Kamloops. We could feed them on the train, all of them, but some of the guests were anxious to find something else to do in Kamloops other than just go out for dinner.

TRACY LAKEMAN: It was pretty hairy. That night, by the end of the two hours, a number of the restaurateurs actually stood up and congratulated us and talked to the others: "This is a good thing for our community and we should be supporting them." A couple of them wrote letters to the editor on our behalf. We finally got approval from council. Then we had about 29 days to put it together.

A RIVER RUNS THROUGH IT

Tracy hired six local musicians (four of whom were still performing or helping to stage *Two River Junction* in 1999), and they conceived a revue based on local history, complete with native entertainers drumming and dancing in full regalia. It was housed in a tent 66 by 164 feet, seating 300 guests, pitched in Pioneer Park beneath a bridge—right beside the rapidly rising South Thompson River.

TRACY LAKEMAN: They were predicting floods bigger than 1979; I had no idea what they were talking about. But sure enough, here come the floods. We went to the community and said, "The tent's going to be flooded out. We need your help." I had found the one private guy in town with a sandbagging machine, and volunteers started making sandbags. Then we got inmates from Raleigh Correctional to come out, too— about 20 of them from the minimum-security jail at a time—and at one point had about 30 volunteers from the community. I was so touched—

Two River Junction *began life in a tent, seen here under construction.*

but that's this community. The first year we were able to hold off the water. We had to do it the next year as well, and the water started to come under the sandbags. I got a pump.

The second year, I was learning how to control the weather elements far better. We were battling with wind and rain—and, of course, the guests are older and all they can hear is this *Whoosh!* of the tent and they were terrified. The first year, we'd put in two air conditioners. It would get up to 40 degrees in the tent and there were a lot of complaints. We put chunks of ice in swamp coolers, ran the water over the ice, and blew air through the ductwork into the tent. The following year, I increased the ductwork.

And then we were hit with maple bugs from the maple trees that surrounded the tent. In the fall, the maple bugs were attracted to the white of the tent. They look like little brown cockroaches with antennae. We couldn't spray because they would just come back. In fact, the staff were instructed on how to remove them should they fall on a table—swoosh them off and step on them. They landed on some guests and we had to tell them they were perfectly harmless.

We moved to the Italian cultural centre in '98.

ROSEMARY PAHL: By the time I'd arrived in '96, *Two River Junction* was losing a bag of money. We tried to fix it up two years in a row. Doug Kelsey and I had both done a business case and felt very strongly, based on feedback, that it was eroding the brand name of the *Rocky Mountaineer*. Quite frankly, my advice was to get out of the business and to find some other way of pre-selling reservations in the city. Peter would not get out of the business, so the alternative was to get out of the tent.

TRACY LAKEMAN: In the first year we lost over $300,000, in the second $100,000. We've got this huge infrastructure and now we're trying to fill the seats to pay for it. And we never do catch up. Then we found Columbo Lodge [the Italian centre] and changed the inside to look a lit-

The full cast of Two River Junction, *who captivate* Mountaineer *guests in Kamloops.*

tle more rustic but still keep a classy atmosphere. The guests didn't want the wood floor and the *Whoosh!* of the tent. We're halfway through the second season [1997] and they're thinking of pulling the plug completely on *Two River Junction*. I said, "We'll make it work." We laid off some of the performers, the guys doing sound and lights, and servers. We turned it around; it lost a minimal amount of money.

The third year, it was touch-and-go. We had to convince the COO, Rosemary, because she was ready to pull the plug, and we cut back again. We hired a producer, Alan Askew, and introduced a Billy Miner theme in 1998. I spent hours in the museum looking up story lines about Miner [who on September 10, 1904, at Silverdale, B.C., became the first armed bandit to hold up a train in Canada]. I think we made some money that year, and halfway through our fourth year, it looked like we were going to make a lot more.

In the first year, we'd attracted an average of around 15 percent to 20 percent of the people riding the train; in 1999 it was about 50 percent. And that still leaves 35,000 people over the course of a season going to the local restaurants.

ROSEMARY PAHL: I was glad I was wrong and that it got turned around.

BOB MCMILLIN: Rosemary gave the company some framework and taught them how to run a business in a formal sense. She taught them about scheduling, about making and monitoring plans, and all of the proper things that big businesses do that little businesses don't when they are just reacting to a phone call. And I think if you asked James or Murray or Earl—who I'm sure were wondering why a health-care professional was in the train business—they would tell you, as they told me a year later, "Rosemary is running the train and that's fine by us."

THE LONGEST EVER

Another of Rosemary Pahl's responsibilities during her first eventful year with the *Mountaineer* was overseeing the Day of the Longest Train. Until 1996, the lengthiest passenger consist ever to run in Canada had been Canadian Pacific's Dominion Train #3, which on July 13, 1965, operated from Regina, Saskatchewan, with 27 cars. (At the time, consists seldom exceeded 26 cars because of technical restrictions.)

ERIC BELANGER: I remember the days when 324 people on board was a huge train for the *Rocky Mountaineer* and we would all come down and pitch the luggage—everyone, including Peter, would roll up their sleeves. In '96 I get pulled into Peter's office with the executives and they say, "Do you realize that on September 12, you have over 1,200 people leaving Vancouver on the train—and what are you going to do to promote this?" My job is to make it news. We had about a three-month lead. We went on a manhunt to scour the archives and found out that the troop trains in the war carried more passengers, but not by much. But we *were* able to boldly say that we were the *longest* passenger train in Canadian railway history. The biggest trains on record had 27 cars—the braking system was deemed less reliable beyond that number—and here we had 37 [which included three locomotives, 25 Signature service coaches, the bi-level GoldLeaf dome coach, a single-level SilverLeaf coach, three power cars, three baggage cars and one lounge/smoking car.]

So that was the hook, and it worked beautifully. The first thing we did was create a huge sign over the doors to the platform that told guests they were embarking on the longest train in history. Everyone was given a nice little Canadian flag; we had onboard literature so that everybody knew what was going on; and we hired our own camera crew and had our own reporter. We were in fact packaging our own report, with Peter being interviewed about the success of privatization. The regular media were there, too: television, radio, the *Globe and Mail,* the *Financial Post.* In Kamloops we invited the whole town to come down for some cake and a band. We got phenomenal coverage about the Little Train That Could—we got picked up on the news in 25 cities across Canada.

ROSEMARY PAHL: There weren't enough bedrooms in Kamloops for over 1,200 people. Four passengers were to sleep over at this little place in the country. James [Terry] and I decided to go check it out. The owners were lovely but had never ever run a bed and breakfast before: there were no drapes on the windows, there was a shared bathroom down the hall. The fellow was young and to him it looked like a palace, but it wouldn't be suitable for a paying passenger. So one set of guests got my hotel room in Kamloops and the other set got James's.

ERIC BELANGER: The timing of the event could not have been better. Later in October Peter was going before the Standing Committee on

The first of the Longest Trains.

Transport in Ottawa, meeting with the prime minister and a lot of his constituents, and presenting a case for the *Rocky Mountaineer* at the time VIA Rail was announcing that it wanted to increase its services.

JESS KETCHUM: The minister of transport, David Collenette, urged the Standing Committee on Transport to conduct hearings in Ottawa on the future of VIA Rail and how to revitalize passenger-rail services in Canada. We decided to spend our time encouraging them to understand that VIA Rail runs right across the country coast to coast and they should get out of Ottawa, listen to some other people, and come on the *Rocky Mountaineer*. Instead of having two hours maximum [at a hearing in Ottawa], we had two days with them. We put the Parlour Car on the train and spent virtually all of two days just letting them understand the product, experiencing what the guest experiences. In Kamloops, we arranged for them to have a presentation by three councillors and the city manager about how important the *Rocky Mountaineer* was to the city in economic activity. Then, on the last day, we got them on board the Parlour Car—they didn't know we had this rolling boardroom—where Peter made a presentation.

And their report, when it came out, was very complimentary to the *Rocky Mountaineer*. I don't think there is anyone in Ottawa in government circles today, regardless of party or department, [who] would tell you that privatization will ever go ahead without the Great Canadian Railtour Company being consulted or involved.

On October 7, 1999, the company would surpass its own record by running an even longer train, with 41 pieces of equipment: three locomotives pulling 38 passenger, baggage and power cars, including six GoldLeaf dome coaches—carrying a total of 1,144 passengers.

TAKING ON VIA—AGAIN

Planning for the first of the Longest Trains had gone on against the background of the fresh threat from VIA Rail, which still smarted at the victories Great Canadian Railtour had won—not the least of which was its success in the marketplace. The hostility behind the subsidized Crown railway's latest foray had been brewing for a long time, as a VIA insider recounts.

MICHAEL SHAMAN, who was then VIA's regional director of maintenance in western Canada: Peter is having lots of problems contractually with VIA Rail and I'm hearing this on the sidelines, about a settlement of the dispute and not paying bills, and VIA threatening not to operate the equipment. . . . There was a lot of discussion throughout the company of the poor relationship between VIA and the Great Cana-

On September 12, 1996, the longest passenger train had 37 cars.

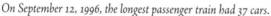

dian Railtour Company. My direction was to treat Peter Armstrong as a customer but at the same time take a very cautious approach, because of his willingness to expand his market and take away from the VIA market. I gave him what he paid for, and what he paid for, he received—nothing more and nothing less. And at the same time, I struck up what I would call a good business relationship with the company. I was a tough negotiator and my policy was honesty, and at the end of the day we shook hands and had a beer together, because business was business and my allegiance was to VIA.

As time went on, there was a change in the presidency. Terry Ivany came in [as president, in September 1993, for four years] and at the same time the battle was really heating up for VIA to expand its network of services, in particular between Vancouver and Jasper. VIA had a strategy to introduce additional train services in what we call the peak periods, between May and September, to accommodate ridership between Jasper and Vancouver, which was a high-potential market and a sector where we could make some very good profit. The mediation that had taken place said that VIA would have to stay out of that market until such time that the agreement with Peter Armstrong and VIA expired. In other words, VIA could not introduce any parallel services directly in competition with Armstrong's train, despite the fact that Mr. Ivany in his wisdom

challenged that—in terms of getting ready for the service and preparing people and moving the company in that direction and getting ready to have the right things in place.

I think at this point it became personal between Mr. Ivany and Mr. Armstrong.

DUGAL SMITH, the Price Waterhouse management consultant who advised Peter: There's a story that Peter tells that he's touring some big shot from New York around the [Vancouver] station and Terry Ivany is there. Peter introduces the fellow to Terry and Terry shakes hands with him—but will not shake hands with Peter.

MICHAEL SHAMAN: Let me say this: there's a certain history in VIA Rail for dislike of Peter Armstrong, not as an individual, but his ability to take that product and turn it into something that is a winner. And I think that a lot of employees who still reside in VIA today or who have left VIA have a distaste for Mr. Armstrong because he accomplished a lot. Total resentment. You know, I have to take my hat off to Armstrong. It wasn't given to him. He built it to what it is today. It wasn't done with energy alone. It was a huge capital investment.

TERRY IVANY: What I said to Shaman and these guys was, "Look, a lot of our people are very upset with Peter, very upset." People in the maintenance centre and people in the station—because Peter said some very unkind things about these people, let alone me. When he went about doing his thing, he really conveyed the impression that people at VIA were incompetent and they shouldn't be getting these subsidies. Anyhow, it was really bad. So I said, "Look, guys, we have to be very careful here. We have a contract with this organization, and I want to make sure that you live up to it. Simple as that, but you don't have to go beyond that, I gather." . . . I mean, Mike [Shaman] did a good job for me for the time that he was there, then we had some disagreements in the end—that's why he's not there any more.

MICHAEL SHAMAN: There were things in my relationship with Mr. Ivany that were directly related to the *Rocky Mountaineer* contract where he and I had very conflicting views. And the way that he wanted me to administer the contract, there was no way I could look at myself in the mirror and say I am getting up in the morning to do this—and as a consequence, I am no longer with VIA. I left in May 1997, after being with the railway for 29 years. A meeting was convened with Mr. Ivany and we parted company. We had a very heated discussion and agreed to disagree, and approximately six weeks later the board of directors of VIA Rail Canada met in Vancouver. I got all sorts of praise and reinforcement for the good job I was doing in terms of managing the business: high quality, low cost, bringing in external revenues for the company. I did the *West Coast Express* contract myself [for the Vancouver-region commuter train]. . . . When I left there, I was bringing about $5 million in gross revenue to the company in external revenue. And after the board of directors' meeting, my vice-president called on me in my office and threw a letter in front of me and I was told my services were no longer required.

TERRY IVANY: VIA, you see, cannot operate in a purely commercial way in the marketplace because of its political attachments. Any time that you try and make any kind of proactive move from a marketing standpoint, you get bus operators yelling, the airlines yelling, Armstrong yelling. . . .

[At VIA] I could sense some horrendous hostility towards Peter Armstrong and the *Rocky Mountaineer*. I didn't know anything about this, so I said, "Well, the guy's a businessman and let him go." So I guess I was Peter's defender at VIA for a couple, three years. I thought that he had a nice little business there. [But after Ivany decided to increase Jasper-Vancouver frequency], that's where it kind of fell apart. We had a deal with Peter: we had to inform him that we were going to do this, which we did. He didn't like the idea that we did it in that way. I faxed him and said that we are going to go for this [increased frequencies]. . . .

Our trains are always full during this tourist season. Well, I thought, *You've got to make hay when the sun shines here.* Peter was doing very well, so I said, "Let's put six frequencies on a week from Edmonton or Jasper to the West." I didn't particularly see it as competition, because my view on it—and Peter disagrees with me on that, that's okay—is that we had a different-type service. . . . Peter's noncompete clause is that we will not operate a service between Calgary and Vancouver during the daylight hours that competed directly with him. . . .

We went to our [transport] minister, [David] Anderson, and initially he thought it was a great idea. Then we informed Peter and things started to change. He was very upset about it. He thought we should have talked to him about it. Yes, I talked to him personally about it. Then we got into running wars and things. That's when I really started to divest myself from Peter and really got into some problems, because I didn't like the way in which he conducted himself.

Among the people from whom Peter sought advice was David McLean, who had been chairman of Canadian National Railways since

David McLean

1994. He was part of the team—along with president Paul Tellier and director Ed Lumley— who privatized CN in '95. A champion of entrepreneurship, McLean is chairman and CEO of the McLean Group, which developed award-winning urban properties, and of the Concord Pacific Group, the developer of the former Expo 86 waterfront lands in Vancouver. As a friend of Prime Minister Jean Chrétien, whom he had come to know as president of the Alberta Young Liberals three decades earlier, the Vancouver-based businessman was well positioned in both politics and the rail industry to offer Peter counsel.

DAVID MCLEAN: The first time I met Peter, we were both on the board of St. George's School when he was just about to start the *Rocky Mountaineer*. I certainly could see he had an entrepreneurial gleam in his eye. The railway [CN] always looked upon him with favour because he was an entrepreneur, somebody who we always felt could do something with passenger service.... He had a problem with VIA, which wanted to go into competition with him. They had sold him what they really couldn't do properly, and then they turned around a few years later and wanted to get into it again. I guess the role that I played in that was just to ensure that the government treated Peter fairly: when you sold somebody something, you can't come back through a government-subsidized company and compete with them. That just didn't seem fair....

Peter made a good case. He saw the opening and made sure who he had to see, spent a lot of time in Ottawa talking to the right people.... It was lobbying, but he had a good, logical case and a case that everybody was prepared to see the rationale of. David Anderson was the minister of transport and that didn't hurt us any; we had a B.C. guy. He understood the issues of a start-up company. I don't think Peter cares about competition—but not subsidized by the public. I think that's wrong, and I think everybody thinks that's wrong. The people I've put Peter in touch with regard him as a guy who's really good for B.C. and Canada and tourism.

Peter's political supporters have included Jim Gouk, the Reform Party critic for transportation, and fellow B.C. Reform member of Parliament Jim Abbott. Among the people Peter approached in Ottawa was Calgary-reared Randy Pettipas, who was an advisor on western Canada to Prime Minister Jean Chrétien when he met Peter for the first time in 1994. (Following his political career, Pettipas became a partner in Global Public Affairs in Ottawa; one of his clients is Great Canadian Railtour.)

RANDY PETTIPAS: I had been travelling at great length and had come in very, very late the night before and had early meetings the next morning—the first one being Peter Armstrong, whom I had never met. He was shown to a boardroom and then I arrived and it was all very friendly and we had coffee. As Peter would tell the story, as I took a mouthful of coffee, I actually spit it at him. That's not true. It's *only* not true because he was sitting at the other side of the table. This is the one and only time I've ever done this in my life, but for some reason, with a mouthful of coffee, I proceeded to speak and the coffee spilled all over my shirt and my tie. And what was the most remarkable part of the whole meeting is that Peter sees it all happening and doesn't miss a beat in his presentation. He just keeps on talking like this is an everyday occurrence: people always sit in front of him and spit coffee all over him. And he says very gracefully, "Can I get you a napkin?"

At this point he's just educating me on the service he has. The nice thing about a meeting like that—other than the embarrassment of spitting coffee—is that Peter wasn't in asking for anything. He was simply there to say "Here's who we are." As he went through it, I was just waiting for the common question people in government receive. But Peter said, "Oh, and we don't need anything." It's sure a nice way to start the day. He was back a number of times, keeping up a very regular contact: "We've purchased new equipment, we've expanded our routes, we now employ more people." It's a success story, and everyone likes to become close to a success story.

Then Peter had some issues with government when VIA decided to double their frequency from Jasper to Vancouver, which is an obvious threat to Peter Armstrong. All of Peter's work paid off in the sense that when he wanted to raise this issue with government and get a hearing, he wasn't coming in cold. People knew who he was, they knew the history, and had come to know him and trust him. At that point I was the executive assistant to the minister of transport, David Anderson, and the person Peter would call when he wanted to meet with Mr. Anderson or make sure he was up to speed on Peter's views of that situation. The minister had to take a very neutral position. Ultimately the decision was his, and he needed to sit back and get views from both sides, take recommendations from the department and his staff, and then come to a conclusion. It wouldn't be proper for me to say what my recommendation to the minister was.

JESS KETCHUM: I think Peter and the *Rocky Mountaineer* have in fact benefited by VIA Rail being so obstinate—in that it gave Peter a reason to get up earlier every morning. He had a cause and it also created the opportunity for us to go out and generate a tremendous support for the company beyond what most private-sector firms get to do. I mean, wouldn't Canadian Airlines or Air Canada love to have people so willing to write letters to editors and the politicians and make phone calls on their behalf?

Kamloops was the key for one reason. The *Rocky Mountaineer* makes quite an impact in Vancouver because of the employees, the purchases made here and all of those things, but the impact in Kamloops is huge. You see all those *Rocky Mountaineer* buses roaring around, taking people out to their hotels and back to the station. The company is well thought of because it has made such a major contribution to diversifying the economy. So we needed to generate some public reaction to VIA Rail's attempt to come back at us.

DAVE DEOL, the Kamloops hotelier: We supported Peter with telephone calls and letters to our MP, Nelson Riis (his son was my bellman once), and the minister of transport. I said I didn't think it was right, because the government sold off a piece of VIA to a private company and they're doing well; now VIA wants to get back into it. And when the government had it, they still subsidized it. A guy's doing well, he had his hurdles he had to overcome, and they're going to crush him because the government sees a good opportunity? Nelson was supportive all the way. I think he did some lobbying to the other members of the government.

FRED OAKLEY, who had known Peter as the Hotel Vancouver doorman, ran Tourism Vancouver before becoming tourism manager for the city of Kamloops in 1991: When I first arrived here, you would never hear tourism mentioned, period. They thought tourism was visiting your aunt. But now there's debate going on in the community on the building of a convention centre with banquets for about 1,500 people. One of the impacts has been the *Rocky Mountaineer*, which made them conscious of the value of the tourism dollar and the number of jobs it creates. Particularly now when we've had so much closure in the mines, for instance, which was the backbone of our area, and with forestry in decline. Yes, the *Mountaineer* brings millions of dollars' worth of revenue into our community. Yes, they have not only 30 or more people permanently employed, but through the use of our facilities likely employ hundreds of others. When I first came here, there were about 1,400 hotel rooms, and today there's somewhere around 3,000—it's more than doubled.

I was involved through the tourism advisory committee, which supported Peter's suggestion that this would be unfair competition. The city was very much behind the *Rocky Mountaineer* and what Peter was trying to do. And that all goes back to the way he treats people, which is upfront and honest, and if he's got a problem, he tells you about it and works to straighten it out. That's why the support was there: because the groundwork was done over a period of years. Peter came personally to talk to people in the community. People get used to seeing the *Rocky Mountaineer* buses go by and realize they're seeing dollars and jobs go by.

CLIFF BRANCHFLOWER, who was then the mayor of Kamloops: Great Canadian Railtour put the *Rocky Mountaineer* on the map. They've done a great job here. The idea was there, but Peter is Mr. Marketing, and he's not afraid to hire good people. They keep adding trains and features, like their overnight western-style cabaret in one of the nicest venues in the city. He has the credibility to lobby at the highest levels. Peter has made such a success of it, and this subsidized Crown corporation was trying to get back in. VIA keeps their people on the train at night, whereas the Great Canadian Railtour people get off and stay in the community to help our hospitality industry tremendously. So the city and council, including myself, did join in the lobbying. The chamber of commerce and various business associations also went to bat for the Railtour people.

JESS KETCHUM: The people of Kamloops were wonderful. I mean not just city council but the hoteliers, the restaurateurs—they recognized that what VIA Rail was trying to do was a threat. I had a senior official in David Anderson's office phone and ask me to turn off the tap. They were getting hundreds of letters, phone calls, people wanting meetings. Not just the transport minister but other ministers were getting enquiries from the governments of British Columbia and Alberta. [Premiers] Mike Harcourt and Ralph Klein were supportive. This was an issue that created more heat in Ottawa than just about anything else in B.C. Nelson Riis was on the radio one day and made some statement that may have inadvertently sounded like he was not supportive of the *Rocky Mountaineer*. That was cleared up in about two hours; by nightfall he was supporting it. We had Friends of the Train, a pretty exhaustive database that we still maintain to this day, ever growing.

DAVID MCLEAN: One of the challenges Peter faces in the future is to look at ways of being as independent as possible so he doesn't have to depend on other companies. He'll always have to depend upon the rail lines—he's not going to be able to put in his own lines—but he's done a good job in Kamloops, developed a huge business there by putting in his own infrastructure. . . . No one can ignore him now; he's a factor. He's been able to prove something that VIA couldn't do and make it very successful.

TERRY IVANY: I would have to give credit to Peter, tremendous credit, for his political savvy. He did a tremendous job of lobbying, not only the minister and his political aides, but the Reform Party. He did a great job with publicity out on the West Coast. Then as they went through the gyrations, and [our minister] heard a lot from his constituencies, in the end he still felt VIA's plan was a pretty good idea, but he was afraid that it would impact negatively on Peter's operation and he didn't want in any way to have it that VIA put some undue hardship on Peter's operation. In the end, the answer was no.

RANDY PETTIPAS: Mr. Anderson took advice from many people—and the decision he made, Peter was very happy with.

TINY B.C. FIRM BEATS OUT
RAILROAD GIANT FOR BANFF RUN

OTTAWA—An upstart B.C. company has won its battle against the federal Crown corporate giant VIA Rail for the lucrative Vancouver-Banff–Jasper rail tour business, the *Vancouver Sun* has learned.

Transport Minister David Anderson is scheduled to announce today [February 14, 1997] that VIA, which will receive a $250-million taxpayer subsidy this year, will not be allowed to double its capacity from three to six trips a week that it sought to operate this summer.

Anderson's decision represents a huge victory for Vancouver-based Great Canadian Railtour Co., which operates the *Rocky Mountaineer* tourist train on the scenic route across B.C. through the Rocky Mountains to Banff and Jasper. . . .

"I can't tell you how relieved we are," Peter Armstrong said in an interview. "I think David Anderson has listened to the people out West. He recognized the depth of our support."

Helping the Train
Come In: The Mountaineers

Greet the World ¶ In 1997 Great Canadian Railtour was at-

tracting so many passengers that it had added three new custom-built

bi-level dome coaches to its GoldLeaf service and doubled the frequency

of its runs with the addition of a second train that offered 54 new depar-

tures during the season. That was the same year it expanded into the

corporate-meetings and incentive travel market, introducing two spe-

cialized multi-purpose coaches called the Parlour Car and the Club Car.

. . .

Left: A winter train amid the Rockies' snowy splendour.

Such success was being built on the professionalism and concern of all those Mountaineers, behind the scenes as well as on the front lines, who realized that they were doing so much more than operating a train service. As Brian Porter of Mansfield, England, wrote Peter about his trip between Banff and Vancouver, which had surpassed all of his experiences riding with CP, CN and VIA: "The train was superb and it was all enhanced by Gerard [Burke] and his colleagues. They were much more than 'staff' to us all. They were 'friends.' No one could have been more attentive. The meals, too, were perfectly prepared and presented." With employees like that, it's no wonder that when one train was delayed recently during a trip, none of the passengers would leave on the buses quickly dispatched to pick them up—they were just having too good a time on board.

BEHIND THE SCENES WITH THE ONBOARDS

JAMES TERRY: We had 400 applicants for the 35 onboard-attendant positions in 1999. We look at the resumé first and, based on a matrix giving one point for languages, one for tourism experience, one for food and beverage experience, one for something that proves that they've done commentary or something similar, we then cut off at those who get 7 out of 10. And then we do about a half-hour telephone interview with them. Only as a stage one—you've really got to see these people. A good number speak more than one language. In 1999 we had our best year ever— about a fifth of them might know another language. Probably most common would be French and German; Japanese, because a lot of people in our industry have found it valuable; and then we just happened to have hired a couple that have six languages (including a reservations supervisor). But I'm not going to have someone that speaks six languages yet is dead from the neck up.

CHRIS MURPHY points out that even those passengers who speak English have very diverse characteristics: Collectively the Brits can be quite funny and maybe even a little bit risqué, but individually they are very reserved. And if you're going to give them a cup of tea, you put the cup down and they say, "Thank you." Now you give them the milk: "Oh, thank you very much." You give them a stir stick: "Thank you, thank you, thank you." They say "thank you" so many times. They are generally so

The lounge car is a place to relax and mingle.

impressed with the country and the scenery and *ooh* and *ah* at all the right times. Just give me one in my coach and they get everyone on-line for a really good trip—they're infectious with it. Yet you have to deal with the fact that they are never upfront when something is bothering them. I guess they think that it's not polite.

The Americans will tell you what's bothering them, all right. Very demanding of the service industry in general, and I think that's because theirs at home is very friendly, very helpful, and they're just used to that. And Americans very much ask personal questions and call you "Honey" right away.

Australians are like Americans, but they sound more like a Brit. They are still very upfront and demanding, but not as confident about being demanding as an American is.

Canadians are very quiet. In fact, you usually don't know if you have a Canadian on board until halfway through the trip when they'll pipe up and say, "Yeah, I'm a Canadian." Very quiet, but they're filled with pride to be sitting in the coach and seeing people from all over the world going *Wow!* And they are proud of you and the job you're doing.

ANGELIQUE MACGOUGAN, who at age 19 in 1997 was the youngest onboard attendant the company had hired, talks about the weather the train travels through: In my first season, getting up to Hope my passengers are saying, "Is that dead salmon?" I've fished lots in my life, and the banks of the Fraser River on both sides were black with so many thousands of dead salmon that couldn't make it across Hell's Gate. The water was up too high in '97, causing all the flooding. Last season [1998], the water was at an extremely low level, a very dry season. We had about 3,000 different forest fires. Salmon Arm alone lost 6,400 hectares of forest and $4 million was spent killing the fires. You could see little helicopters, one after another, that come down into the water, scooping it up with what looks like a big bowl, and taking off. From June all the way through September, there were no animals.

This year [1999], it's all flooding. We get really shocked, because we know this land like the back of our hand. We go by Saddle Rock, at about Milepost 26, right before Hell's Gate, where a log flipped up onto a rock in '93. This season you can see only about three feet of the rock, and last year you could see almost 12 feet, the water was so low. There's a bridge near Kamloops we cross over, and the water was so close this summer that you could hear it under our wheels. Then it just dropped 10 feet last week. . . .

And the heat in Kamloops can be insane. I've told my passengers they're not getting off the train until their bus is right there beside us. One day we went swimming in an outdoor pool at our hotel and got out and in not even three minutes, my hair was dry, the heat was so hot. We had a high of almost 45 in Kamloops last year.

OJAY MATIAS, a Philippines-born attendant in his second season in 1999: Going north from Kamloops, around Barrière, we had 93 feet of snow this year, and when it melts, you can see the floodwaters. I was telling my guests, "Ladies and gentlemen, I'm going to show you my dream house." And I'm looking, there's water on both sides, under the track. I'm saying, "The house has got four acres of land, planted with Christmas trees." The next thing I know, it turned out to be oceanfront property—water right up to the treeline. "That's a nice house," I told them. "You can have a sailboat and a powerboat."

One innovation that has made the attendants' lives easier is the Palm Pilot, a compact hand-held computer that tracks guests' purchases on board the train.

SCOTT REMILLARD: In the early days a train would come in and the staff went into the boardroom in North Vancouver and spread the cash out all over the table to count it. It would take three or four people hours and hours. It was silly. In 1998 Roman Pendzey, the coordinator of our MIS department, put in the Palm Pilot system, that was so state-of-the-art that it was on CTV national news. Before the train leaves, the passengers' names get downloaded into each attendant's Palm Pilot.

CHRIS MURPHY: I love the Palm Pilots. My wish list with this company is slowly coming true. When we used to report to our train, we'd get a stack of papers, because the office really had no idea what we did on the train, so they just gave us everything on people—from when they got on their plane in Florida to when they arrived back home. Through the years we got them to scale it down a bit, and now, because you get a little stack of paper and a Palm Pilot, cashing out is really quite easy. It has a list of everyone and their seat numbers, so if you get a tour group and they want to change seats, we can track them.

GARY GERVAIS, the carman-mechanic, expresses a recent concern: With our new bathroom system with holding tanks, we have these air-driven, computerized toilets. We put up signs saying "No paper towels, no napkins," but people just put the stuff in there, and the toilets aren't made to handle them. They plug up, and most of the time you just reset them to get them going, maybe use a plunger, but at other times you have to tear the whole thing right apart on the road. We can do a lot during a run, like changing small motors on the fridges. We have brushes for the motors and the blower fans.

The major things are done in the new maintenance yards in Kamloops. We have people to look after the air conditioning, to do the inspections, change the brake shoes, and there are jacks available to change wheels. We have five locomotives now, so we can do our own switching in

GoldLeaf Service combines luxury with a wide-open view.

the yard, and enough track that we don't have to ask permission from CN. We can do the maintenance ourselves, and a lot of the staff have been with the company for quite a few years now: electricians, carmen, air-conditioning people and a plumber. It's made a huge difference.

ERIC BELANGER mentions the lengths to which all the staff will go to help a guest: One summer, an older fellow was leaning out of the vestibule trying to get a picture and he lost his hearing aid. He advised the train manager that he had lost it, he thought, a few miles west of Boston Bar. Very graciously, [CN personnel agreed] to look for it and couldn't find it. For whatever reason, I think they looked for miles in the other direction of Boston Bar—and found it along the track.

NORMAN KURCK of Southampton, Ontario, who had lost the hearing aid, later wrote a letter of thanks to Peter for returning it: I was amazed to receive it. Such a small item to find along double tracks on a mountain, and have a freight train stop so a crew could search for it.

You must be very proud of your employees. Christine Murphy was excellent, and very efficient in calming me and getting action started to retrieve my lost hearing aid. She did seem very concerned for my situation. Pierre Drouin was very professional and kept me informed. . . . What a wonderful response from people (very touching) in a world that seems to be getting more economic-inclined.

NOT-SO-GREENER PASTURES

Exporting the *Mountaineer* brand of hospitality to other tourist locales has always been in the back of Peter Armstrong's mind. Some of the most exciting possibilities would result from the full or partial privatization of VIA Rail or public-private franchising partnerships to operate various rail systems VIA now runs. Among them might be tourist versions of the Toronto-Vancouver and Montreal-Halifax routes. Over the years, Great Canadian Railtour has also looked south and across the Pacific for other opportunities. So far none of the prospects have materialized, but the research has been intriguing.

EARL SIMONS, now vice-president of corporate development, about his trip to Mexico with Peter in 1994 to look at the *South Orient Express* running there: We got the president to walk us through the train. We went into the baggage car and there's baskets of fresh oranges. We pick one up and there's an Uzi sitting under the basket. "Oh, put it down," the president says. "I don't know if you've noticed, but we've got three *federales* [undercover government police] on board, and they've buried guns all over the place because apparently we're going to get robbed this trip." [They weren't, but the incident did put a damper on any thought of running a railroad in Mexico.]

Three years after the Mexican trip we went to Australia, where they were privatizing their trains. We looked at it with a banking company, and because of our timeline and because we had to see the entire route of every single train, we had only three weeks to do it in. It was just go, go, go. It was very hard, it was hot, it was enjoyable. Peter took some of the trains, I took the others. We kept wondering why the bank people were spelling off each other. They were tag-teaming us because they knew how tiring it would be. They knew what they were doing. Then Peter went back to Australia later with Bev and Dugal Smith [the management consultant]. We did put a bid on it.

DUGAL SMITH: One of the things that they were looking at is Australian National Rail, which basically has three rail lines: a commuter line, a middle-distance line, and then a long-distance line that went right across Australia, the equivalent to a cross-Canada trip.

BEV ARMSTRONG: The privatization deal, just like ours, got done by a group of investors led by an Australian investment group with rail investors from all over the world, from the U.K. and the U.S. (and we're still talking to them). There was a classic dinner in a hotel when we met some of the proposed investors in the deal, and everybody had different ideas as to what the deal would look like. We were uncomfortable with what the other people thought, so that actually killed it for us. We then made a second trip to Australia about a month after that to continue discussions and were told that people had come around to our way of thinking. An hour into the meeting, we noticed that nothing had changed, so Peter and I immediately got back on the plane and flew home. Thirty hours of flying.

EARL SIMONS: What we did learn is that we would like to be in Australia. We liked the Gold Coast, we liked Adelaide and Melbourne. There are some good tourist possibilities down there.

MARKETING TO THE WORLD
The marketing budgets have mushroomed as the company targets the United Kingdom, Europe and Asia as well as the United States. As marketing and sales VP Murray Atherton notes, "My *increases* in budgets now are what Rick [Antonson] had to work with as *full* marketing budgets in the early years."

MURRAY ATHERTON: Today we have not only Mike Leone [doing public relations in the U.S.], but Klieber Public Relations in Germany and Affinity in the U.K., another PR company, opening up what's called non-traditional opportunities for us, working with Debbenham's, a huge department store in London. They did a mailing to 1.4 million of their card holders with a program of *Rocky Mountaineer* and got an amazing response. And Klieber in Germany had a program where people would fill in a form in a subscription travel magazine and enter to win a trip on the *Rocky Mountaineer*. They had over 120,000 entries—they've never had that kind of response on anything before.

In the beginning, we used to get 50 percent of our passengers from the U.S. and 50 percent of that from California. (We didn't have any money, and it's easy to get down to California because Canadian Airlines was—and kept being—wonderful partners with us.) California remains a huge portion of the market, but the U.S. has gone down to about 40 percent, which is nice. The U.K. is now running around 20 percent. Germany is coming on very strongly: we will probably do about 3,000 from there this year and it's growing exponentially. Australia/New Zealand combined are about 8 percent. Japan is coming on from 2 percent to 4 percent. We're getting more and more family and company incentive groups. Japanese people are now looking at western Canada on the Internet. Michele de Rappard works very hard in ensuring that if somebody looks under *Travel, Rockies, Train*, then *Rocky Mountaineer* will pop up on the screen.

A cameraman hangs around the train.

In September 1998 Sarah Jones opened our European sales office in London. She originally worked at the Pacific Palisades Hotel in Vancouver as sales manager, looking after the *Rocky Mountaineer* account. At any trade show I'd be attending, she would have the Palisades booth directly opposite me, so I would see what a hard worker she was. We hired her in 1993, and her move to England has resulted in a huge increase in business out of the U.K. and Europe.

Recently, under marketing director Graham Gilley (whose background was in product sales and marketing with Nintendo and Gillette)—and working with Vancouver advertising agency Bryant Fulton &

Shee—the marketing thrust has been shifting. It has edged away from the long-lived line "The most spectacular train trip in the world" to slogans such as "The only way to see the Rockies" and "No one ever wrote a folk song about a mini-van."

MURRAY ATHERTON: And we've been developing infomercials on TV. We did a little bit in northern New York state and California. Viewers phone our 1-800-665-RAIL telephone number. Unfortunately, infomercials go in the middle of the night, so you have to have a telephone staff to answer the phones. We had pizza parties at 4 in the morning. And we get a deluge of phone calls. The first time we ran it, we got something like 900 calls in 27 minutes.

MICHELE DE RAPPARD: Recently we did a follow-up direct-mail campaign to 15,000 people who have contacted us for brochures. It had a Billy Miner theme. The cover said: "Take a trip back in time when train robbers would have prevented you from receiving valuable mail like this." We did different test mails where we'd include the *Two River Junction* show if they booked before a certain time. We included a survey—How often do you take a vacation? How far in advance do you typically plan it?—with a sweepstakes offering 10 *Rocky Mountaineer* fleece vests. We had a 12-percent response rate. The people at the mailbox in Point Roberts, Washington, would phone and say, "What's in this package? You have another 800 responses here!" We found we were on track knowing the age groups of our passengers, knowing that people are getting more into two- and three-day escapes maybe four times a year.

MURRAY ATHERTON: We had four companies from Japan who came to us and said, "We want you to run a winter train—one day between Kamloops and Banff." The Canadian Tourism Commission kicked in $100,000 towards advertising. The Japanese tour operators all committed $25,000 each. So there was $200,000 worth of ads in Japan to promote this whole program. We put up $100,000, which was our operational cost of running the train in December 1997. We had Dal Richards and his band on board, Stuart Ellis-Myers as a British Santa Claus and some entertainers for the kids. Two hundred people, all Japanese, and a few North American travel-agency people.

The Kamloops-Japan Business Community greeted them. We decided that we would give them a true western Canadian experience, so we

Santa Claus surprises the Mountaineer's *winter guests.*

had a bonfire by the train station and people on horseback, community groups singing Christmas carols, hot chocolate. Unfortunately, the wind was blowing just so amazingly that all the sparks from the bonfire were going right towards the heritage station, so the fire was just sort of glowing embers. All the people came by motor coach from Vancouver up to Kamloops, sleeping on the way after flying from Japan that morning. In Kamloops they all huddled in their heavy coats and the buses immediately left to drop off their baggage at the hotels. We had a number of dignitaries from Kamloops speaking, but they hadn't arranged to have any translation. So all of these poor Japanese people are standing there listening to all these speeches in English, having no idea what it's all about. They were given hot chocolate that they've never tasted before. And after the festivities were over, I had this one dear little lady come up to me and say, "Our program over now?" When I said yes, her eyes brightened up and she said something in Japanese, and all the people turned around and headed towards the buses—but there are no buses. And these people are just so beat; they've been up for days.

The next morning, we take them to Banff, where we meet another group taking the train westbound. The sun was out all the way and it was a totally magical experience. It just solidified the fact that we had to offer this as part of our overall product. In Kamloops that night, I'm introducing Stuart as our travel-agency sales manager—"Some of you may have met him earlier as Father Christmas"—and this one dear little 70-year-old Japanese lady said, "You are Santa Claus?" We thought that she was going to hug him. Instead she gave him the biggest goose you'd ever seen.

Peter and I are committed to the program. We'll have to expand it to about a minimum of six to eight departures and run it into January and maybe even February.

VERY 'INTERESTING' PEOPLE

By definition, the most important passengers travelling on the *Rocky Mountaineer*—the true VIPs—are the everyday, low-profile guests who are the lifeblood of the company. They are the people who make the *Mountaineer*. Occasionally, though, there are other, higher-profile individuals

Pierre Berton

on board, such as actor Morgan Freeman (*Amistad, The Shawshank Redemption*), Canadian author Pierre Berton (*The National Dream*, about the building of the Canadian Pacific Railway), and even large groups from major corporations who book entire cars—as Great Canadian's ex-senior business analyst relates.

SCOTT REMILLARD: A few years ago, the owner of a large construction company in Germany came to us and said every year he took his best clients and their wives on a trip. "We have two weeks and $75,000. What can you do for us?" We rented a special mahogany railcar out of the States and put them on it as their exclusive coach, arranged suites in the best hotels, helicoptered them up to the top of Whistler [ski resort] and transferred them by limo everywhere. There were six people and they had a great time.

MURRAY ATHERTON: Our first major incentive program was through Maritz Corporation, the biggest incentive company in North America.

The client was Citgo Petroleum Corporation, an American gas retailer. As an incentive, for reaching certain sales levels, their distributors could win this trip on the *Rocky Mountaineer*. They came up to see the train, Scott Graf from Maritz and the client from Citgo. We're walking down the train and the client says to Scott: "I want this."

"What do you mean?" Scott says. "You haven't even seen inside the train yet."

"I want this for my people. I see all these people coming off this train. They're hugging the attendants; the attendants are hugging each other. Everybody has a smile on their face. That's what I want for my people." I tell that story to the onboard training group, because that's what it's all about. I've spent many, many years working in hotels, and you never see people lining up at a cashier's wicket saying, "Thank you for letting me spend my money with you." *We* get that kind of satisfaction.

SCOTT: At first Citgo said, "We want our own train," and we said, "We can't give you your own train."

"How about if we depart a half-hour earlier than everyone else?"

"That will cost tens of thousands of dollars."

They said, "Yeah, okay."

But CP said no, so Citgo said, "Well, we want a car where we can go smoke our stogies."

"We don't have a car where you can smoke your stogies."

"Can you build one? We'll pay for it."

MURRAY ATHERTON: We gave the challenge to Earl Simons, who with the people in Kamloops reconfigured an entire car into a saloon/smoking coach. There's a brass plaque on the car today that commemorates all the people in Kamloops who went above and beyond to build this. There were 280 Citgo people who took over two domes; they had five individual cars on the train. We set up a travelling kitchen in baggage cars, because they wanted the same food in the domes as in the regular cars.

The Citgo trip was part of an innovative initiative called Meetings in Motion, designed for groups that want to have a strategic meeting, corporate conference or rolling executive retreat aboard the *Mountaineer*. Consultant Ann Coombs mentions one such meeting where the motion added a little drama.

ANN COOMBS: At Coombs Consulting Limited we put together major seminars for companies in very interesting ways. So I began to use the train as a place to conduct creative workshops. Pierce-Phelps Incorporated out of Pennsylvania, the northeastern States' largest supplier of heating and air-conditioning equipment, have been clients of mine for years, so I brought 70 members of their management team and distributors to the *Rocky Mountaineer* for five days. It was a quarter of a million dollars' worth of business—two days on the train.

We were in the dome car, which we used as the meeting room. The microphone was attached to one of the back outlets, and I was at the edge of the staircase with a very tight cord. The train turned a corner, and one minute I'm there and the next I'm gone—in the middle of my presentation. Now, during one of our training sessions with the attendants, we had a wildlife author do a presentation and hadn't covered up all the windows to accommodate the showing of slides. So he threw his hands up in the air and said, "I cannot work with this!" And here is everything that I have said to this onboard team—that no matter what happens, you find a solution. As I lunged my way down the stairs in the middle of my presentation, the two onboards servicing the GoldLeaf car threw their hands up in the air as I came back up the stairs and mouthed the author's words: "I can't work with this!" And I never skipped a beat—I never stopped talking.

SCOTT REMILLARD: We've had some famous people on the train, including a high commissioner from India who travelled with a couple of RCMP bodyguards. We keep these trips totally secret.

One especially secret trip was designed for Microsoft co-founder Bill Gates and his wife, Melinda, in 1997. Getting Gates's people to consider travelling on the *Mountaineer*, rather than with the competition, proved to be an adventure in itself.

MURRAY ATHERTON: I was part of the sales process where we kidnapped Bill Gates's assistant. Bill Gates loves trains. He'd been across China on a train. Now he was moving into his house and had to get away while they were doing a big move, so he was looking at coming across the Canadian Rockies by rail. We were working with our sales rep in Seattle, Michelle Ott. Wendy Langdon, who was one of Bill Gates's three assistants in the office, who does all the travel plans, flew up on Helijet with one of the corporate travel people from the American Express in-plant office for Microsoft. I had a limousine pick them up and bring them to the station. We showed them how we would configure the dome for Bill Gates and had lunch—Peter Armstrong, myself, Michelle, and Ken Erickson, the Canadian Tourism Commission sales manager in Seattle.

They were talking with us, VIA Rail, CN and CP, and somebody had told Wendy that the trip between Vancouver and Kamloops might be a little boring for Bill Gates. This was a Saturday, and after lunch they were going to the matinee of *Show Boat* at the Ford Theatre and then flying back to Seattle. About half an hour into the lunch, Peter asked, "So, Wendy, what do you have going on tomorrow?"

"Oh, nothing really, just doing some laundry."

"Good. You're going to stay here in Vancouver tonight, be on the train tomorrow morning at 7 in the morning. We're going to take you up to Kamloops so you can experience the whole trip, and Michelle Ott is going with you." (Michelle was going through cancer chemotherapy treatments.)

They had not planned to stay. Peter raided the ATM in the lobby of the train station to get $600 and bought them a wardrobe so they could have a change of clothes. He phoned Mark Andrew at the Hyatt and got his suite (Mark had just moved out of the hotel into his house.) I called Ray Greenwood, who is the chairman of Symphony of Fire, and got them invited down to the opening of the fireworks show that night. They had a special dinner at the English Bay Café. The next morning they went on the train to Kamloops and then flew back to Vancouver, where we had a limousine laden with food for their drive back to Seattle for dinner. Needless to say, Bill Gates did that route.

GERARD BURKE, the senior GoldLeaf service manager, was aboard the train with the Gateses: It was a *Rocky Mountaineer* dome car and a CP club car being pulled by two CP engines—two in case one broke down. He had the dome with a smaller galley, and we took out a couple of seats upstairs and built in a huge table to give him and his wife, Melinda, the option to eat upstairs or downstairs in the dining room.

When they got to Kamloops, we had rented the biggest limo in town and took them out to the South Thompson Guest Ranch, where he'd booked the whole golf course for himself—18 foursomes just so he and

Melinda could play by themselves. The next morning, Ole Nichum, then our executive chef, and I met them back at the train. That was the day David Mitchell spent some time with them. *(See Side Trip: Riding with Bill Gates, page 231)*. When we stopped in Field, Bill Gates and his wife got to ride the head-end engine in the cab with the driver to the Continental Divide, where we stopped and they got out and took pictures. Then they came back on to Lake Louise, which is only about 10 miles, and said "Thank you" and shook hands and that was the end of that. To be honest, it was a boring trip with just two people, but it was a thrill, though.

TRAINING FOR THE TRAIN

In the first few years, as the company just tried to stay alive, the training for onboard attendants was minimal. But by mid-decade, Peter and his people realized that the high quality they were promising on the *Mountaineer* demanded a more sophisticated training program. They called on Ann Coombs, the service-excellence specialist who had done the secret surveys of the train's onboard operations.

ANN COOMBS: We started out doing on-line training for the reservations agents to deal with the consumer—how to stay focused in a call centre after eight hours on the phone. We did the onboard-attendant training a year later and ran it for three years. We got really creative and broke every rule there was. Over two weeks we took them off-site for experiential training rather than just product knowledge. We took them through team-building games, took them outdoors, let them put together theatre skits that showed their talents to one another and built an amazing bond between them. We involved the management team so that it wasn't a we/they situation. The company had some serious problems with morale and union issues—and it was all about communications. And in a very short period, that training mended this in a very powerful way.

GAIL HEEZEN, who left the Reservations department in 1998 and now returns every year to continue training staff, remembers the spirit that she and Ann helped instill in employees: When I was in Res in '95, we had these two ladies from New Zealand who arrived on the wrong day—they'd missed the train completely. Somehow they got through Reception and ended up sitting at my desk for three hours. We got them hotels, sent them on a tour, and they got on the train two days later. But it was so heartwarming when they wrote a letter saying, "We got the best deal because we got to see the inside of a reservations centre working." I had such fabulous staff back there in Res. I hate to hear "Oh, that's not my job," which I'd always heard at other companies. One night I was going out to my car and saw two of my staff who speak Spanish going to a hotel with a Spanish-speaking couple who they overheard saying they had no place to stay.

ANN COOMBS: The training evolved because there were so many on-board attendants who started to return that we had to increasingly improve and excite. So we started to involve them more in the actual design—modules on safety training, team-building, service excellence, procedures and communications [such as reading body language]. In their business they have to be incredibly intuitive and sensitive, because they're dealing with a lot of overseas passengers who don't always speak English. . . . The most important thing to understand is that for them it's a job, and for the passengers it's a life experience.

James Terry has since taken over the training program and runs it with J. J. (Jean-Jacques) Belanger, the Montreal-born, fluently bilingual former hotel and restaurant manager he hired in 1998 as director of train and station services. At the end of the sessions, Peter traditionally gives a little speech, and then leads the trainees in a ritual that has become part of the corporate culture: the wave-off, in which the staff line up in a row and wave to all the guests as the train leaves the station. By the time Peter has them practising the wave-off, the energetic James and J. J. have helped instill in the attendants the required keenness to make their guests happy from departure through arrival.

J. J. Belanger (left)
and train manager
Tony Pellegrino

JAMES TERRY: J. J. brings infectious enthusiasm—up for the challenge, don't care how hard it is, never says no. There are 100 staff who report to him. A lot of the train managers are pretty strong characters. They need to be: they're in charge of a huge responsibility. Some of them are not very easy to manage, and J. J. has done a good job. He's hugely responsible, with me, for the whole training program we put together. We had two weeks of pre-season training with the train managers, and once, in trying to empathize—with them all listening to his every word—he said, totally unintentionally, "I can make a mistake, but I'm not human." Now everyone says, "But yes, of course, J. J., you're not human."

GERARD BURKE, who had worked with Belanger and tipped him off to the job opening at Great Canadian Railtour, points out just how human his friend is: J. J.—he's a big fellow—got up on stage at the 1998 staff party in Kamloops and belted out "Mustang Sally" and Sinatra's "New York, New York." He blew our people away.

BAD TIMES

Among the real-life, on-the-road situations the training sessions have to anticipate is the possibility of death or near-death on the tracks—as these stories from the recent past reveal.

SCOTT REMILLARD: We've had a few accidents. One happened on a Sunday morning in Coquitlam [in Greater Vancouver] where the train is coming around the corner, the level-crossing gates go down, and a man drives in an S around them—but gets caught in the middle. One of his passengers died. In another incident, a man was killed near Langley, B.C., when he purposely parked his truck on the tracks to commit suicide.

GAIL HEEZEN was on board with a familiarization tour of 42 travel agents at the time: We'd almost finished the trip after five days of bonding. And after the train hit the truck, they stood up in the car and did a prayer circle, these southern American travel agents. They were also praying aloud for the onboards who were outside helping. It was really emotional, because a few days ago these agents didn't even know each other.

SCOTT REMILLARD: Then there was a logging truck in 1997 that was caught on film. (Some level crossings have cameras on them.) You can see the logging truck stall on the tracks, see the driver jump out of it really fast and run down the tracks, shouting "Stop! Stop!" But the train can't stop in time and spins the truck around. He wasn't hurt. And it just dented the locomotive a bit, but the brakes get ruined, because the engineer slams on the brakes and that blows them out.

Some of the best times have sprung from the camaraderie, the family-like bonding, that has developed among the Rocky Mountaineers over the years. Marketing manager Michele de Rappard, who has been with the company since 1990, suffered an aneurysm in 1997 and was on sick leave for five months before being enthusiastically welcomed back to work. In recounting the sometimes-intense relationships among co-workers, she tells the story of a hospital encounter with Stuart Ellis-Myers, who was then director of travel-agency sales, and follows up with a description of Earl Simons, vice-president of corporate development.

MICHELE DE RAPPARD: We're excellent friends at work and they all signed a card for me after my aneurysm. And Stuart Ellis-Myers—whom I had a love-hate relationship with; we drove each other nuts—dropped it off at the hospital. Well, Stuart walks into intensive care. I'm supposed to be in the dark and my parents are saying, "Who's this man barging in?" Because when you have an aneurysm, you have to be basically comatose for 10 days. Here I am looking like a big Q-Tip and there Stuart is. I'm thinking I'm dying—and that's the last person I'm going to see? He asks if he can read the card to me. The nurses come in and say, "I think you'd better leave." [Miraculously, Michele came through her ordeal and returned to work and her on-again, off-again work relationship with Stuart.] . . . .

Uncle Earl [Simons] doesn't have any kids of his own. Our kids are everything to him. When my son was little, he'd come into the office and Earl would be hiding around the corner with a water gun shooting him. Earl always had toys and cookies in his office. The first couple of Christmas parties, he'd go out and buy presents from Santa. We didn't even know who was doing it at first. Now even if he's away at Christmastime, he leaves the money and makes sure the kids get the toys.

VICKI HALLER: One day Earl says, "We're going shopping, so get your coat." Off we go and buy toys for all the employees' little kids. Christmas party day arrives and all the kids are there and every single toy made noise, everything jumped and moved. Michele's little guy and a receptionist's boy, both about 3½, got a fire truck and ambulance with sirens and red lights. Earl brought me to the washroom and on the other side of the door you can hear: "Let us out. It's dark in here." Max and Nathaniel were locked in there. They'd wanted to see the lights in the dark.

My Antony was only about 13 and had come into the office after going to the movies with a friend. Earl was writing something and I was helping him proof it, and when the kids came back, they didn't know he was there. They were in the front office giggling and fooling around when all of a sudden over the intercom comes this voice: "This is God speaking. Everybody sit down." Well, they just froze until my son said, "That's just Mr. Simons."

MAKING HIS MARK

Earl Simons was in a playful mood when Mark Andrew arrived in April 1998 as senior vice-president and chief operating officer, replacing Rosemary Pahl. "I sort of initiate everybody with a squirt gun when they first come," Simons recounts. "I initiated Mark and I actually bought him a gun, too, and, of course, Peter wants to get in on this. Mark being the new guy on the block has to act a certain way—and here's the president of the company and the vice-president of corporate development with water pistols, chasing each other all over the place. And Mark is saying, 'Oh, my God, what have I joined?'" The North Carolina-reared Andrew (who has never lost his "y'all" drawl) had spent nearly two and a half decades in the hotel industry, most recently as general manager at Vancouver's Hyatt. At the hotel and as chairman of Tourism Vancouver, he'd known Peter for many years—had in fact turned down jobs from the persistent president of Great Canadian at least a couple of times before accepting the COO position. Andrew initiated his own enhancements to the *Mountaineer*'s operations.

BOB MCMILLIN: Mark will tell you that, in terms of issues and process, a train is like a hotel on its side. It's all about guest service and integration of services, about people and relationships. Mark had done all the jobs in the hotel—the kind of general manager who walks the hall every day. He knew what was going on and felt the beat and knew the tempo of his hotel, and I'm sure he knew all the housekeepers by their first names and all their kids' names, too. He is very much an operations type of a fellow, and that's what Great Canadian needed to tighten it down.

MARK ANDREW: When I first got on the job, it was three weeks prior to the first train going out for the season and it was frantic trying to get things done. It reminded me of opening hotels. The guest service in the hotel and the train is the same: a guest is a guest, and you treat them as if they are God because they *are* God. And that's what this company has brought to this industry—the focus on the guest as well as the focus on the employee, the onboards, making sure that they are well trained, happy. I was really adamant that we didn't start my second season with the same frantic, seat-of-the-pants operation we did the year before.

I did an opinion survey of all the employees through an outside company, which gave them a list of 500 questions. From that I learned that this company is beyond reproach when it comes to employees being dedicated to guest service and safety, to helping each other and believing that they're part of a finely tuned machine looking to keep getting better. And also that there was a real communications problem—a real Kamloops-versus-Vancouver division in the company. We could see we had a definite problem with Kamloops, and that was a precursor to some of the changes that we made. We adopted some new management styles up there and [when Doug Kelsey left] hired Peter Casement, who had 29 years with Canadian Airlines as director of operations. He has been a general manager of various facilities and currently ran the Calgary, Edmonton, Winnipeg and Whitehorse airports. A real people person but also the kind who will roll up his sleeves and crawl under the train and look at the problem.

Mark Andrew gets down and dirty.

After we did the opinion survey, we asked all the employees what their biggest problems were. Then the executive team had a little retreat and put together a mission statement for the company: *We are committed to developing and offering unique quality vacation products in Canada for our guests.* And a vision statement—*to be the premier provider of Canadian tourism travel experiences*—along with a values statement: *We are committed to achieving excellence together based on the values of Attitude, Integrity, Accountability, Quality and Communication within the company and the communities in which we operate.*

We needed more training and hired a training coordinator, who is Michele Ng, and we spent a good deal of money to create a training centre. Michele is continually doing training, whether it's time management, lifestyles, good eating, stress management, how to use the computer system. And we increased the number of training days for the car attendants from seven to 10 and increased their time in Kamloops, where they now get a full week of training, including narration on the train during what we call the Onboard Olympics.

Meanwhile, Norma Rattray [a certified general accountant with several years in the tourism industry, including financial management of Whistler Mountain] has been a great addition as a hands-on director of finance. We brought in a very knowledgeable director of human resources, Aila Morgan, who's all fired up and adding a lot of fresh ideas.

And my second season started far smoother than any other ever. The night before the train went out, people were going home at 6 or 7 o'clock instead of staying all night to make things ready—and that just didn't happen before.

Mark Andrew would go on to a fresh challenge in November 1999 with Westin Hotels, to be succeeded as chief operating officer by James Terry—the former vice-president of guest and station services, who would bring his own highly involved and involving style to the position.

GOING SOLO

"How have things changed since the beginning?" asks veteran onboard attendant Chris Murphy. "Peter has grey hair. He didn't have any grey hair when I met him." Another change in the past decade has been his attempts at sharing the burden of management with chief operating officers. ("He is the epitome of the founder-owner-operator—the classic entrepreneur who can't pull himself out of the operation," Mark Andrew maintains.) What Peter really hasn't wanted to share—with anybody but his brother—is ownership of the company. In 1998 he decided to buy out all the remaining partners but Bev.

MIKE PHILLIPS, current chairman of Great Canadian Railtour: Peter built this company and in the beginning he had about 5 percent of it because all of the money came from everybody else. He lived with that, but I think he also had a master plan that he would like to own the company one day. So Rick Browning left and we paid him out and we all got a few more percentage points in the company—all the shareholders, including Peter. It started to be time to think about getting some money back to the shareholders, because it had been a long, hard investment for everybody. And Peter made a very deep personal decision that, number one, he didn't want to take the company public, and then he really didn't have it in him to sell the company either. He wanted some things that entrepreneurs want, which the board was a little slow in giving him. So he arrived at a board meeting and said, in tears—well, right on the edge of tears—"Guys, I've reached a decision that essentially I either buy you out or I'm going to quit and we have to get rid of the company."

As financial consultant Glenn Munro says, "Jim Houston is the nicest guy in the world, but he's a hard-assed businessman. The Working Opportunity Fund were a little softer around the edges." After Munro did an evaluation of the share values, negotiations over the next six months required two third-party appraisals, one commissioned by Peter and the other by Houston and WOF.

GLENN MUNRO: It's like a son living with his parents: you rely on their shelter, advice and guidance, but at some point you just grow up and you leave home. And both Jim and Mike appreciated that they were like parents—that they'd nurtured Peter and come to his rescue. Now it was time for him to embark on his own. Once they realized that Peter was serious about this, they both said, "Fine, let's work out a fair deal."

But there were a lot of tense moments. Everybody was getting on everybody's nerves. Jim was getting mad at me. I was getting frustrated. Peter was really frustrated. He finally said, "Here, take it or leave it." And we ended up finalizing a deal that was in between the other appraisals— pretty close to what I'd originally come up with. During all this we had been carrying on discussions with the Royal Bank to secure our financing. Eventually we went right to the top floor of the bank in Vancouver, dealing with the most senior people in the Royal in western Canada. But the vendors had to take a larger [financial] takeback than what we'd originally anticipated. They both deserve a lot of credit for that. And we needed some extra working capital in the deal before the bank would sign off. I went over to see Mike Phillips at the Working Opportunity Fund, and he put up that amount as a backup line of credit. We've never touched it.

MIKE PHILLIPS: It was the largest dollar return on any investment we [at WOF] ever made.

GLENN MUNRO: So the deal is signed, the lawyers looked at all the documents and said they could now release the cheques to the vendors. Well, it turned out that the lawyers handed the wrong cheques to the wrong people. The vendors went to the bank and they're standing there with cheques for big amounts of money—in the millions of dollars—trying to deposit them. The teller says, "You've got a cheque made out to someone else." Ten minutes later there's a great shuffle and everybody comes back saying, "You've got my cheque, you SOB."

JIM HOUSTON: We don't own a train any more, but Peter owes us a lot of money, so we are vitally interested in his success.

GLENN MUNRO: About a month later we had a big party on the train cars for the lawyers and everybody involved. We all went down there, climbed aboard, drank too much, had a lovely dinner and told a lot of lies. It was a real party. Peter had been a young guy with no money, and at one point he was down to 4 percent of the company. Without putting much money of his own in, he and his brother now own 100 percent. He's created a company that no one knew or cared about, but now it's a company that in 1999 won him the Canadian Venture Capital Entrepreneur of the Year Award. The train has come in.

WENDY ARMSTRONG: Peter has been talking about this [the early hard times] more recently with other people, and I'm listening in and don't remember all the details. I knew there were problems. Peter wouldn't be around very much, be very tense, we didn't take any holidays. It was one thing after another: VIA, the Jackson thing—like, when does this end? I know it was a struggle for us at home. The kids really know. They see what we can do now and compare what it was like then and say, "Is it really okay, mom?"

"Yeah, it's okay, we can do this."

We've always had this saying about the train coming in. It probably started back in those tough times. "One day the train will come in—we'll be able to do the family holiday." So the kids are now saying, "Well, I guess the train's coming in now, eh?" The girls have just done a trip to Europe. And the kids are very appreciative, because it hasn't always been like that. They've seen how hard their dad's worked. We don't think the train's here yet, but it's definitely coming in.

SIDE TRIP: RIDING WITH BILL GATES

David Mitchell is vice-president and chief development officer of Simon Fraser University. But it was in his role as a historian and author—among his books is *All Aboard! The Canadian Rockies by Train*, which Great Canadian Railtour commissioned—that he accompanied Mr. and Mrs. Bill Gates on a *Rocky Mountaineer* trip in the summer of 1997. What follows is his account of a fascinating 24 hours he spent with the Microsoft multi-billionaire and his wife.

DAVID MITCHELL: "Let me tell you about the very rich," F. Scott Fitzgerald wrote in the 1920s. "They are different from you and me."

"Yes, they have more money," Ernest Hemingway responded a decade later.

This famous literary exchange came to mind after I spent a day with the world's richest man, Microsoft co-founder Bill Gates, and his wife, Melinda, on a train trip through the Canadian Rockies. As we travelled aboard the *Rocky Mountaineer*'s spectacular GoldLeaf dome car and two historic Canadian Pacific railway coaches, I was delighted to discover that they're as down-to-earth as the couple next door. Is it possible that the very rich aren't really very different after all?

On the first leg of a vacation, they were enjoying some rare downtime away from the frenetic pace of running the most dynamic company in the most dynamic industry on the planet. There's probably no better way to escape an impossibly hurried existence than to board a train and

Gerard Burke, Ole Nichum, Bill and Melinda Gates.

simply let the world roll by. And that's especially so when touring through the breathtaking scenery of the Rocky Mountains.

Bill Gates has a reputation as a futurist, but he's also been a keen student of history. In addition to being conversant with the details and patterns of America's past, he's a storehouse of knowledge about business history. But he was thirsty for information about Canada.

He was curious about the nation-building role that railways had played in our history. And, like most people who tour the Rockies by rail, he was simply awestruck by the remarkable achievement of building a rail line more than a century ago with primitive technologies through such forbidding territory. Mr. Gates was inquisitive about the origins of railways and their initial impact on travel and commerce. He seemed intrigued when I suggested that railroads were actually the Internet of the mid-19th century, at that time representing a revolution in communications and transportation by means of a growing web of train tracks around the globe. A World Wide Web of an earlier era.

In a relatively brief career, 41-year-old Bill Gates has put his stamp on an industry that has transformed the way most of us work and play. And that's because at the age of 19, he foresaw the day when we'd all be using personal computers. Today, every time Microsoft stock rises even a single point, he significantly pads his lead as the wealthiest person alive. . . .

He pointed out that, in Vancouver before boarding the train, he was actually surprised when a few people approached him for his autograph. Wearing a baseball cap, he didn't expect to be recognized.

The couple are avid readers and had bulked up on a good selection of contemporary fiction for their vacation. They also travel with their own collection of CDs. What do they listen to? John Lennon, Bette Midler, soundtracks from popular musicals and movies.

And following their train tour through the Rockies, they were looking forward to playing golf and tennis and relaxing with each other. Just like any other yuppie couple from the baby boom generation. Yes, they have a lot more money, but it's refreshing to note that they aren't really different from you and me.

Marking a Momentous
First Decade: The *Mountaineer's*
10 Extraordinary Years ¶ Two great Canadian rail-

roaders, celebrated a century apart: William Cornelius Van Horne and

Mac Norris. And on Friday, April 30, 1999, launching its 10th season of

operation, Great Canadian Railtour Company memorialized both men

by christening its original dome cars in their honour. Van Horne, the

visionary builder of the original line through the Rockies. Norris, the

railroad veteran who reshaped British Columbia Rail into a profitable

. . .

Left: Stephanie Pember-Johnson, Gerard Burke and Scott Barker.

enterprise and then became Peter Armstrong's mentor in making the *Rocky Mountaineer* the success it is at the start of a new millennium.

It was a full, fascinating day of celebration, which began that morning with the first graduating class of the newly named Rocky Mountaineer Railtours University—RMRU. A record group of 88 novice and returning onboard attendants had completed two and a half weeks of training in everything from delivering lively en-route commentary to a government-prescribed exercise in handling that most unlikely of events, a railway hostage-taking incident. And to put a final, romantic spin on the celebrations, a vacationing couple from Australia—marking their own 10th anniversary of being together—had appeared the day before in the company's headquarters in Vancouver's Pacific Central Station. Rail buffs exploring North America's most famous trains, they asked James Terry, director of guest services, if they could be married on board the *Rocky Mountaineer* the very next day. They could, and late the next afternoon they were (with James as their best man)—on the observation deck of 9501, the dome car freshly dedicated as the *W. C. Van Horne*.

Just another day in the life of Great Canadian Railtour Company at the end of its remarkable first decade.

PADDLE LIKE A DUCK

On that last morning in April, the graduating onboard attendants and the train managers were assembled in a huge tent behind Pacific Central Station to celebrate the end of their comprehensive training sessions, with the guest services director as host for the convocation.

JAMES TERRY: Welcome to the graduation ceremony of RMR University. . . . A process that started in a small room in the Hotel Vancouver and culminated this year, the start of our 10th season, with a *train* training session, a real live moving experience with more staff involved in the process than the average size of a trainful of guests in 1990. [We've gone] from poring over a road map of B.C. in 1990 to a full-scale, total-involvement training experience over two and a half weeks aimed at guest service excellence. From two-day St. John's first-aid courses to a week of intensive training at the Vancouver Trade and Convention Centre, where we examined the very philosophy of service-excellence and best-practice standards, learned commentary through practical educational sessions

Peter congratulates the 1999 graduating class.

intermingled with confidence-building teamwork sessions and work-shops. Then it was on board our own *Rocky Mountaineer* buses for three intensive days of safety and procedure training. A visit to *Two River Junction* to witness a truly excellent entertainment spectacle. [You learned about] emergency procedures manuals. The essentials of communication on the rails. Evacuating down ladders from bi-level dome cars. Controlled evacuations of train cars filled with fake smoke to imitate a real fire. Smashing out a breakout window to evacuate 40 guests and staff. . . . Today 88 RMR onboard attendants are graduating—53 returning, 35 joining up for their first year with *Rocky Mountaineer*.

PETER, noting that the company would be welcoming its 300,000th passenger in 1999: Now I look forward to where we are going to go in the future. And I look forward with a lot of confidence, because I know we have a true commitment to exceptional guest service. That's what has been driving this company right from the very beginning.

MARK ANDREW: Congratulations, Class of '99, the first official RMR University graduating class—kind of apropos for our 10th season. . . . I want you to remember one word: sunscreen. [The crowd erupted in laughter.] Wear your sunscreen. Everything else, you heard when you

The classy Class of '99, the first to graduate from Rocky Mountaineer Railtours U.

graduated from high school and college. You truly are the best class, not only the first class, of RMRU ever. For the past two weeks y'all been trained: you know safety, you know service, guest name usage, commentary. . . . You know how to smile (not that we taught you that). You know the history of B.C. and Alberta, of Rocky Mountaineer Railtours—and you *are* the history, part of where we go forward from here. . . . Remember the sunscreen.

ROD HARRIS, president and CEO of Tourism British Columbia: You are joining not just an incredibly innovative and tremendously successful company, but you are also joining an essential and—I'll be so arrogant to say—an *elite* sector of the British Columbia economy. And that is the tourism industry, which last year generated $8.7 billion in gross revenue. It currently employs 235,000 individuals in more than 15,000 businesses throughout the province. It's growing more rapidly than virtually any other sector but electronics. We have the same number of people employed as they do in the forest industry and we are now the second-largest export industry, just after forestry. We're expecting through the great work of organizations such as yours to surpass it. . . . And as you deal with unexpected, unanticipated events, the secret to good customer service is to be like a duck. If you look at ducks, they're swimming on the surface and everything is calm—but underneath they're paddling like hell. So just maintain that level of customer service and I know you'll do a great job.

IT'S ALL IN THE RECOVERY
After the graduation ceremony, the staff and guests met to mark the 10th anniversary of the company and to dedicate the company's first two dome cars in honour of a pair of influential rail pioneers.

RICK ANTONSON, president of Tourism Vancouver and GCRC's first vice-president of sales and marketing: I remember the thrill of the day Peter came into the office and said, "We've got a departure with 200 people—can you believe it?" And it seems like yesterday. What saved us then was Peter's vision and the fact that we didn't know what we didn't know. And every time we stubbed our toe on something, Mac Norris would say, "It's okay. It's all in the recovery." What a corporate philosophy. . . . When we started, Peter said, "Forty-three years and nobody's ever made any money taking passengers by train through the Rockies." So when I left, he said, "Rick, thanks, you've extended the record to 46." He's often asked why I didn't leave a year or two earlier. . . . It's been thrilling and I guess we say to Peter, "Thanks for the ride."

LYN TAIT, who was then deputy minister to British Columbia's Ian Waddell, minister of small business, tourism and culture: There's such energy and enthusiasm as you talk to the staff here. It's wonderful to see. Just think, in 10 short seasons this firm has gone from a dream—from being the first private operator in Canada to take over what was a money-losing route from VIA to becoming North America's largest privately owned passenger-rail operator. And I understand you have further ambitions, eventually, to go transcontinental. I know everyone in the room here today wishes you well in that fabulous vision. . . . Imagine what this firm could do if it took over the entire VIA operation.

PETER: Looking back, it would seem quite easy to take over a train and make it profitable—that's what I kept telling Rick. It has a personal side to it: my brother, who's been suffering through this problem for 10 seasons with me, is my partner. He may recall that our mother would walk the seawall in West Vancouver with her lady friends, who'd ask her, "What's your younger son doing?"

"Well, he's running a train through the Canadian Rockies."

They'd look at her and think, *Oh, dementia's coming on.* She got so upset about this that when they asked her what I was doing, she would say, "Oh, I don't know."

Mom, we hope you can now tell your friends that we're doing well. . . .

I would just like to say how appreciative I am of all the people who have contributed to the *Rocky Mountaineer*—by our calculation there will be over 800 people directly and indirectly who've been employed in this company right from the very beginning. And 800 people all working for the same goal, the same shared vision . . . and that vision has always been very simple, very easy to understand: we're going to move ahead with exceptional guest service and we're going to make sure every one of our wonderful guests is an ambassador telling the world. And it's paid off for us, because 75 percent or more of our passengers tell us that the reason they're here is that they've heard from a friend or relative.

MARK ANDREW: Our first year, 100 people would be a big train. Leaving in two days (actually less than 39 hours from now, James), we

From left: Mike Phillips, Peter, Mark Andrew and Tourism BC's Rod Harris.

will have 500-plus thrilled passengers leaving Pacific Central Station heading to beautiful Kamloops and then off to Banff and Jasper and Lake Louise and on to Calgary. For our first train out, that's going to be a record. In keeping with the theme that it really does keep getting better, we've got four beautiful dome coaches and we just ordered two more—they'll be here in September—and we're hoping to have more next year.

MIKE PHILLIPS, chairman of the GCRC board: Don't get the wrong idea about why this company is a success. It is not the Rockies; the Rockies do not sell themselves. When you think about it, the Rockies are just dumb bits of rock. And even the train is just steel—now don't tell that to

Mac Norris (third from left) takes delight in the GoldLeaf dome car named in his honour.

Earl [Simons, vice-president, corporate development], because he thinks it has a soul. In the range of the spectacular, they are second and third compared to the spectacular efforts of the people who have got this company here today.

RICK ANTONSON: In the second year, Mike offered to help with the brochure and stuff, but when he sent in the line "the Rockies are just big dumb rocks," we asked if he could go work on the board or something.

The first of the dome cars was dedicated to Sir William Van Horne of the Canadian Pacific Railway, described as "a man of great organizing abilities and relentless drive—the CPR line was completed on November 7, 1885, in 54 months... years ahead of schedule. It was a feat of construction that amazed the world." More than a century later, Peter Armstrong introduced another rail giant, Mac Norris.

PETER: As a director of Great Canadian Railtour Company since its inception, Mr. Norris is being recognized today for his devotion and commitment to both Rocky Mountaineer Railtours and the Canadian rail industry. GoldLeaf Dome Coach 9502 will carry Mr. Norris's name on the exterior of the coach and a bronze plaque will be erected inside, which will read: "Mac Norris, director of Great Canadian Railtour Company. Mr. Norris has had a distinguished career in the railway industry, which includes positions throughout Canada with Canadian Pacific Railway and the Pacific Great Eastern Railway, and as president and chief executive officer of British Columbia Railway from 1978 to 1989. The opening of the northeast coal line and the establishment of the *Royal Hudson* excursion trip are among his numerous accomplishments. Since 1990 Mr. Norris has had a pivotal role in the development and success of Great Canadian Railtour Company."

MAC NORRIS: Over a long railroad career I experienced many challenges, but I must say that the first three years of Great Canadian Railtour Company offered some new and *interesting* ones. It was fascinating for me to become involved with a group of entrepreneurs—with a background like mine from Canadian Pacific and then a government railroad. A group of entrepreneurs who, convinced of Peter's idea that a daylight passenger train through the Rockies could be profitable, backed the proposal with their money and expertise and saw it through. . . .

Through it all, Peter was the driving force which brought the company to its present success, and Vicki Haller [his executive assistant] was the driving force behind Peter, keeping him organized (and there's a lot of truth in that). . . . I'm honoured indeed to have a dome car dedicated in my name. Incidentally, Peter, the name Mackenzie Charles Norris probably would have been more dignified. But my name in the railway industry is Mac Norris, and it's appropriate and it's a damn sight less pompous. . . .

Peter, I don't think you realize the awesome responsibility you've taken on in making this very kind gesture in dedicating a car in my name. From now on, that car has to be kept clean, and it can't get any dints in it . . . and we can't have any irresponsible actions like breaking champagne over the train.

There were no champagne bottles broken over the *Mac Norris* that day, but there certainly was plenty of bubbly poured in front of the two dome cars later in the afternoon. Russell Burling and Cheryl Hoskin had come all the way from the New South Wales town of Gloucester, Australia, to get married aboard one of the renowned North American trains they had longed to ride. Russell, a lanky, drawling grader operator who'd once worked for a steam railway, had been with Cheryl for a decade. Their impromptu ceremony on the *W. C. Van Horne*, the dome car 9501, would be the first wedding ever performed on the *Rocky Mountaineer* (but theirs was not the first romance to have blossomed onboard—see *Side Trip: Love on the Line,* page 247).

CHERYL HOSKIN, speaking minutes before her marriage ceremony: Russell and my late husband worked together for 19 years, and we've been together now for nearly 10 years. He's just going to make it legal. I already got the ring. Why would I need the paper? But we're both agreed. It's mutual. We've been talking about marriage for a long time, but we have never set a date. We were going to get married in Wisconsin and then we thought, *Why not get married on the* Rocky Mountaineer? We were booked to go on their first departure. It's always been a dream holiday of mine to go through the Rockies by train. Then we said, *Why not do it before we go on the train?* It was this morning we thought we'd go out and find out what we have to do, what paperwork. A tour bus driver yesterday said to go to [the provincial vital statistics] office on Robson Street. And they said, "Yes, come back and give us some money and we'll give you a licence." Just like that. The lady gave us a list of names of marriage commissioners, so we rang them from the hotel. Then we came down here and spotted the *Rocky Mountaineer* parked in the station and came up and saw James.

JAMES TERRY: They asked if they could get married on the train. I said, "Well, certainly you can, but you'll need a justice of the peace, from my understanding." So they said, "What if we go get a justice of the peace and do it in two hours? Let us think about it." And I said, "Call me and if you want to do it, we'll do it." I got a call from them this morning: "Yeah, we're doing it."

RUSSELL BURLING: We had to rush off downtown to the marriage place and get our certificate and all—$100 Canadian. Then we couldn't

Cheryl Hoskin and Russell Burling with a marriage commissioner. They were married aboard in a last-minute ceremony on April 30, 1999.

get a cab out of our hotel and I offered a bloke $1,000 to rush us back to the terminus. He wouldn't take it. In the end I hailed a cab outside the hotel. I said, "We're trying to get to the railway station. We've got a train to catch and quick." He put the hammer down and we got over here awful quick.

The *Rocky Mountaineer* staff had swung into action, ordering champagne, wedding cake and a photographer. There were flowers and a red carpet left over from the dedication of the dome cars. Peter Armstrong and many of the head-office employees were on hand to witness the ceremony. A motorized people-mover drove the couple—she bearing a big bouquet of roses and he with a yellow-daisy boutonniere—down the station platform to the *Van Horne*. There they climbed onto the observation deck with a female marriage commissioner and James Terry in his role as best man and ring bearer.

COMMISSIONER: We are gathered at this place to witness a formal joining in matrimony of this man and this woman according to the custom prevailing and under the authority given me by the Province of British Columbia. The state of matrimony as understood by us is a state ennobled and enriched by law and honourable tradition. . . .

RUSSELL (to Cheryl): Don't you start crying now.

COMMISSIONER: . . . . Now, for as much as you, Russell, and you, Cheryl, have consented in legal wedlock and have declared your solemn intention in this company, before these witnesses, and in my presence, and have exchanged these rings . . . I now pronounce you husband and wife. Russell, you may kiss your bride.

CHERYL, standing on tiptoes out of her shoes to reach up to Russell as she wipes away her tears to the applause of the Rocky Mountaineers: Oh, thank you!

RUSSELL, sipping champagne on the platform afterward: This is a holiday that Cheryl's wanted to do for a long time. She said, "Well, let's go first class"—which we are. It's a dream come true. I only expected to walk onto the platform here, jump up on the car, say "I do" and walk off again. This will remain with us for the rest of our married life. . . . In the meantime, we've got a lot of trainspotting to do.

Like 300,000 voyagers before them, they were embarking on the Trip of a Lifetime.

SIDE TRIP: LOVE ON THE LINE

Anything can happen aboard a train: merrymaking, melodrama, mystery—and, of course, romance.

MIRIAM KORFHAGE: I was going to be in Walla Walla, Wash., in August for a family reunion and for some time knew I wanted to take the Rocky Mountain Triangle trip. It took a lot of courage to sign up as a single. I had never done that before.

On August 12 my tour started with an afternoon bus tour of Vancouver. When I went to the area in the Vancouver Hotel to wait for the bus, there was one other person there—a man. We got on the bus together and sat together. We had dinner together. The next day we rode in the same taxi to the station. Our seats were opposite each other on the train, so many times we sat together. Well, the rest of the trip we had our meals together and took all the tours together. By the end of the trip we realized that somehow or other love had blossomed and now what? After one day at home away from each other, we realized we had something that was special and have now decided to marry. We feel it was fate that we met. Mr. Harold H. Schlintz lives in Fresno, CA, and I, Miriam S. Korfhage, live in Jackson, LA. He is coming here on Sept. 8 and we are going to make all our wedding plans. He is 76 and I am 72. We never realized that at this age it was possible to meet someone and fall in love. We hope that sometime we can come back to Vancouver and take another trip on "our" train.

APPENDIX

GREAT CANADIAN RAILTOUR
BOARD OF DIRECTORS, PAST AND PRESENT

BEV ARMSTRONG, Director, 1990–present

PETER ARMSTRONG, Director, 1990–present

RICHARD BROWNING, Chairman, 1990–December 1994

SAM GUDEWILL, Director, June 1998–present

JAMES HOUSTON, Director, 1990–1994;
Chairman, December 1994–July 1998

GEOFFREY LIPMAN, Director, November 1998–present

MAC NORRIS, Director, 1990–present

MIKE PHILLIPS, Director, 1991–1993, June 1994–June 1998;
Chairman, July 1998–present

SANDY SLATOR, Director, February 1996–April 1997

FRANK STACK, Director, July 1993–February 1996

JOHN ZAOZIRNY, Director, April 1991–February 1996

Chona Abao

Darryl Abate

Marie Abbott

Khaled Abdel-Barr

Evill Ake

Corazon M. Alamar

Shaanaz Ali

Chris Allan

Clay Allen

Elena Allen

Todd Allison

Keith Alston

Cameron Althrop

Debbie Anderson

Mark Andrew

Gizella Andrews

Stephen Andrews

Marilyn Angus

Christina Anselmo

Arthur Anthony

Rick Antonson

Suzette Argo

Peter Armstrong

Wendy Armstrong

Sylvia Arneson

Andrea Arnold

J. J. Arsenault

Anda Asaoka

Douglas Ashby

Christie Atherton

Murray Atherton

Scott Atherton

Rosemary Atkinson

Michael Austin

Joseline Avendano

Terri Axani

Najia Azmat

Michelle Babiuk

Antony Bainbridge

Scott Baker

Walter Bakker

Dale Balanski

Lara Balcaen

David Baldwin

Susan Ball

Tom Ballantyne

Fiona Barclay

Scott Barker

Wendy Baron

Krishna Barrett

Valerie Bartram

Robbin Basra

Craig Battersby

Shannon Bauer

Leslie Baxter

Kate Beasley

Margaret Beaton

Brent Beaumaster

Reg Beebe

Eric Belanger

Jacques Belanger

Brad Bell

Montgomery Bell

Britt Bennekou

Kirsta Bentley

Lesley Berry

Bruce Bertolotti

Dana Beschorner

Wendi Biberdorf

Lori Biglow

Maria Bitamba

Kevin Black

Tracy Blair

Karen Blaquiere

Darrell Bliault

Brigette Bliskis

Sofia Bliss

Adrian Bois

Kristina Bone

Joseph Bongard

Maria Boni

Daniela Bordignon

Cara Boshko

Elizabeth Bothwell

Jeremy Boulding

Anick Bourbonniere

John Bourgeois

Jerome Bourgon

John Bowers

Paul Bowes

Tracy Boyd

Michele Bradley

Clint Braithwaite

Cindy Bratkowski

Kevin Brennan

Carmen Bressanutti

Dana Brewza

Heidi Bricknell

Nigel Brooke

Greg Brooks

Terry Brooks

Monica Broscheit

David Brown
Stacey Brown
Joseph Bryan
Peter Brydon
Sonja Brynelson
Ian Buchanan
Jaquelyn Buchanan
Gerard Buckley
Linda Budeau
Suzanne Buffam
Michelle Buglioni
Norm Bulloch
Karen Burdon
Gerrard Burke
Tina Burke
Phillip Burton
Wade Bush
Crystal Bushau
Robert Butchart
Julie Butler
Michelle Butler
Simon Caindee
Claire Calvo
Heather Cameron
Megan Cameron
Marlene Camile
Tracey Campbell
Ted Campmans
Manon Cardin
Rodney Cardoz
Mark Caredda
Glenda Carlson
Robert Carpino
Leah Carrigan
Mike Carroll
Vance Carroll
Jean Cartelier
Peter Casement
Pat Castle

Susan Chalmers
Brian Champoux
Vincent Chan
Angela Chand
Alison Chaplin
Jennifer Chaplin
Carla Cherkas
Helen Cho
Brandy Cholin
Janice Chong
Agnes Chow
Grace Chow
Peggy Chow
Darcy Christo
Kim Citton
John Clark
Scott Clarke
Michael Clayton
Rob Clermont
Robert Clibbon
Sarah Collier
Morgan Collins
Lee-Anne Coltart
Barbara Colussi
Angela Connors
Jennifer Connors
Gina Cooper
Lawrence Cooper
Elizabeth Coppens
Fiorino Corsi
Elizabeth Cortes
Stephen Cosper
Joanna M. Cossey
Carie Costin
Betty Cowling
Kerry Lynn Coxon
Tracey Cramer
Jeff Crane
Melissa Cranwell

Kelly Crawford
Zachary Creer
Rodd Cruikshank
Elizabeth Crump
Max Cu
Elizabeth
   Cunningham
Roberto Damian
Phung Dang
Richard Darisse
Katy Dastoor
Chuck Davies
Randy Daye
Adie Deeks
Brian Deeprose
Kirsten Degenhardt
Jaime DeGuino
Krista Dennett
Michele de Rappard
Sharlene Dickson
Leanne Dilks
Dana Y Dilling
Thomas Dixon
Jaime Dizon
Tina Djurectic
Anita Don
Louise Donahoe
Nancy Donaldson
Mike Donchak
Helen Dosdos
Cintia Dos Santos
Alex Douglas
Arshia Dowlati
Greg Doyle
Nicole Draheim
Tammy Drake
Pierre Drouin
Jean Francois Dube
Tiana Dunham

Michelle Dupas
Don Eaton
Susan Eberhardt
Lori Ebl
Wesley Eccleston
Gillian Edmunds
Rachael Edwards
Chris Eggleton
Phillip Elliot
Bruce Elliott
Sharon Elliott
Stuart Ellis-Myers
Kiersten Enemark
Tasha Enemark
Kyle Erickson
Katie Ernst
Erie Estampador
Bern Euler
Anthony Evangelista
Derrick Evans
Gareth Evans
Susan Everts
Brenda Fanning
Nancy Farenholtz
Zahra Faritous
Jennifer Farrell
Marg Fartaczek
Janice Fawcett
Marci Fear
Jason Feng
Tim Fentiman
Kathryn Ferguson
Marsha Ferguson
Armando Fernandez
Terry Fiddick
Matthew Fischer
Ken Fisher
Norm Foisy
Megan Foley

Glenn Forkutza
Dallas Forsberg
Jaylene Forth
Angela Foster
Fawn Foster
Angelina Fowler
Julia Fowler
Karen Franks
Alexandrea Fraser
Edith Fraser
Lisa Fraser
Melanie Fraser
Scott Fraser
Lisa French
Tim French
Tereza Frymire
Tim Furniss
Nancy Gabrielse
Terry Gainer
Gary Gamble
Tina Gardner
Jerri-Lynn Garlough
Allen Gascon
Gerald Gatchalian
Akiko Gavac
Heidi Gawehns
Gary Gervais
Darren Gibbons
Michael Giesbrecht
Ruth Gilchrist
Manjinder Gill
Graham Gilley
Issac Giroux
Clay Gjernes
Stewart Glen
Byron Glynoa
Niki Gnissios
Ray Goddard
Roberta Gonzalez

Frances Goritsas
Scott Gorrebeek
Melvin Gott
Brent Gough
Wendy Gouk
Susan Govia
Jaclynn Grad
Brazil Graham
Maxine Graham
Thomas Graham
Karla Green
Janice Greenwood
Brent Griffiths
Amy Guan
Gregory Guitard
Patti Hackman
Dawn Haering
Andy Hagel
Dwayne Haire
Paul Halder
Janet Hale
Allen Hall
Emery Hall
Sheila Hall
Vicki Haller
Petra Haluska
Carolyn Hamilton
Rob Hamilton
Kimberly Hand
Donna Hanna
Sara Hansen
Kayoko Harada
Vincent Haraldsen
Robert Hargreaves
Nina Harju
Stephen Harris
Marica Harrison
Brenda Harvey
Tricia Harvey

Joanne Hasell
Sharon Hasse
Michael Hassler
Kira Haug
Jean-Philippe Hauray
Eleanor Healy
Jarita Heer
Gail Heezen
Kerri-Lynn Heise
Robert Henderson
Alistair Henry
Elizabeth Henshaw
Bryce Herman
Maeghan Herman
Shauna Hetherington
Catherine Hikawa
Barbara Hill
Jay Hindle
Trevor Hinton
Blair Hirtle
Sara Hodgson
Keith Holgren
Stuart Holland
Brad Holler
Cathryn Holler
Robert Hollick-
    Kenyon
Stephen
    Hollingsworth
Karen Holms
Ryan Holowaychuck
Joanne Honeygold
Cathy Hornsby
Sarah Rose Horsfall
Rod Horychuk
Jim Howard
Helen Huang
Jackie Hubrick
Ning Hum

Erica Hummel
Michael Hungerford
Randall Hunter
Amanda Hyde
Karen Hyde
Susan Ibbott
Mellissa Ing
Irene Lau
Laura Jackson
Dana-Lynn Janeson
Cathie Jarrel
Robert Jenkins
Craig Jensen
Lori Jensen
Tricia Jerome
Shane Jeurissen
Keith Jewers
Kelvin Jobson
Lesley Johnson
Lionard Johnson
Lisa Johnson
Lou Johnston
Jim Johnstone
Brenda Jones
Sarah Jones
Evie Jordan-Knox
Howard Jules
Rick Jupiter
Brian Kadoski
Sandra Karbovszky
Darren Kawamoto
Cameron Kay
Petr Kazda
Lesley Keetley
Adama Keller
Douglas Kelsey
Jayson Kennedy
Kim Kennedy
Jody Kennett

Randy Kerley
Michael Kevany
Monisha Khanna
Di Kilbridge
Anna Killian
Jin-Hee Kim
Kim Kingston
Mark Kinskofer
Manfred Klassen
Ursula Klein
Pauline Kooner
Kirsten Koppang
Karina Kosoloff
Lorna Kozak
Janice Kurylowich
Renata Kubica
Nina Kumar
Janice Kurylowich
Miki Laakso
Ronald W. Lacoursiere
Bob D. Lake
Bill Lakeland
Tracy Lakeman
Joyce Lam
Mei Lam
Jan Lamirande
Darron Lampreau
Barbara Lane
Martina Lange
Doug Langford
Roland Langille
Lionel Lanoie
Michelle Lanzo
Brian Lapensee
Grace Lapuz
Catherine Lara
Jean Laramee
Michelle Lardizabal
Locelyn Larkin

Anita Larsen
John Larsen
Chris Laursen
Vernon G. Lavis
Melissa Law
Grant Lawlor
Rebecca Lawrence
Shand Lawson
Christine Leblond
Daniel LeCamp
David Leclerc
Louise Leclerc
Andrea Lee
Gerry Leonard
Martin Leonard
Angie Leung
Jennette Leyland
Victor Lind
Mike Lister
Erin Little
Iain Lock
Tony Locke
Vickie Locke
Robb Logan
Sean Long
Marcus Louie
Susan Lowery
Brenda Lozada
Thomas Lozza
Lily Lu
Amanda Lugsdin
Dave Lyle
Bernadette Lynch
Jeann Lyons
Natasha MacBride
David MacEntee
Angelique MacGougan
Melanie Machnee
Don MacKinnon

Dolores Maclean
Loretta MacMahon
Kelly Madden
Lorna Magill
Richard Magill
Timothy Magill
Eleanor Mah
Kyla Mahoney
Carmel Malet-Veale
Barbara Maloney
Clifford Maloney
Kristin Malthe
Erin Manahan
Jill Manahan
Andrew Manke
Bill Manning
Constantine Maranis
Michael Marsh
Kim Marshall
Lydia Marsi
Anita Martin
Paulo Martins
Terry Maslasz
Daniel Mason
James Mathieson
Ojay Matias
Brandi Matthews
John Matthews
Naomi Mayede
Jeffrey Mazo
Greg McBroom
Natalie McCall
Janet McCartney
Lisa McCaskill
Mark McChesney
Richard McDonough
Shelby McDowell
Christine McEachern
Dan McGarrity

Terence McGillion
Colleen McGiverin
Gabriela McGreal
Karen McGregor
Andrew McIntosh
Melodie McIntyre
Michael McKay
Jacqueline McKee
Kelly McKenzie
Greg McLean
Sacha Mclean
Lori McLenna
Reece McNaughton
Daniel McPahil
Laura McRitchie
Allison Meade
Karen Melnechuk
Sonia Merlo
Shane Metcalfe
Linda Michlacci
Laura Mickleson
Calvin Milenk
Alison Miles
Wendy Milloy
Leslie Mills
Monique Mirault
Ellen Mochizuki
Donna Moffat
Sonia Moioli
Tam Moira
Melissa Montague
Paul Moody
Farion Moore
Sharon Moore
Tyler Moore
Claude Morency
Aila Morgan
Greg Morhart
Clarise Morris

Richard Mott
Leslie Mounteney
Susan Mueller
Yvette Mulder
Karen Mumby
Christopher
 Muncaster
Wing Mung
Christine Murphy
Peter Muth
Michel Nadeau
Sandra Nadeau
Rosita Nadela
Trisha Nakagawa
Karim Nanji
Laila Nazarali
Amanda Neale
Phillip Neathway
Lisa Neilsen
Cindy Nelson
Rob Nelson
Brian Ness
Caroline Newman
Henry Newman
Michele Ng
Lina Nichol
Ole Nichum
Ken Nidle
Christine E. Nilsen
Juanito Ninalga
Laura Noakes
Ted Noakes
Craig Noble
Randall Noble
Dorothy Nooshin
Leanne Norden
Bonnie Norton
Laurel Norton
Lou Novosad

Brad Noyes
Otto Nupponen
Paul Nursey
Margaret Obaze
Ron O'Brien
Nosa Oghomo
Linda Oliveira
Miriam Olivia
Michael Ologhola
Tom Olsson
Todd Ono
Glen Ovenden
Keiko Ozeki
Pervin Ozelmanglu
Ana Pacheco
Krista Page
Silvana Pagnotta
Rosemary Pahl
Karen Palmar
Perry Panchmatia
Amarjit Panesar
Rosetta Parente
Bob Parker
Dave Parker
Erica Parker
Wesley Parker
Leona Parker-Elliott
Lesley-Anne Parsons
Gordon Partridge
Jim Paton
Darren Pausch
John Pavlovich
Tony Pellegrino
Stephanie Pember-
 Johnson
Roman Pendzey
Krista Penner
Bruno Perron
Ken Petel

James Peters
Kate Petipierre
Christine Pfeiffer
Christine Phillips
Douglas Phillips
Alexander Pickett
Christine Pidman
Anita Pioja
Janine Plag
Doug Planidin
John Poole
Bonnie Popowich
Tony Potopilnyj
Robert Power
Ranjini Prasad
Peter Primgaard
Tony Prothero
Daylene Randall
Norma Rattray
Peter Ray
Phil Reambeault
Selena Redenbach
Terry Reeb
Erin Reid
Scott Remillard
Roman Rendzey
Tracey Rezansoff
Marion Rhodes
Carol Richard
Lloyd Ripplinger
Cynthia Roa
Christian Roberts
Christine Roberts
Jennifer Roberts
Denise Robertson
Joanne Robertson
Lee Ann Robinson
Tanya Robinson
Erin Rochfort

Naomi Roddick
Bryan Rodrigues
Diana Roemer
Carolyn Rogers
Doug Rogers
Bill Romaniuk
Paul Romanowski
Cameron Rombough
Brenda Roscoe
Darlene Ross
Carrie Rotenburger
Jess Rothenburger
Christine Rowley
Dan Rowley
Michael Rowley
Brenna Rudd
Linda Rumi
Lea Ruuth
Shamim Sachedina
Vaclav Safarik
Jennifer Safronick
Mala Sahan
Susanna Sama
Jette Sandeford
Brigitte Sanderson
Melissa Sansom
Janice Sapergia
Ivan Saunderson
Colleen Sauve
Hermann Schaad
Jason Schaak
James Schimpl
Chester Schmal
Michael Searle
Kim Seaward
Adela Semora
Grant Setter
Kenneth Shapkin
Paul Sharp

Sandra Sharples
David Shawcross
Helen Sheehan
Timothy Sheena
Michelle Shepard
Jason Sherlock
Calinda Shiells
Vuro Shimomura
Philip Shupe
Robert Sidney
Debbie Silva
Susie Silversides
Gordon Sim
Earl Simons
Caitlin Simpson
Jaysun Sinclair
Nile Sinclair
Jason Sirianni
Steven Skaar
Sonia Skelly
Michelle Skrenka
Samantha Slade
Allison Small
William Smedley
Cami Smith
Christina Smith
Joyce Smith
Kirk D. Smith
Ron Smith
Ryan Smith
Scarlett Smith
Shannon Smith
Starrett Smith
Bob Snowdon
Thaddee Sobolewski
Jane Sonneberg
Janet Southwell
Matthew Spice
Penny Squinas

Candice Staford
Tom St. Clair
Bill Steacy
Don Steeson
Bruce Steffan
Sandra Steinhoff
Bud Stirman
Frederick Stirman
Kirstine Stolle
Greg Stout
Chistine Strehike
Kristi Strickland
Kimberley Strome
Monte Strong
Nicole Strosyn
Terry Sturdwick
Arnold Sturgeon
Ivana Styles
Ellen Suarez
Ronald Suchell
Salma Sunderji
Blanca Swan
Chad Swan
Judy Swan
Lupita Swan
Teo Swee
Corinne Sweetin
Laura Syms
Betty Tang
Kirti Tanna
Jennifer Tanton
Amanda Taylor
Sandy Taylor
Scott Taylor
Carol Terretta
James Terry
Randy Terry
Gerald Thibault
Douglas Thiessen

Tina Thomas	Nicole Vogel	Ann Winter
Dave Thomson	Hien Vu	Sharon Winter
Judy Thomson	Petra Wagner	Kevin Witherspoon
Pamela Thurston	Caronne Wagstaff	Barbara Wochowska
James Tobin	Ed Walker	Martin Wojtula
Jane Tom	Patrick Wallace	Michael Wolfram
Jennifer Tomlin	Kathleen Walsh	David Wolstenholme
Monica Tong	Janet Wang	Adeline Wong
Antonio Torchia	Lisa Wang	David Wong
David Trant	Sophia Wang	Leonard Wong
Jon Treichel	Steve Ward	Neil Wong
Louis Trempe	Jon Wasnock	Mark Wood
Carla Trenholm	Lisa Watson	Frances Woodcock
Bozo Trklja	Brent Weaver	Doug Workman
Georgia Trousdale	Nora Weber	Suzi Wortman
Joanne Tsang	Suzanne Wehrli	Edward Wu
Wanda Tse	Danny Weisbeck	Rhonda Yam
Ellie Tseng	Lucas Wells	Yas Yamamotot
Kate Turley	Susan Werner	David Yano
Murray Turnbull	Sharlet Wheating	Jinkee Yap
Christine Turner	Samantha White	Marilou Yap
Doug Turner	Tammy White	Flora Ye
Virginia Turrin	Elizabeth Whitelaw	Madeline Yee
Van Tuyen	Tracey Whiting	Danley Yip
James Tworkowski	Erin Whitty	Jessica Yong
Carlito Ugay	Steven Wickens	Heather Young
Farzana Unwalla	Larry Wilberg	Leah Marie Yutiamco
Karl Valaitis	Dean Wilkins	Jennifer Zakaib
Paulina Valledor	Erin Willems	Ken Zaleski
Karlina Van der Weij	Catherine Williams	Carin Zanon
Louise Van Hoven	Mary Williams	Anrea Zaslov
William C. VanVeelan	Monica Williams	Gregory Zayadai
Crystal Vehse	Peter Williams	Rami Zein
Tanya Velasque	Trevor Williams	Larisa Zenjin
Bonnie Venus	Peta Williamson	James Zerebeski
Maria Verdicchio	Jaqueline Wilson	Jennifer Zimmer
Kumar Verma	Jeff Wilson	Murray Zimmerman
Tim Villa	Kirsti Wilson	Heidi Zurbrugg
Harakh Vimlesh	Lisa Wilson	Antonietta Zuzolo